THE DEAD VOLCANO

THE DEAD VOLCANO

The Background and Effects of Nuclear War Complacency

Stephen J. Cimbala

PRAEGER

Westport, Connecticut
London

Library of Congress Cataloging-in-Publication Data

Cimbala, Stephen J.
   The dead volcano : the background and effects of nuclear war complacency /
Stephen J. Cimbala.
     p. cm.
   Includes bibliographical references and index.
   ISBN 0–275–97387–5 (alk. paper)
   1. Nuclear warfare.   2. Cold War.   3. World politics—1989–   4. World politics—
21st century.   I. Title.
   U263.C4832   2002
   327.1'747—dc21   2001034578

British Library Cataloguing in Publication Data is available.

Library of Congress Catalog Card Number: 2001034578
ISBN: 0–275–97387–5

First published in 2002

Praeger Publishers, 88 Post Road West, Westport, CT 06881
An imprint of Greenwood Publishing Group, Inc.
www.praeger.com

Printed in the United States of America

The paper used in this book complies with the
Permanent Paper Standard issued by the National
Information Standards Organization (Z39.48–1984).

10 9 8 7 6 5 4 3 2 1

To my Mother and Father

Contents

Acknowledgments

The author gratefully acknowledges the following persons for insights and evidence contributory to the completion of this study: John Arquilla, U.S. Naval Postgraduate School; Pavel Baev, Oslo Peace Research Institute; Stephen Blank, U.S. Army War College; Michael Crutcher, U.S. Army War College; Charles Dick, Royal Military Academy, Sandhurst; John Erickson, University of Edinburgh; William Flavin, U.S. Army War College; Colin Gray, University of Hull; James Holcomb, U.S. Army War College; Jacob Kipp, Foreign Military Studies Office, U.S. Army; William Martel, U.S. Naval War College; George Quester, University of Maryland; Keith Payne, National Institute for Public Policy; David Sorenson, U.S. Air War College; and Timothy Thomas, Foreign Military Studies Office, U.S. Army. I am also grateful to the Arms Control Association and to the Center for Defense Information for citations and use of data previously published by both organizations. I thank Dr. James Scouras for permission to use some models and data for my purposes.

I acknowledge with special emphasis the encouragement given to me to complete this study by James T. Sabin of Greenwood Publishing Group and his helpful suggestions. Penn State Delaware County Campus, Office of Academic Affairs, contributed administrative support without which it would not have been possible to complete this project. In that regard, I thank Charele Raport for her exceptional efforts in the face of great adversity.

I thank my wife, Betsy, for her love that has made possible all of my achievements and carried me through all of life's most important passages.

Introduction

This introduction is deliberately brief. My reason for writing this book is to address my students, colleagues and other interested audiences on a subject of considerable concern to me. The concern is prompted by what I consider to be wrongheaded optimism on the part of policy makers, theorists and lay observers with regard to the future of nuclear weapons, war and politics. This misplaced optimism is described below. We are, in essence, like the peasant farmers who till the slopes of a dead volcano, assuming that it will never erupt because it hasn't.

The end of the Cold War and the demise of the Soviet Union were welcome historical passages. But these events had some undesirable side effects. One of those side effects was complacency, both intellectual and political. Intellectual complacency or, perhaps, excessive euphoria, assumed that the end of the Cold War and the disintegration of the Soviet Union spelled an end to large-scale wars among military great powers. The twentieth century had been a century of total war: wars fought "to end all wars" (World War I) or for the unlimited purpose of imposing "unconditional surrender" (World War II) on the defeated. Combatants were required to mobilize virtually all of their societal and economic resources: the line between military and civilian was pushed into the background as "civilians" engaged in partisan warfare and as their homes and factories were subjected to unprecedented air bombardment.

World War II seemed to have (at least temporarily) exhausted the appetite of heads of state for total war. At least, it produced a postwar balance of power that was bipolar (two-sided) instead of multipolar (many-sided): the United States and the Soviet Union were the only states capable of sustaining a global military influence for the next 45 years or so. Their rivalry was at times intense, but it required them to engage in a form of bloc consolidation (NATO in the West, the Warsaw Pact in the East) that kept other potential sources of conflict in Europe under wraps.

For example, commentators often remarked during the Cold War that NATO had three purposes: to keep the Americans in Europe, the Russians out of Western Europe, and the Germans down from another go at England, France or Russia. For its part, the Soviet Union saw continuing control over the politics and militaries of Eastern and East Central Europe as its protective glacis against another incursion from the West. In fact, the Soviet Union's leadership, while fulminating in public diplomacy against NATO's alleged threat to legitimate Soviet interests in Europe, actually came to welcome NATO's contribution to stabilization of the Central Front marked by a divided Germany.

Nuclear weapons grew up with a divided Germany, a divided and pacified Europe and a bipolar international system militarily dominated by two "superpowers" based outside of Europe. These were all exceptional political and military conditions. Europe remained out of the immediate danger zone of major war unless someone was willing to run the risk of nuclear self-destruction in order to change borders or acquire additional resources. Even Stalin, in the earliest years of the nuclear age, could not get a brief from his general staff advising that he overturn the European balance of power by a direct military thrust at NATO's vitals. Instead, he probed (as in Berlin, in 1948) or supported proxy wars outside of Europe (as in Korea, in 1950), but he stayed short of posing to the United States and its European allies a threat without an exit strategy.

Interpretations of the Cold War, and of the role of nuclear weapons in United States and Soviet Cold War strategy and politics, have not infrequently suffered from either of two errors of exaggeration. The first error is to assume that nuclear weapons were, despite their enormous destructive power, of little actual military or political importance in maintaining the long peace of 1946–1991. The second, and opposite, error is the argument that during this same time period, nuclear weapons were so overriding of other military considerations that they precluded any serious likelihood of large-scale warfare, inside or outside of Europe. The beginning of wisdom about nuclear weapons then and now is to recognize that both these arguments extend a grain of insight into a dangerously compelling misjudgment.

The first error of emphasis assumes that nuclear weapons were not necessary to avoid any World War III between 1946 and 1991. The devastation caused by World War II in Europe was sufficient to improve the memories of at least a generation about the unacceptable costs of total war. The Soviet Union, having suffered historically unprecedented casualties in World War II (numbering as many as 27 million military and civilian deaths, by some estimates), would be even more reluctant than the United States and allied Western powers to fight another war that might bring renewed devastation to its homeland. Related to this argument about the pacific character of enduring memory in Eurasia was a strategic one: the Russians would recognize that the power of American economic mobilization for protracted war, demonstrated so conclusively between 1941 and 1945, would carry forward into the postwar world. Thus, the Kremlin could not expect to start any conventional war in Europe without a guarantee of a rapid and decisive victory over NATO. In any protracted war, the military advantage lay with the West because the United States and its allies were the richer coalition of states; the Soviet Union and its allies, the poorer.

This first error of emphasis in explaining the role of nuclear weapons in the Cold War peace is, therefore, actually an error of de-emphasis: it depreciates the relevancy of nuclear power and attributes the long European peace to other causes. These other causes, let it be said here, were not irrelevant: proponents of the "lingering memory" thesis and of the Russians' realistic fear of American economic strength told a true tale. But they told the tale out of context. Their insights unduly deemphasized the significance of nuclear weapons by omitting the level of analysis that political scientists call *structural realism*. Structural realism is a perspective that emphasizes the constraints placed upon states or other international actors by the international system. The international system is shorthand for the *distribution of power and values* among states and other actors, and for the *balance of power* among the same actors. The distribution of power and values among actors influences the kinds of interactions that actors have with one another. For example, the values of the Nazi regime in Germany after 1933 included overthrow of the existing balance of power in Europe. But Hitler lacked the military power to do so until 1939, when his invasion of Poland kicked off the Second World War.

Structural realists looking at the Cold War would emphasize that nuclear weapons were important but not only, or mainly, on account of their awesome destructive power. Killing, after all, can be accomplished in large lots without nuclear weapons. It was the distribution of power and values between 1946 and 1991 that made nuclear weapons especially influential in world politics, for several reasons. First, the two largest nuclear arsenals (by far) were held by the two geopolitically dominant state actors: the United States and the Soviet Union. Second, on account of this global military bipolarity, allies were expendable and containable: they could not go off on their own and start a war which would bring in the superpowers despite themselves, as Austria and Serbia did on the eve of the First World War. Third, because bipolarity was combined with ideological hostility, as between Washington and Moscow, the United

States and the Soviets knew with unusual clarity where to target their military intelligence gathering efforts. The probable source of mischief was not in doubt; only the modus operandi was. Fourth, the nuclear weapons technologies available to the superpower duopolists during the Cold War favored a defensive strategy over an offensive one. The last point deserves further comment because it has been muddled in some accounts of Cold War strategy and arms control.

Nuclear weapons mated to ballistic missiles were offensive weapons against which no effective defense capable of intercepting those missiles and their warheads was available, at least not prior to the end of the Cold War. The lack of any defensive *technology* to preclude the success of missile attacks enforced the priority of a defensive *strategy* on the two nuclear superpowers. The usual historical condition of perpetual competition between offensive and defensive technology and tactics was, at the highest possible level of warfare, suspended in a frozen status quo. Unless and until either side concocted an effective defense to blunt the attack of the other side, neither side could launch a nuclear first strike and hope to escape the total destruction of its own homeland. Mutually assured destruction (nicknamed MAD) was a fact of life enforced by bipolarity and technology, regardless of the whims of particular Soviet premiers or American presidents. There is some irony, therefore, in the arguments made by some military strategists and by at least one former Soviet president, to the effect that nuclear war was so terrible that it had repudiated Clausewitz. In fact, Clausewitz had emphasized in his now classic study *On War* that the defensive was the stronger form of war: if we make the perfectly reasonable substitution of defensive war avoidance by means of the balance of nuclear terror for Clausewitz's version, he remains undated.

If the first error of emphasis was to fail to credit nuclear weapons and the systemic forces that gave them especial impetus, the second error of emphasis was to credit nuclear weapons and nuclear deterrence with a self-sufficient ability to pacify all of Europe and the U.S.-Soviet relationship during the Cold War. The gist of this argument goes as follows. We had the correct number of nuclear wars between 1946 and 1991—none. We had the correct number of wars among major powers during the Cold War—none. We had the correct number of wars between the Americans and Soviets during the same time period—none. If we contrast the first 45 years of the twentieth century with the second 45 years, the contrast between the first period (two world wars originating in Europe) and the second (as above) is so remarkable that it cries for singular explanation. And that explanation, in the minds of those who attribute much to nuclear causes, lies in the singular fear of total annihilation that the Americans and Soviets were able to bring to bear against one another and, by implication, against their respective allies and partners.

As in the case of the first error of emphasis, there is some significant truth to the argument on behalf of nuclear fear. There is no doubt that a certain amount of extra caution was often practiced by the Americans, by the Soviets and by others in the face of the possibility of nuclear war or of escalation from conventional to nuclear war. The Cuban missile crisis gives evidence of the careful maneuvering that Kennedy and Khrushchev engaged in, once the United States had discovered the Soviet missiles deployed in Cuba and had publicly demanded their removal within a short time. Kennedy was determined to reach his political objective short of war, and to do so he had to practice deterrence and coercive diplomacy by alternating carrots and sticks in dealing with the Soviet leadership. Too many sticks would back Khrushchev into a corner from which he might lunge desperately into a nuclear first strike at North America. We now know that a significant danger in the crisis was that, apart from a deliberate if desperate Soviet *first strike*, there was the additional possibility of a deliberate or inadvertent Soviet nuclear first *use* in Cuba. The Soviets had deployed with their group of forces in Cuba tactical nuclear weapons, including FROG (Luna) nuclear-capable surface-to-surface missiles for their ground forces, as well as tactical anti-ship cruise missiles intended to assist in denying U.S. invading forces easy access to Cuban shores.

Worse than having deployed to Cuba both tactical and strategic missiles capable of being armed with nuclear charges, Khrushchev also placed the group of Cuban forces under the local theater command of a former cavalry officer—Gen. Issa Pli'yev, a crony of Khrushchev's from the Second World War. This is pertinent to the nuclear danger of the Cuban crisis because, at one stage during the summer of 1963, Khrushchev flirted with the idea of delegating to the local theater commander in Cuba the authority to use nuclear weapons first if the Americans invaded Cuba and if communications with Moscow were cut off. Khrushchev later thought better of this idea and rescinded Pli'yev's authorization to initiate tactical nuclear war. Had the Americans invaded Cuba as they were preparing to do until the crisis was resolved on October 27 by Khrushchev's agreement to American demands, they might have encountered Soviet resistance that included tactical nuclear strikes on U.S. ground troops or ships. One can only imagine where the ladder of escalation would have gone from there.

The Cuban missile crisis, among other experiments in brinkmanship between the Cold War superpowers, showed that crisis management in the nuclear age required a certain competency in balancing both *threats* and *reassurances*. Threats by themselves created only fear that might backfire into shared disaster. Crisis-time reassurances were necessary in order to persuade the other side that, if it complied with the threatener's demands within a reasonable time or otherwise satisfied the threatener's objectives, it would be spared the consequences of noncompliance. Carrots and sticks again. This need for reassurance along with deterrence sounds commonplace now, but it was a lesson learned slowly and painfully by the Americans and Soviets as they invented together the applied and uncertain science of nuclear crisis management: in Berlin from 1958 through 1961; in Cuba, in 1962; in the Middle East, in 1973; and at other, if less conspicuous, times.

The experience in the Cuban missile crisis and in other Cold War confrontations showed that the structural or static features of the international system did not guarantee a loss of control over the dynamics of actions between or among states. The insights of structural realists, alluded to earlier in our discussion, provided important explanations for those aspects of the system that were continuous or stable across time. But those structural factors can only amount to preconditions or predispositions, relative to the actual behaviors of political leaders and commanders in time of peace, crisis or war. The multiple causes of their behavior include other factors, including their perceptions and expectations, needs and desires, images of themselves and of the enemy, among many candidate variables. Because the dynamics of leaders' behavior cannot be predicted only on the basis of the static background within which they must decide, structural realism cannot stand alone to explain why nuclear war did not happen between 1946 and 1991. In other words, neither nuclear danger by itself, nor nuclear danger coupled to a bipolar distribution of international military power, suffices to explain the long peace of the Cold War.

One dynamic or behavioral element that must be added to the explanation for the long peace is the *nuclear learning* that took place on the part of political leaders and their foreign offices and military bureaucracies. Whereas there was considerable uncertainty among all hands in the early years of the nuclear age with regard to the singularity of nuclear weapons, and with regard to their impact on diplomacy and crisis management, by the last two decades of the Cold War the U.S. and Soviet arms control communities were speaking in a commonly understood subtext. This subtext carried across their professional military and diplomatic communities despite the day-to-day disagreements among their heads of state with regard to particular issues of policy. Soviet and American diplomats and soldiers engaged in nuclear arms control became a "regime" of a sort: a subset of institutions, procedures and expectations that influenced policy by enlarging the context within which the nuclear debates were conducted. Some, especially American political conservatives, mistook this development of transnational nuclear community as a Soviet intelligence deception to exploit U.S. gullibility (granted that intelligence, policy and strategy cannot be neatly separated either analytically or in practice).

On the other hand, the development of a transnational regime of nuclear arms control experts, including not only Americans and Russians but also others, helped to establish a common means of calibrating the international arms race. In turn, moving toward agreed measures of calibration was helpful in imposing international restraint on the spread of nuclear weapons. If we could all agree on what to count and what to look for with regard to nuclear weapons manufacture and deployment, then we had improved our chances of persuading or coercing others into stopping their military research and development efforts below the nuclear threshold. One of the more remarkable accomplishments of the Cold War, to which the transnational community of nuclear arms control experts contributed, was that nuclear weapons spread much more slowly among states than early Cold War pessimists had predicted or feared.

Recognizing that the structure of the international system could not guarantee against an eruption of nuclear fire, the Americans and Russians engaged in two forms of nuclear learning that we have already cited: adaptive crisis management, mixing deterrence with coercive diplomacy, and shared understanding on the dangers of uncontrolled nuclear proliferation. There was a third aspect to the two states' nuclear learning during the Cold War, and it grew unexpectedly out of their need to develop organizations and procedures for new kinds of military forces.

Because nuclear missile weapons promised to accomplish so much devastation within such a short period of time against which no defenses were foreseeable, special thought had to be given to the command and control of nuclear forces. The Americans and Soviets were motivated to do this for somewhat different reasons and for some similar ones. The Americans did not fear the possibility of professional military disloyalty to the prevailing political order; but the Soviets, as a matter of principle and ideology, did so. Any threat to the primacy of the Communist Party control over security, including military, questions was not acceptable. Bonapartism was even more dangerous if rebellious generals got hold of weapons of mass destruction and decided upon their own version of Soviet military enlargement in Europe. The United States had other concerns. Interservice rivalry and shared power over security policy, between the legislative and executive branches of government, ensured that the issue of who would operate nuclear forces, and how, would migrate to the top of the policy ladder.

In addition to these political rationales for new thinking about the problem of nuclear command and control, the realities of nuclear force operations imposed special requirements on force commanders and politicians. A nuclear war could begin under conditions of very short warning and great surprise. Forces had to be highly responsive to authorized commands for retaliation (in order to deter), but not so trigger-happy that they would go off on account of a false provocation. Building nuclear command and control systems that could provide reliable retaliation when authorized, but also preclude accidental or inadvertent war when not, was no small challenge to American and Soviet political leaders, military commanders and scientists. In the American case, for example, organizations (e.g., Strategic Air Command) were purpose-built for the nuclear retaliatory mission. More important, the United States recognized in the 1950s the need for organizational separation between the functions of *attack warning* and *nuclear retaliation*. The former function was entrusted to the North American Aerospace Defense Command (NORAD); the latter, to SAC and other components of the U.S. missile and airborne nuclear strike forces. The validation of attack detection, in other words, was set apart organizationally from the authorization to strike back and from the physical capability to do so. (For more on this topic, see Chapter 6.)

We know less about the nuclear command and control arrangements on "the other side of the hill" in Moscow compared to the American side. The Soviets were, and the Russians are, secretive about nuclear command and control, whereas the American media and other investigators have exposed many aspects of the U.S. system to public view. Despite this difference in the available data base, we can say that both sides recognized the unique challenges that nuclear weapons posed to pre-nuclear command and control arrangements, and they also recognized that something had to give. Each state in its own way, and according to its own traditions and regime style, adjusted to the nuclear revolution in military affairs and the command and control revolution that came along with it. (Chapters 1 and 2 trace this evolution.)

Now we are definitely living in a post–Cold War era, but are we living in a post-nuclear one? This question anticipates part of what will be covered in the interior chapters that follow and in the concluding chapter; let us leave something unanswered for now in the interest of keeping alive reader curiosity. But everyone knows that, in military affairs as in all else, we have crossed over into the "information age" or perhaps into the age of "information warfare." Some feel that this leaves the nuclear age behind, or of interest only to professional historians of the Cold War. Others, like this author, are worried about the shotgun marriage between weapons of mass destruction and cyberwar. War, as well as deterrence, has always been about information to some extent. But information warfare as conceived by some of its proponents and practitioners would, perhaps inadvertently, create chaos in the reconnaissance, communications and command/control systems of putative enemies. This kind of cyberwar is a potential "force multiplier" against opponents not armed with usable nuclear weapons, as Saddam Hussein was not in 1991. However, against an opponent with nuclear weapons and short fault-tolerance for failed command and control, could cyberwar provoke the very crisis or war that it was intended to prevent? (Chapter 7 goes into this issue in more detail.)

Optimism about the cohabitation of cyberwar and nuclear deterrence is argued against in Chapter 7. Optimism about the spread of nuclear weapons to additional state or other actors is contested with equal fervor in Chapter 8. Cold War success in holding back the spread of nuclear weapons, together with the presumed status of the United States as a singular global military power in the new world order, has created a diminished state of vigilance about nuclear weapons spread. It is not all bad news. The United States did get a big win when participating states agreed to indefinite extension of the Non-Proliferation Treaty in 1995. The Clinton administration also took the lead in pressing for a ban on nuclear testing and mobilized a strong international consensus on its behalf. On the other hand, the U.S. Senate rejected the Comprehensive Test Ban Treaty (CTBT) in October 1999, dealing a setback to the administration. Despite this ill-considered vote, U.S. funding for the international nuclear test monitoring system supported by the Comprehensive Test Ban Treaty Organization (CTBTO) remained intact. The system is intended to provide a network of 321 test monitoring stations in 90 countries in order to detect nuclear explosions and a global telecommunications network to share the data.[1]

The Clinton nonproliferation policy also promised to develop a left hook as well as a right cross. The problem was not only to reduce the incentives of potential sellers of nuclear and other weapons of mass destruction. It was, in addition, necessary to diminish the appetites for nuclear weapons on the part of not yet weaponized states or, failing that, to reduce their ability to acquire nuclear and other WMD and long-range delivery systems. There were a variety of possible approaches to this second track of discouragement or prevention of buyers. One approach has already been mentioned: the multilateralization of regimes for the prevention of nuclear testing. A second option was counterproliferation, in both active and passive forms. Active counterproliferation might include military strikes against existing or developing nuclear weapons storage or production facilities. Active counterproliferation might also take the form of the threat of force, backed by the promise of economic aid if the state were willing to forego the option of nuclear deployment. A deal of this sort was cut with North Korea in 1994 under the so-called Framework Agreement. The Clinton administration used coercive diplomacy that combined tacit but strong threats of military intervention with reassurances that economic aid would be provided to reconstitute a non-weaponized North Korean nuclear power industry.

Passive counterproliferation on the other hand operates more through diplomatic maneuver than by means of overt military threat or coercive diplomacy. Passive counterproliferation on the part of the United States and others helped to change the intentions of some states aspiring to nuclear status, including Brazil, Argentina and South Africa. However, these cases of nuclear appetite, followed by ultimate nuclear indigestion, were more the result of regional or domestic political factors as opposed to international pressures. One cannot infer any necessary precedents from these cases about the willingness of other aspiring nuclear powers to stop short of fulfillment of their ambitions. (Chapter 8 provides additional discussion of the problem of nuclear proliferation.) The more probable prognosis is one of additional nuclear armed states with intense regional rivalries, with governments of uncertain accountability, and with officer corps as concerned about their domestic political status as they are about the nuances of nuclear command and control. When some of these regionally assertive states acquire both the nuclear fire and the means of long range delivery against targets of opportunity (as India and Pakistan have done, and as Iran is trying to do), then regional containment of proliferation may resemble the problem of bottling up the diplomatic crisis of July 1914.[2]

NOTES

1. See *Arms Control Today* (November 1999): 28.

2. For assessments of the relationship between deterrence and proliferation, see Stephen J. Cimbala, ed., *Deterrence and Nuclear Proliferation in the Twenty-First Century* (Westport, Conn.: Praeger Publishers, 2000). See also Paul Bracken, *Fire in the East: The Rise of Asian Military Power in the Second Nuclear Age* (New York: HarperCollins, 1999) and Colin S. Gray, *The Second Nuclear Age* (Boulder, Colo.: Lynne Rienner, 1999).

THE DEAD VOLCANO

Chapter 1

The Nuclear Revolution and American Military Strategy

INTRODUCTION

Detonation of the atomic bombs over Hiroshima and Nagasaki in 1945 announced to a stunned world the arrival of a new and frightening technology for mass destruction. No longer would it be necessary for states and their armed forces to first defeat the armed forces of their enemies before imposing unacceptable economic and human costs on enemy societies. As the numbers of nuclear weapons available to the Americans, the Soviets and others grew during the Cold War years, so too did the diversity of means for delivering these charges over intercontinental and shorter distances: missiles and bombers of various ranges and payloads. It became clear to U.S. and to allied NATO leaders, as well as to Soviet ones, that the price of shooting out differences of opinion over the status quo in Europe or other issues would be disproportionate to any anticipated political effects. Especially after the arrival of de facto nuclear-strategic parity between the United States and the Soviet Union in the latter 1960s, the resort by NATO or Russia to major war in Europe was checkmated by the possibility of escalation of any conventional war into something far worse.

In this chapter, I consider the problem of adjusting Cold War strategy, arms control and defense policy to the nuclear revolution, mainly from the U.S. or allied NATO standpoint. The next chapter covers the same ground from the Soviet perspective. The possibility of mass destruction in nuclear war imposed some discipline on the two Cold War "superpowers" insofar as the willingness to run risks in pursuit of unilateral advantage was concerned. Brinkmanship could only be pushed so far and, after the near-miss of the Cuban missile crisis, crisis avoidance was judged to be preferable to nuclear crisis management. A number of qualitative and quantitative arms control agreements were reached by the Americans and Soviets which showed that, despite differences in military-strategic thinking and in geopolitical objectives, the mutuality of shared nuclear danger was as transparent in Washington as in Moscow. U.S. and allied efforts to adjust to the reality of nuclear plenitude and to the future possibility of nuclear weapons spread left a legacy which is anticipated in this chapter, but given more direct consideration in a later chapter.

THE DEVELOPMENT OF NUCLEAR STRATEGY

It took at least a decade after Hiroshima before a consensus began to appear among U.S. political leaders and their military advisors that nuclear weapons, especially once they had been deployed in large numbers, had revolutionized traditional military strategy. The object of traditional military strategy had been the use of armed forces to obtain victory in combat. On the other hand, the "social contract" on which nuclear deterrence rests is based on the exchange of hostages. It is a relationship between states which is based on terror as a medium of exchange. The lives of innocents, and on an unprecedented scale, are placed at immediate risk should either side stray over the boundary between peace and war. If this hostage relationship is what makes nuclear deterrence as one form of military persuasion seem so horrible, it is also what makes nuclear weapons credible as instruments of coercion.

It seemed to some that nuclear weapons had severed the connection between war and politics.[1] The truth was more subtle: nuclear weapons had changed the grammar of the relationship between force and policy, but the relationship itself still had to hold good. For that to happen, political leaders and military planners had to learn the arts of coercive diplomacy and crisis management in addition to the pre-nuclear means of managing military forces for political influence. Now the ability to manipulate threats and to provide offsetting reassurances appropriate to the dispute in question, and with a nuclear backdrop, became a necessary component of leaders' political tool kits. The end of the Cold War and the rebirth of Russia cast further doubt on the political utility of nuclear force, and perhaps, on the threat of force. Without a global opponent and favoring regionally oriented military strategies, U.S. military planners are left in great uncertainty about the relevancy of nuclear weapons except as weapons of last resort.

Nuclear weapons appeared to reverse the traditional relationship between offensive and defensive military strategies, in which the making of attacks was thought to be more risk laden and problematical of success than the conduct of a successful defense. On the other hand, the speed and lethality of nuclear weapons made offensive technology look more imposing, but not necessarily an offensive *strategy*. Weapons which could be protected from a first strike could be used to execute a retaliation of unprecedented destructiveness against the attacker. Unless the attacker could obtain preclusive protection against retaliation from the victim, the difference between the attacker's and the defender's postwar worlds might be politically and militarily insignificant.

The paradoxical implications of nuclear weapons for military strategy, as noted above, led to military planning solutions that followed one of two paths. First, planners could put all their eggs in one basket, emphasizing the certainty of a massive retaliatory response for almost any aggression, including attacks using conventional forces only and those attacks launched against allies protected by a U.S. or Soviet nuclear umbrella. Second, and opposed to the first, planners could emphasize the use of nuclear retaliation in selective doses, including strikes by tactical and theater nuclear forces stationed outside their home territories and by specially tasked strategic nuclear forces aimed at targets in a particular theater of operations.

It turned out that massive retaliation and flexible nuclear response became sequentially preferred attempts by U.S. policy makers and planners to square the nuclear circle. Massive retaliation, as a one variant strategy, made less and less sense as the U.S. nuclear monopoly, and later relative superiority, were overturned by the Soviet attainment of nuclear parity. Massive retaliation faded from declaratory policy by the end of the 1950s and was eventually supplanted in the 1960s by the less hubristic "assured destruction" in declaratory, but not in operational, policy.[2] Massive retaliation and flexible response also had the vices of their virtues: inflexibility that might freeze leaders into inaction for all but the gravest provocations, in the first case, and seduction into what was expected to be a small war but turned out to be a larger one, in the second case. Accordingly, the Eisenhower administration by its second term had begun to recognize the virtues and vices of both massive and flexible nuclear retaliation, although it produced no actual war plans which placed serious constraints on the geographical scope or societal destructiveness of U.S. retaliatory attacks.[3]

Despite a considerable U.S. superiority in numbers of delivery vehicles and warheads during the latter 1950s and early 1960s, U.S. leaders expressed little confidence in the stability of nuclear deterrence and approached the idea of nuclear brinkmanship gingerly. During the Cuban missile crisis and despite a favorable ratio of approximately seventeen to one in deliverable nuclear weapons, President Kennedy pulled back from invasion of Cuba or the bombing of Soviet missile sites in Cuba, disregarding strong urgings from military and other advisors.[4] Concerned about the danger of escalation which might get out of control during the crisis, Kennedy and his advisors held back their conventional military sword in favor of coercive diplomacy.[5] Instead of seeking military victory below the nuclear threshold which the Soviets were powerless to prevent, Kennedy sought to give Khrushchev a face-saving exit from a preestablished path of mutual confrontation. U.S. nuclear options and war plans were relevant to management of the Cuban missile crisis not because they promised to provide victory at an acceptable cost, but because they created a zone of uncertainty through which Khrushchev and Kennedy were determined not to move.

Although the Kennedy administration would subsequently begin a process of refining U.S. nuclear war plans with the objective of creating a larger spectrum of military options, neither Kennedy nor his successors could escape the limits placed on strategy by the upper end of the ladder of escalation. Successors to Eisenhower were able to discard the rhetoric of massive retaliation but not the reality that any feasible plan for U.S.-Soviet nuclear war would of necessity involve massive nuclear responses and unacceptable collateral damage for both sides.[6] Additional refinements to those SIOPs subsequent to those of the Kennedy administration did not change this condition of nuclear rigidity. Accordingly, critics of U.S. nuclear strategy and of NATO nuclear dependency for the deterrence of war in Europe fought a rearguard action to establish credible options short of massive nuclear response, from the 1950s through the 1980s.

The U.S. strategy of massive retaliation invited dissatisfied analysts and policy makers to borrow from pre-nuclear thinking and from disciplines other than military history and political science. During the "golden age" of U.S. strategic nuclear theorizing (from the latter 1940s through the middle 1960s) operations researchers, social psychologists and economists contributed important new insights to the field of U.S. military strategy.[7] Although these insights revolutionized the way in which the field was conceptualized in academic studies, they provided no consolation to policy makers and planners who sought to overcome obstinate nuclear technology that stood in the way of proportionality and discriminate uses of force. Not only technology stood in the way of nuclear proportionality as a pathway to the reestablishment of the connection between war and politics. Politics were even more important; ends became as controversial as means became unyielding. NATO members other than the Americans were never completely sold on the advantages of nuclear flexibility, and in Paris leaders opted for nuclear unilateralism as a guarantee that French national interests would not be hostage to graduated deterrence.[8]

It soon became apparent that the case for flexible nuclear response would be politically controversial in the U.S. policy debate and among

NATO allies. Once former Secretary of Defense Robert S. McNamara had abandoned counterforce and damage-limiting strategies in favor of a declaratory emphasis on assured destruction, traditional military strategy seemed to have been sold out in favor of nuclear stalemate. McNamara argued that assured destruction described a condition as much as it summarized a preferred policy, although assured destruction was also appealing to him as a metric for establishing minimum force sizes against the more ambitious demands of military services.[9] A classical strategy, for the credible use of nuclear offenses and anti-nuclear defenses for victory, was judged by McNamara as both unattainable and undesirable.

Growth in U.S. and Soviet strategic nuclear forces during the 1960s, and McNamara's persistent advocacy in U.S. and alliance policy debates, drove out of the realm of political feasibility a damage-limiting strategy based on offensive force modernization combined with ballistic missile defenses. By the early 1970s, as the conclusion of the SALT I treaty demonstrated, the Soviet leadership as well as the American had accepted the anti-classical logic that mutual deterrence could be based on offensive retaliation combined with limited defenses incapable of nationwide protection.[10] The acceptance by both nuclear superpowers of this condition increased the difficulty of U.S. officials in selling nuclear flexibility to a justifiably skeptical European audience.[11] (See Appendix 1.1 at the end of this chapter for a summary of major developments in U.S. ballistic missile defense research, development and deployment through 1990.)

If SALT codified the death of any feasible search for classical strategy by means of defenses and offenses combined, there was still the possibility that additional military feasibility could be introduced into nuclear strategy by tinkering with offenses alone. The policy innovations from 1974 through the present in U.S. doctrinal guidance for strategic target planning were based on this search for an exit from the apolitical strategic impasse of assured retaliation, judged by the standards of classical strategy. Advocates of flexible nuclear response, from the 1950s through the 1980s, argued from basic premises which constituted modified versions of pre-nuclear thinking applied to nuclear strategy.[12] The term "neoclassical" is more appropriate for these modifications of classical strategy for victory because they acknowledged the futility of traditional war-winning strategies applied to a situation of mutual deterrence. Instead, the neoclassicists attempted to modify assured destruction at the edges by adapting offensive forces to the exigencies of bargaining and coercive diplomacy. Neoclassical reasoning combined psychological arguments about the influence of perceptions on deterrence or escalation control with traditional aspirations for military superiority or favorable outcomes in war. (Table 1.1 summarizes the variations of neoclassicism.)

The neoclassical arguments for nuclear flexibility had two principal variations. The first variation was that, while U.S. officials actually rec-

Table 1.1
Varieties of U.S. Nuclear Strategy

I. Assured Destruction/Assured Retaliation
II. Neoclassicism (nuclear flexibility)
    A. Perceptions of Russian strategy
    B. Intrawar deterrence
        1. Escalation dominance
        2. Manipulation of risk

Source: Author, based on various works by Colin S. Gray, Robert Jervis, George H. Quester and Thomas C. Schelling. See, in particular: Gray, *The Second Nuclear Age* (Boulder, Colo.: Lynne Rienner, 1999); Jervis, *The Meaning of the Nuclear Revolution* (Ithaca, N.Y.: Cornell University Press, 1989); Quester, *The Future of Nuclear Deterrence* (Lexington, Mass.: D.C. Heath and Co., 1986); and Schelling, *Arms and Influence* (New Haven, Conn.: Yale University Press, 1986).

ognized that nuclear war was politically pointless and that nuclear flexibility was of little or no value, for deterrence to work Soviet leaders must also believe those things. It was argued that the Soviet leadership did not share these convictions about the absurdity of nuclear war or about the disvalue of selective nuclear options. Therefore, it followed that the ability to deter a massive Soviet attack against North America did not necessarily deter a lesser provocation, such as an attack on Europe or selective strikes against U.S. territory.[13] Psychologist Steven Kull has referred to arguments of this type as "greater fool" arguments: U.S. officials acknowledged the futility of nuclear flexibility, but suggested that the possibility of Soviet belief in nuclear flexibility required equivalent U.S. preparedness for similar options.[14]

The second version of neoclassical nuclear flexibility called for the United States to improve its offensive forces in order to deter escalation to advantage by the opponent, i.e., for intrawar deterrence. Although unprecedented societal destruction could not be avoided in nuclear war, there were, in this view, meaningful distinctions among postwar outcomes, including postwar states of affairs which could be characterized as victory or defeat. The second version of nuclear flexibility sought counterforce capabilities, but not in numbers or in quality sufficient to make possible a credible first strike against Soviet forces. Counterforce capabilities were useful as part of a strategy of bargaining and coercion during war.[15] Two rationales were advanced for improved counterforce on behalf of intrawar deterrence in this variant of neoclassicism: escalation dominance and risk manipulation.

Escalation dominance means that one side can establish through favorable exchange ratios, in one or more components of post-attack nuclear forces, a position so superior that the other side is forced to yield to its demands.[16] Escalation dominance is a form of limited nuclear re-taliation or warfare. The ability to prevail in a nuclear endurance contest below the level of all-out war is a necessary condition for influencing the wartime behavior of the opponent.[17] In contrast, the manipulation of risk approach does not depend on the ability to prevail at any level of actual nuclear exchange. Manipulation of risk gets both contestants into a com-petition in brinkmanship and nerves.[18] The purpose of higher levels of destruction is not to impress the opponent with the damage already done, but with the possibility of unlimited and uncontrollable escalation which might follow.

Whereas escalation dominance was more relevant in the case of a war which was begun by means of deliberate attack, the other variation was more appropriate for nuclear wars which resulted from accidents or from inadvertent escalation.[19] The escalation dominance approach presup-posed that rational actors would continue their utility-maximizing cal-culations after nuclear war had already begun. Manipulation of risk approaches were based on a more skeptical appreciation of rationality in the actual conduct of nuclear war. Manipulation of risk actually de-pended upon a "threat that leaves something to chance," as Thomas Schelling explained it.[20] A process of nuclear brinkmanship or a two-way competition in risk taking left open the possibility that both sides would lose control over events, thereby suffering greater than expected or greater than acceptable losses. The possibility of losing control over events was the element which created the shared interest in restraining the level of violence and in moderating political objectives.

Arguments for flexible nuclear response were stigmatized by their use in the U.S. policy process as ingredients in force-building rationales. In addition, the Soviets showed little apparent interest in flexible nuclear response as a means of bargaining, especially in the case of strategic nuclear weapons exploded on Soviet territory. Nevertheless, the con-struction of a Soviet adversary determined to exploit any relative coun-terforce imbalance was all too often perceived by policy makers as a necessary part of the case for counterforce and nuclear flexibility.[21] While Soviet military doctrine in its politico-military aspects (grand strategy) remained essentially defensive and potentially open to the concept of limitation in war, the military-technical level of Soviet military doctrine offered little in the way of encouragement to those U.S. scholars who sought to find Politburo or General Staff interest in limited nuclear war or controlled nuclear exchanges.[22]

NUCLEAR WEAPONS AND THE COLD WAR

The Cold War is now seen by many, combining hindsight with nos-talgia, as a period of political peace and military tranquility. The rela-tionship between nuclear weapons and the long peace from 1945 to 1990 was a peculiar one. Nuclear weapons were not incorporated into a traditional military strategy for attaining victory at an acceptable cost. Instead, they were part of an experiment in applied psychology in which the leaders of states, the designers of weapons and the operators of forces and command systems played roles knowingly and unknowingly. The experiment did not really work as intended, but war was avoided anyway. The avoidance of war was overdetermined by other forces between 1945 and 1990, so that nuclear deterrence, dangerous as it was, left the relationship between the United States and the Soviet Union more or less as it would have been without those weapons.

Subsequent to the Cuban missile crisis of October 1962, U.S. and Soviet leaders perceived a mutual interest in strategic arms limitation, in the avoidance of accidental or inadvertent nuclear war, and in preventing the spread of nuclear weapons. Agreements concluded during the 1960s included the Nuclear Test Ban Treaty of 1963 and the "Hot Line" (Direct Communications Link) for emergency discussions between heads of state. Discussions between Moscow and Washington about strategic arms limitation got under way during the latter years of the Johnson administration, continued under Nixon and culminated in the SALT I (Strategic Arms Limitation Talks) agreement of 1972. SALT I provided for (1) a treaty of indefinite duration limiting each side's anti-ballistic missile defense systems (the ABM Treaty) and (2) a five-year interim agreement placing ceilings on the numbers of land- and sea-based (submarine-launched) missile launchers (ICBMs and SLBMs respectively) of the two sides. SALT I was a significant diplomatic as well as military milestone. It codified military-strategic parity between the Soviet Union and the United States and supported Soviet diplomatic efforts to obtain U.S. and allied NATO acceptance of the political status quo in Europe. Washington and Moscow also concluded in 1971 two agreements on the prevention of accidental/inadvertent war and the avoidance of unnecessary fears of surprise attack.[23]

The interim agreement on offensive arms limitation embodied in SALT I was superseded by SALT II, signed in 1979 and carried forward (although never formally ratified by the United States) until it was transformed into START (Strategic Arms Reduction Talks) during the Reagan administration. The ABM Treaty remained as the cornerstone of U.S.-Soviet strategic arms limitation until the end of the Cold War. As amended by a 1974 protocol signed at Vladivostok, it limited both sides' national missile defense systems to one site of no more than 100 defensive interceptors. The United States chose to deploy its ABMs at Grand Forks, North Dakota, and the Soviets around Moscow. (The U.S. system was eventually closed down by Congress in the mid-1970s.) The ABM Treaty became a powerful symbol of affinity for the advocates of mutual deterrence based on offensive retaliation. When the Reagan administration proposed its Strategic Defense Initiative (SDI) in 1983, opponents of the deployment argued that it would overturn the ABM Treaty of 1972 and reopen the race in offensive weapons hitherto capped by the SALT/START process. Even after the Cold War, the U.S. and Russian efforts to arrive at an agreed definition of an acceptable threshold between permitted "theater" ballistic missile defenses for overseas forces and allies, versus impermissible "strategic" ballistic missile defenses of their respective state territories, were based on awareness of the diplomatic fallout of any attempt to circumvent the ABM Treaty.

Even more shock resistant than the ABM Treaty was the Nuclear Nonproliferation Treaty (NPT) ratified in 1970 and supported by both the United States and the Soviet Union. The agreement was intended to prevent the spread of nuclear weapons or weapons-related technology from the nuclear "haves" to the "have nots." Non-nuclear states were offered the promise of support for verifiably peaceful uses of nuclear energy, under an inspection regime conducted by the IAEA (International Atomic Energy Agency, an affiliate of the UN). The ABM Treaty surprised its parents by living to the end of the Cold War (after which its political, if not military, relevancy came into question). The NPT not only outlasted the Cold War but has become even more relevant since. The NPT was extended indefinitely in 1995 by near unanimity, with the important demurrals of India, Pakistan and Israel. The favorable climate established by the NPT extension carried forward into the 1996 multilateral agreement on a comprehensive test ban (CTB) on nuclear weapons testing, extending and deepening the impact of the original Test Ban Treaty and the subsequent Threshold Test Ban and Peaceful Nuclear Explosions (TTB and PNE, respectively) treaties.

Not all U.S. or Soviet governments gave equal emphasis to arms control, but despite fluctuations in attention span, enduring benefits matured. First, continuing arms control negotiations educated both sides during the Cold War about one another's strategic and defense cultures. Second, the strategic arms limitation agreements of the 1970s and 1980s (SALT/START) did provide a framework that allowed both sides to avoid expensive deployments of systems that would have been militarily superfluous, or eventually obsolete in the face of improved technology. Third, cooperation between Washington and Moscow to limit the spread of nuclear weapons technology helped to limit the number of nuclear aspiring states during the Cold War and set a useful precedent for multilateral cooperation against proliferation after the Cold War. This U.S.-Russian post–Cold War cooperation against nuclear weapons spread included the Cooperative Threat Reduction (CTR) authorized by the U.S. Congress in 1991 to encourage denuclearization and demilitarization within the states of the former Soviet Union, especially within the four successor states (Russia, Belarus, Kazakhstan and Ukraine) that inherited the former Soviet nuclear arsenal.[24]

Efforts to limit the significance of nuclear weapons during the Cold War were complicated by the role of nuclear weapons in U.S. and allied NATO strategy for the prevention of war in Europe and for the establishment of a credible defense plan if deterrence failed. Some U.S. and European analysts and policy makers doubted that conventional deterrence was feasible; others feared that it might be. Those who doubted that conventional deterrence was feasible tended to see a viable Soviet threat of invasion, absent NATO military overinsurance. Those who feared that conventional defense was feasible noted that a conventional war in Europe would involve very different sacrifices for Americans and Europeans. A conventional deterrent for NATO might not be as convincing as a conventional defense, backed by nuclear deterrence. Lawrence Freedman explained the painful dilemma with which NATO policy makers were faced, even if they were inclined to credit conventional defenses with more credibility than official NATO doctrine acknowledged:

Whereas the threat of nuclear war would make the risks of war too great, if the threat was only of conventional war the risks might be tolerable. Thus the problem with a nuclear strategy was that it was hard to demonstrate why the U.S., as the only power which could implement such a strategy, should be willing to risk nuclear war in the event of a conventional invasion of Europe: the problem with a conventional strategy was that it was hard to demonstrate why the Russians would be deterred.[25]

The Soviet Union might easily have been deterred by the prospect that even victory in a short conventional war in Europe, however victory might have been defined in Moscow, could not have been sustained. In a protracted non-nuclear conflict between East and West, the likelihood for most of the Cold War was that the United States and its allies would have defeated the Soviet Union and its allies.[26] The United States and its allies in Europe and Japan marshaled economic and industrial power far superior to that of the Soviet Union and probable wartime allies. Stalin, whose brutal terror industrialized the Soviet Union between the world wars, knew as well as anyone the significance of comparative industrial and technological power. In addition, in a protracted war the maritime superiority of the United States and its NATO allies would have forced upon the Soviet Union a Hobson's Peace in Western Europe, even assuming the most favorable wartime cooperation of the Soviet Union's East European "allies."

NATO's willingness to settle for an active duty deployment in Western Europe of about 30 ground forces divisions was not forced by the economics of defense, as some politicians contended. NATO could have created conventional forces capable of credible deterrence against massive and protracted, as well as limited and short, Soviet conventional probes. The point was proved to reluctant Europeans by McNamara's "whiz kids" when the latter recalculated the relative strength of Soviet and U.S. (plus allied NATO) divisions in the 1960s. Taking into account the different organizations of the U.S. and Soviet forces, Pentagon analysts recalculated the relationship between Soviet and NATO force sizes, firepower indices and other attributes related to probable performance in war. By 1965, McNamara's staff felt they had convincing evidence that a Soviet division force cost about a third of the cost of a U.S. division force, that the Soviet force had about one-third as many personnel, and that the Soviet force was about one-third as effective as the U.S. division force (U.S. division forces were larger and in the early 1960s included a great deal of division force combat power outside the division itself, compared to Soviet forces).[27] As Adam Ulam has argued, NATO's psychology of conventional inferiority was based on the circumstances of its origin in 1949:

There was no reason why the assumption of NATO's conventional arms inferiority, reasonable in 1949, should still have persisted in 1965. It was then fully within the capabilities of America's European allies more than to match the Warsaw Pact's forces; yet they continued to profess (though ever less confidently) their reliance on the U.S.'s now increasingly porous nuclear umbrella to save them both from the Russians and from having to spend more on defense.[28]

These calculations did not prove that NATO's then available conventional forces were adequate deterrents against truly desperate Soviets, nor were they insurmountable conventional defenses against all of NATO's political and military vulnerabilities. The calculations did show that NATO's deployed forces were sufficient to deny the Soviets victory in a short war without running an unacceptable risk of protracted military stalemate, or nuclear escalation. Nuclear weapons added a component of uncertainty and risk to Soviet calculations, but they were as much a curse as a blessing for any NATO approximation of rational strategy. As the numbers of nuclear weapons deployed with tactical air and ground forces multiplied, the problem of command and control, including NATO nuclear release, became more intimidating. NATO's apparently hodgepodge theater nuclear force structure was not entirely coincidental: it was not designed to fight efficiently a sub-strategic war in Europe prior to, or in lieu of, a larger war including attacks on American and Soviet homelands. Instead, NATO's nuclear command system was *intended*, and made quite obvious to the Soviets, as a waltz toward Armageddon:

The NATO strategy of relying on nuclear weapons is politically and militarily credible because the governing command structure is so unstable and accident-prone that national leaders would exercise little practical control over it in wartime. What other command mechanism could possibly be built to invoke a nuclear conflict that, for all practical purposes, is tantamount to a regional doomsday machine?[29]

Professor Bracken may be charged with overstatement in a good cause: the alliance nuclear command and control system was not *intended* to fall apart on the night. But pessimism about its resilience in the face of all but token nuclear strikes was prudent, and the situation was not strategically foreordained. A nuclear dependency was not forced on NATO by its inability to spend money for ground divisions or tactical air wings compared to the Warsaw Pact. NATO was unwilling, not unable, to do so.

The second argument for NATO's nuclear dependency pivoted on the exposed position of West Germany, and especially of West Berlin, as a symbol of Western anti-communist resistance to Soviet communism. The United States and its NATO allies arguably could not have defended West Germany, and definitely not West Berlin, with conventional forces under any set of assumptions. Berlin could not be defended by conventional forces, but Soviet pressure against Berlin might be mitigated by nuclear coercion.[30] And the Germans' insistence that NATO corps be deployed close to the inter-German border in a "forward defense" posture meant that any Soviet penetration of about 100 km or more into the FRG would have unhinged NATO's short war conventional defense plan. Germans rejected a rearward-leaning instead of a forward-leaning strategy for political reasons, and the French left NATO's military command structure in 1966 for their own political reasons. The result of German enthusiasm and French abstinence was that neither the head nor the tail of NATO's conventional defenses could be fitted into a plan for victory in a short war without nuclear escalation.

In sum, the Cold War experience with nuclear weapons taught that, at least with regard to conflicts among major powers, nuclear weapons were unlikely to redeem a failed or implausible defense strategy. Fortunately for posterity, the Soviet Union from 1945 to 1990 had no plausible attack strategy against Western Europe at an acceptable cost to Moscow's political or military leadership. If nuclear weapons could not serve as war winners or war stoppers, could they perhaps be war preventers?

CRISIS MANAGEMENT AND NUCLEAR WEAPONS

Crisis management prior to the nuclear age was less important to planners and to policy makers than military preparedness for actual war fighting.[31] It was assumed that preparedness for actual combat was the best deterrent. Admittedly this assumption was not always correct: some historians thought that the July crisis of 1914 had ended in a war because the war preparations of the various sides stimulated countervailing preparations by their enemies. A conflict spriral of increasing tensions and suspicions had resulted in an August 1914 outbreak of war which none of the sides really wanted, according to this argument. Whether World War I is an exception to the general rule, or whether historians have misread it as an example of failed crisis management, it remains the case that before nuclear weapons, crisis management was less important because the costs of war were not obviously catastrophic for all concerned.[32] Nuclear weapons changed that calculus, and changed it forever. Now even small military exchanges by forces holding these powerful weapons could inflict historically unprecedented damage on their enemies, and nuclear weapons made it obvious to even the most obtuse leaders that this was so.

The choices facing crisis-ridden political leaders and military planners are usually an array of bad and worse options. The point of no return may not have been passed and the crisis may still be resolved short of war. A crisis resolved short of war is going to be resolved in favor of one side or the other, so the outcome from a political standpoint is not one which distributes post-crisis rewards and punishments equally. For example, the Cuban missile crisis of 1962 was resolved because Soviet Premier Khrushchev realized that his Cuba missile ploy had overextended his strategic reach. He backed off after having been reassured against further U.S. escalation of the crisis once Kennedy had received a guarantee that Soviet missiles would be removed from Cuban soil.[33]

Because the outcomes of crises can distribute benefits unequally, it follows that leaders may prefer a larger risk of war, by means of continued crisis, to a peaceful settlement.[34] Leaders can always persuade themselves that one additional demarche or a little more arm twisting can bring the opponent around without actually stepping over the brink that separates coercion from violence. Leaders might mistakenly infer, for example, that the other side, lacking in military power compared to its opponent, would not dare to start a war. Therefore, the other side must back down. During the Cold War as well as prior to it there were important examples of states without nuclear forces which were willing to attack a nuclear-armed state or to threaten its vital interests. Egyptian leader Anwar Sadat, as a case in point, launched his attack against Israel in 1973 despite the near certainty that Israel already had nuclear weapons and the certainty that Egypt and its allies did not.

An article of faith by some policy makers during the Cold War, for example the influential U.S. former Secretary of Defense Robert S. McNamara, was that strategic nuclear weapons served only to deter one nuclear-armed state from attacking another. They served no other useful purpose; in other words, they were irrelevant to the deterrence of conventional war.[35] McNamara meant to say that the threat of escalation from conventional to nuclear war could not be manipulated *deliberately* by the Soviet Union against the United States, or vice versa, because either side could absorb a first strike and still deliver an unacceptable retaliatory strike against the other. But the danger of Cold War confrontation was not only deliberate, but also *inadvertent*, escalation. Both sides might get into a process of bargaining in which the stakes were not entirely clear. One or both sides might not fully understand the military operational details of nuclear alerts, thereby sending signals not intended and generating a process of escalation over which they ultimately lost control. Political leaders and some theorists dismissed this possibility of inadvertent war during the nuclear age because they thought of war as an *outcome* and not as a *process*. An outcome is something concrete that has a clear "before" and "after"; a process is a continuous sliding scale which allows for a mountain climber to gradually fall down a cliff, only recognizing his peril when he hits bottom.

The pernicious interaction of mobilization systems which contributed to the outbreak of World War I was not intended by the leaders of that time. But the crisis management of the Cold War years probably depended, and subsequent nuclear crisis management might very well depend, on leaders' expectations that a deliberately created risk of loss of control over escalation would save the peace. The logic of deliberately created loss of control is thought by strategists to work by frightening one or both sides into some bargain as an outcome preferred to uncontrolled escalation. If uncontrolled escalation is uppermost in the minds of national leaders at a time of crisis, it may turn out that the avoidance of uncontrolled escalation is a priority of such magnitude that further coercion of the other side is forestalled. However, there is nothing to guarantee that forbearance will appeal to leaders because nothing guarantees that fear of uncontrolled escalation will be sufficiently daunting to them.

If leaders in a crisis between nuclear armed states fear uncontrolled escalation more than they desire expected values which can be obtained through additional nuclear blackmail, then they have stronger incentives to end the crisis than to continue it. On the other hand, if continued use of nuclear blackmail seems to be paying dividends and is expected to cause the opponent to yield, then the priority attached to the avoidance of uncontrolled escalation is diminished. Further, nuclear blackmail comes in more than one variety. There is the nuclear blackmail which is intended by the blackmailer, and a nuclear blackmail which grows out of the crisis bargaining between two sides.[36] Even if neither side makes explicit threats of nuclear first use or of nuclear escalation, the presence of nuclear weapons in their arsenals creates an existential risk of wider and more destructive conflict. Both the existential and the deliberate forms of nuclear blackmail were present in the Cuban missile crisis, and both were recognized by Soviet and American leaderships for what they were.

In October 1962, Khrushchev, for example, was able to distinguish between the risk of deploying nuclear weapons covertly and without their having been discovered by the Americans before they were launch ready, versus the discovery of those same weapons in the midst of assembly and preparation. Faced unexpectedly with U.S. premature discovery of his missile ploy, the Soviet leader about-faced and declared that he and President Kennedy should not "tie the knot of war" too tightly lest it become impossible for them to disentangle. Khrushchev was able to communicate this concern to Kennedy, and it was shared by the U.S. president and his advisors.[37] They discovered during the crisis that some of their expectations about how military forces were operated during crisis were mismatched with the actual conditions of those operations. It is not that U.S. military commanders were insubordinate during the crisis; they were not. It is an unavoidable fact that military commanders and policy makers are looking at a crisis from different perspectives and with competing priorities. Policy makers want to avoid inadvertent escalation or war without sacrificing important national values. Military commanders know that they will be held accountable for a surprise strike which catches their forces unprepared, or for failure to carry out efficiently authorized presidential commands.

Khrushchev and Kennedy were able to distinguish in 1962 between controllable and uncontrollable risks because they were aided by advisors trained in the operation of mature command and control systems, and because in neither country was the legitimacy of the ruling political order at risk. Relax either condition—either the maturity of the command and control system or the undoubted legitimacy of the political order—and a crisis, especially a crisis between nuclear powers, becomes much more dangerous. In fact, during the Cuban missile crisis, the transmission of two letters from Khrushchev with conflicting terms for settlement of the crisis almost caused some members of Kennedy's ExComm (Executive Committee of the National Security Council, the president's key crisis advisory group) to conclude that Khrushchev had in fact been the victim of a coup.

For example, in a future crisis between Pakistan and India, or between Israel and a nuclear armed Arab state, neither the stability of the existing political order nor the maturity of its nuclear command and control system could be taken for granted. This is *not* a statement that Third World states are in any fundamental sense less mature politically, socially or culturally than U.S. and Soviet Cold War states were. The comparison is more specific. The Americans and Soviets learned through trial and error how to build into nuclear warning and intelligence systems checks and balances against prompt launch based on mistaken indicators. They also learned how to compensate for the interaction of the two sides' warning and intelligence systems with one another during a crisis. For example, during the Cuban missile crisis the Soviets may have deliberately avoided placing their strategic nuclear forces at higher than normal states of launch readiness.[38] They also avoided dangerous confrontation tactics at sea of the kind which American and Soviet captains frequently engaged in during peacetime maneuvers. Finally, Kennedy and Khrushchev engaged in reciprocal exchanges of reassurance, from head of state to head of state, about the intention of each to resolve the crisis short of war. Had the same crisis happened between the Americans and the Soviets during the early 1950s with their comparatively primitive command and control systems in place, and with leaders probably less insistent upon reassurance than upon brinkmanship, a different outcome might have resulted.

Gordon Craig and Alexander George note that, for coercive diplomacy to succeed, certain conditions must be met. Three conditions are of special significance: the coercer must create a sense of urgency about compliance with its demand in the mind of its opponent; second, the threatener must be perceived by the threatened or coerced party as being more highly motivated to fulfill its goals; and, third, in the mind of the coerced or threatened party a fear of "unacceptable escalation" must exist.[39] The point about unacceptable escalation might seem to support the argument that nuclear weapons are ideal for coercion, and some policy makers, including Khrushchev from the onset of his first Berlin ultimatum until the Cuban missile crisis of 1962, acted as if nuclears were coercive trumps. However, as George has emphasized, coercive diplomacy is essentially a defensive, not an offensive strategy for crisis management. Coercive diplomacy has one of three objects: (1) to persuade an opponent to *stop* an encroachment already begun, (2) to convince an opponent to *undo* an action previously taken or under way and (3) to obtain a change in the opponent's *government or regime* favorable to a desired change in his behavior.[40]

Barry M. Blechman and Stephen S. Kaplan studied the U.S. use of military force to support political objectives from 1946 through 1975.[41] The deployment of many U.S. nuclear weapons with general purpose forces makes it possible that any movement of forces possessing nuclear weapons might send an inadvertent nuclear message. A stricter criterion for isolating cases of intended nuclear signal, adopted by Blechman and Kaplan, was to select cases in which a force that had a designed role in U.S. strategic nuclear war plans was employed to send a political signal.

Table 1.2

Involvement of U.S. Strategic Nuclear Forces in Conveying Political Signals, 1946–1975

Incident	Date
U.S. aircraft shot down by Yugoslavia	November 1946
Inauguration of president in Uruguay	February 1947
Security of Berlin	January 1948
Security of Berlin	April 1948
Security of Berlin	June 1948
Korean War: Security of Europe	July 1950
Security of Japan/South Korea	August 1953
Guatemala accepts Soviet bloc support	May 1954
China-Taiwan conflict: Tachen Islands	August 1954
Suez crisis	October 1956
Political crisis in Lebanon	July 1958
Political crisis in Jordan	July 1958
China-Taiwan conflict: Quemoy and Matsu	July 1958
Security of Berlin	May 1959
Security of Berlin	June 1961
Soviet placement of missiles in Cuba	October 1962
Withdrawal of U.S. missiles, Turkey	April 1963
Pueblo seized by North Korea	January 1968
Arab-Israeli war	October 1973

Source: Barry M. Blechman and Stephen S. Kaplan, *Force without War: U.S. Armed Forces as a Political Instrument* (Washington, D.C.: Brookings Institution, 1976), p. 48.

They tabulated 19 incidents which met this standard, as listed in Table 1.2.

Several conclusions follow from this table. Nuclear threats were used sparingly, and their use was much more common during the early Cold War when U.S. nuclear superiority or relative advantage over the Soviet Union was assumed by policy makers.[42] About one-half of the incidents took place during the first third, or ten years, of the period 1946–1975; three-fourths of the episodes occurred during the first half, or 15 years, covered.[43] These cases refer only to discrete movement of forces which are included in strategic nuclear war plans: other kinds of support provided by presence, military aid or other means were not tabulated in the study. Nevertheless, the Blechman-Kaplan data demonstrate that the apparent U.S. appetite for nuclear coercion diminished, instead of intensifying, as the Cold War lengthened. After the Cuban missile crisis of 1962 was resolved without war, incidents virtually fall off the chart (two incidents in the last ten years from 1965–1975).[44]

Deterrence theory is basically a theory of opportunity: states jump through windows of opportunity to gain some territorial or other prize at the expense of an adversary whose commitment or resolve to defend that commitment seemed weak.[45] It may be equally useful to assume that initiators of crises are motivated by perceived domestic policy needs or strategic vulnerabilities. As Richard Ned Lebow and Janice Gross Stein have argued, when leaders become desperate "they may resort to force even though the military balance is unfavorable and there are no grounds for doubting adversarial resolve."[46] The possibility that leaders may be moved by fear and perceived vulnerability as much as they are moved by perceived opportunity adds an entire dimension to the analysis of deterrence, especially deterrence based on the threat of nuclear escalation.

Leaders driven by need toward objectives which may involve them in war against other states may rationalize away a military imbalance unfavorable to them and favorable to their opponents. This ability of need-driven leaders to rationalize away unfavorable military balances is all the more likely with nuclear weapons, since so few weapons convey so much striking power. The perceived vulnerability of a state's crisis predicament can also be made more acute by nuclear than by conventional threats, motivating the defender to engage in preemption. The problem with nuclear crisis bargaining is not only that the effects of nuclear weapons defy meaningful limitation, but also that the implications of firmness or irresolution for the bargaining process and its outcomes are not entirely clear to the participants.[47]

NUCLEAR PROLIFERATION

A later chapter deals with nuclear proliferation in more detail. The present discussion highlights some aspects of the problem relative to the development of American Cold War strategy and arms control and to ideas and problems carried forward into the post–Cold War world.

The Cold War nuclear powers saw themselves as members of an exclusive club. The Big Five acknowledged nuclear powers (United States, Soviet Union, Britain, France and China) sought to keep club membership small on the grounds that nuclear weapons spread was certain to increase international instability. However, what was to be denied to the ganders was still appropriate for the geese: there was no serious thought to nuclear disarmament among the "haves." The end of Cold War increased the pressure on the nuclear weapons states to limit their own arsenals in the interest, not only of detente, but also of nonproliferation.

The U.S. arms control community was gratified by indefinite extension of the NPT in 1995 and by the approval of a text and release for signature of CTB in 1996. In January 1993, Presidents George H.W. Bush and Boris Yeltsin signed the START II strategic arms reduction agreement. If fully implemented as scheduled by 2007, it would have reduced U.S. and Russian force sizes to 3,000–3,500 warheads each. But START II will never be implemented, for various reasons. U.S. and Soviet/Russian reductions in strategic nuclear forces from the end of the Cold War to 1996 levels are summarized in Table 1.3.

Despite this progress in limiting "vertical" proliferation of American and Russian arsenals, a more dangerous quality is built into the less predictable world of the early twenty-first century. New nuclear armed states (India and Pakistan joined the club of declared nuclear states in 1998) and a variety of regimes aspiring to nuclear status (Iran, North Korea, Iraq) were locked into bitter regional rivalries or held anti-systemic grievances against the prevailing international order. Briefers of new nuclear powers may be able to persuade their leaders, especially leaders intent upon the coercion of a non-nuclear state, that there are winnable and fightable nuclear wars. Regional antagonists who no longer fear American or Russian intervention in theater war might square off until one side reaches for nuclear trumps.

Even if actual nuclear use is avoided, another danger is the use of nuclear threats to intimidate the leaders of states lacking a nuclear arsenal: a few nuclear weapons will look formidable to a non-nuclear state, even if the latter has sufficient forces to prevail in a conventional war.[48] For example, one study of nuclear proliferation concluded that Iran's leadership had made a decision to develop nuclear weapons. According to the study, this decision by Iran will put pressure on Syria, Iraq and Saudi Arabia to create their own nuclear forces; otherwise, those states "would be in a profoundly disadvantageous position in a confrontation with a nuclear armed Iran."[49] Even among new nuclear states thought to have secure second-strike capabilities, deterrence is not necessarily stable: misperception of enemy willingness to carry out retaliatory threats, or of enemy capability to do so, has many historical precedents. As Louis Rene Beres warns:

Even if all of the new nuclear powers were actually able to maintain secure nuclear retaliatory forces, prospective aggressors might, through errors of information, still perceive insecurity. Here, nuclear deterrence could fail in spite of the fact that each nuclear power had "succeeded" in protecting its nuclear retaliatory forces.[50]

The evidence is abundant that even leaders of mature democratic states react to crisis by selecting among a few broad policy options that

Table 1.3
U.S. and Soviet/Russian Strategic Nuclear Forces, 1989–1996

United States

Year	ICBM Launchers	ICBM Warheads	SLBM Launchers	SLBM Warheads	Air Launchers	Air Warheads	Total Launchers	Total Warheads
1989	1,000	2,440	592	5,152	311	5,158	1,903	12,750
1990	1,000	2,440	608	5,216	267	4,648	1,875	12,304
1991	550	2,000	480	3,456	209	3,844	1,239	9,300
1992	550	2,000	488	3,456	158	2,824	1,196	8,280
1993	550	2,000	336	2,688	159	2,840	1,045	7,528
1994	580	2,090	360	2,880	157	2,808	1,097	7,778
1995	575	2,075	384	3,072	122	2,176	1,081	7,323
1996	575	2,075	408	3,264	102	1,808	1,085	7,147

Soviet Union/Russia

Year	ICBM Launchers	ICBM Warheads	SLBM Launchers	SLBM Warheads	Air Launchers	Air Warheads	Total Launchers	Total Warheads
1989	1,378	7,030	949	2,938	161	1,572	2,488	11,540
1990	1,378	6,938	908	2,900	128	1,414	2,414	11,252
1991	1,006	6,106	832	2,792	100	1,266	1,938	10,164
1992	950	5,725	628	2,492	112	1,392	1,690	9,609
1993	898	5,156	520	2,384	113	1,398	1,531	8,938
1994	818	4,314	456	2,320	113	1,398	1,387	8,032
1995	771	3,709	440	2,272	113	1,398	1,324	7,379
1996	755	3,589	440	2,272	113	1,398	1,308	7,259

Source: Natural Resources Defense Council, *NRDC Online*, 1997.

leave open many important details. The perceived threat of an actual attack would not permit more than hastily assembled advisors, broadly packaged options and preliminary data analysis even in the case of the highly developed U.S. apparatus for crisis management. How much less likely is it that a politically unaccountable regime with an untested command and control system could distinguish reliably between valid and false crisis warning, or between deterrence and reassurance signaling offered by the opposing side? As Alexander L. George has noted, at the onset of a crisis a number of complex standing orders come into effect throughout the military chain of command. Lacking detailed knowledge of these standing orders and of the rationales for them, political leaders may "fail to coordinate some critically important standing orders with their overall crisis management strategy."[51] An historical example is provided by the efforts of Russian Foreign Minister Sazonov in the July crisis of 1914 to improvise a plan for partial mobilization only against Austria, as opposed to total mobilization against both Austria and Germany. The Russian General Staff regarded any planning for partial mobilization only as disruptive of the efficiency of general mobilization, and, therefore, no serious planning for partial mobilization had taken place.[52]

There are at least two different issues here, relative to the crisis management potential of immature nuclear control systems: political accountability and operational flexibility. The two issues are closely related: the capability for operational flexibility is indispensable for policy makers who hope to control their crisis-time forces. Political accountability is necessary in order to prevent military usurpation of civil authority in favor of preventive war or preemptive attack.[53] Against proliferation pessimists, Kenneth Waltz argues that the current nuclear powers have solved these problems; therefore, there is no reason to assume that newer nuclear states will not do as well:

All nuclear countries live through a time when their forces are crudely designed. All countries have so far been able to control them. Relations between the United States and the Soviet Union, and later among the United States, Soviet Union, and China, were at their bitterest just when their nuclear forces were in the early stages of development and were unbalanced, crude and presumably hard to control.[54]

In addition to the political fragility of regimes and the disorderly character of newly acquired nuclear command and control systems, a third problem for immature nuclear forces is the potential vulnerability of the forces themselves. Some of the aspiring nuclear states outside of Europe are unlikely to be able to field nuclear forces based on diverse launch vehicles or on survivable platforms. First-strike forces will certainly precede second-strike forces in most nuclear aspiring states. These early generation, nonsurvivable forces offer a temptation to prospective attackers.[55] If those forces can be struck preemptively and disarmed, the attacker can dictate terms to the victim. Vulnerable nuclear forces are even more attractive than conventional forces which are thought to be susceptible to surprise attack. Nuclear preemption removes nuclear deterrence from the equation, limiting the victim to conventional deterrence and war fighting which depend almost exclusively on battlefield prowess, not on skill in coercive bargaining. According to U.S. Air War College analysts William C. Martel and William T. Pendley:

The existence of an Iranian nuclear deterrent invites preemptive attacks. For the states that view Iranian nuclear weapons as an inherently destabilizing development, sooner or later there will be an attempt to destroy those facilities, despite the political and military problems associated with preemptive attacks.[56]

Related to the preceding point, some first-generation nuclear forces, once they have been verified by observation and targeted by enemy planners, may be vulnerable to preemption by an attacker using only conventional weapons. Conventional preemption of a nuclear retaliatory force would be an inviting move for an attacker which could claim to occupy the moral high ground of a disarming anti-nuclear strike, even though its purposes were aggressive and designed to challenge a legal status quo. Menachim Begin's attack against the Iraqi Osirak nuclear complex was widely applauded, although sometimes in sotto voce, by states outside the region which feared the development by Iraq of a usable nuclear arsenal. The Israeli attack was made despite the fact that, at that time, Iraq was in apparent compliance with the Nuclear Nonproliferation Treaty and subject to regular IAEA inspections. We subsequently learned, of course, that the inspections were not foolproof, and this adds retrospective justification in the minds of some observers for Begin's action.

If small states and non-state actors have learned anything from the Cold War, it is that nuclear weapons, whether useful in war or not, carry prestige which opens the door to outside intervention for conflict termination. Thus, another incentive for small-power acquisition of nuclear arsenals will be to neutralize the anticipated propensity of nuclear powers for power projection of their conventional forces, backed by their nuclear weapons. British power projection against Argentina in 1982 was undoubtedly made possible by the backdrop of British nuclear weapons, which the Argentines knew could be used against them should Britain suffer conventional military defeat. Guerrillas have little use for nuclear weapons in their tool kits, but the state actors which back those guerrillas in unconventional wars against foreign enemies might feel less vulnerable to nuclear coercion if they had their own nuclear forces to call upon.

In the case of conventional weapons employed by combatants of roughly equivalent technology and strategic competency, numbers do count. In the case of nuclear weapons, numbers are almost irrelevant once more than "none" have been acquired. This is obviously not true for a state planning large-scale nuclear first strikes against a responsively protected nuclear adversary. But for small states with nuclear mini-forces, the deterrence of the strong by the weak is quite feasible. It is not necessary to threaten the entire destruction of an opponent's society in order to deter him, according to this logic. It is only necessary to threaten the plausible loss of social value or military objectives commensurate with the potential gains of an attacker. Nuclear weapons make the defender's job easy, and the attacker's, difficult, because so very few weapons can cause so much unprecedented, and unacceptable, damage.[57]

The future holds, therefore, the potential for a lethal combination of conventional and unconventional military conflicts with the proliferation of weapons of mass destruction. Some of these weapons may be owned by unaccountable movements with no particular address. Others will be acquired by nationalist or religious separatists who seek a kingdom on earth instead of a territorial state. Other weapons of mass destruction may be found in the hands of formerly celibate Germans and Japanese who feel threatened by neighbors or insufficiently respected by their global and regional peers. Still others will be sought by aspiring regional hegemons, like Saddam Hussein or Muammar Qaddafi, as weapons of checkmate against U.S. or United Nations coercive diplomacy. What some of these new nuclear owners may have in common is unaccountable authority and immature command and control systems, mated to weapons of extreme lethality. Picture Austria-Hungary in July 1914 with short or medium-range nuclear weapons.

A widely held prognosis, popular after the Gulf war of 1991, was that new high-technology conventional warfare strategies would curb states' lust for nuclear forces and for the kinds of terror which can be derived from them. A "Revolution in Military Affairs" based on information age weapons could, in this optimistic view, supersede nuclear weapons and deterrence based on weapons of mass destruction. Military planners were especially interested in precision-guided weapons, automated command/control systems, and real time reconnaissance/surveillance that might make possible improved future Desert Storms. The impact of information technology on warfare is expected to go beyond the improved collection of information. Military experts foresee an emerging competition for "dominant battlespace awareness" based on newer generations of decision aids and models that permit the unprecedented exploitation of knowledge as applied to battle:

A DBK (dominant battlespace knowledge), defined not as data (the transparent battlefield) but as knowledge (a significant exploitable asymmetry) offers pow-

erful implications for the organization of warfare. DBK provides synoptic inte-
grative knowledge, not just data on discrete objects and events. DBK lets its
possessors pierce the fog of war and thus master the unfolding progression of
circumstance, decisions and actions in the battlespace; it puts commanders in
real-time command.[58]

Information warfare or any other emerging war form does not necessarily diminish the significance of nuclear weapons in the new world
order. To the contrary, as "third wave" militaries like that of the United
States and other dominant information powers become more competent
at conventional warfare, weapons of mass destruction could increase in
their appeal to weaker states opposing the international status quo.
"Weapons of mass destruction" includes not only the chemical and biological weapons arsenals available to malefactors, but the distribution
of ballistic missiles and other delivery vehicles of medium and longer
ranges. In addition, there is no reason for complacency in the game of
information warfare. The price of entry or sustained competition in strategic information warfare is not necessarily steep for those well ac-
quainted with the vulnerabilities of their adversaries.[59] A final caveat
against the assumption that the Revolution in Military Affairs will make
nuclear weapons passé is the possibility that precision guidance will allow for miniaturization of nuclear charges down to the "micro" level, at
which users are less reluctant to strike on account of reduced fear of
collateral damage. That would be an especially imprudent and dangerous form of dialectical materialism: combining a nuclear "thesis" with
non-nuclear "antithesis" in order to erode the salience of the nuclear
threshold.

CONCLUSION

During the first nuclear age, coinciding more or less with the beginning and end of the Cold War, U.S. political leaders and military planners learned to adjust to the constraints placed upon traditional military
strategy by the combination of bipolarity and nuclear weapons. The large
and diverse American and Soviet nuclear arsenals placed both sides into
a relationship of mutual hostage taking: i.e, mutual assured destruction
by means of unavoidable and unacceptable retaliation following any surprise attack. The mutual deterrence that resulted from this relationship
precluded an excess of adventurism and blatant imperialism in the
other's sphere of influence: after the Cuban missile crisis of 1962, even
nuclear brinkmanship became odious. Much of the time this led to a gap
between rhetoric and reality in U.S. and Soviet pronouncements about
military strategy and the art of war. Troglodytes on both sides clung to
a desperate hope that some combination of new technology and new

fortitude might restore combined arms warfare, with or without nuclear weapons, to Western and Central Europe. All these hopes were eventually dashed, and leaders became habituated to pax atomica.

All of this theory and experience left open the future of nuclear weapons after the demise of the Soviet Union and the end of the Cold War. Nuclear weapons, justified as the stabilizers of a Cold War confrontation that might otherwise have turned hot, now appeared to some as liabilities that could spread to dissatisfied state and non-state actors outside of the control of the existing nuclear powers. The Revolution in Military Affairs, especially in precision weapons and automated control systems, has as yet unknown implications for the role of nuclear weapons in military strategy. Since few states can as yet play in the league of post-nuclear, high-technology powers, nuclear weapons and ballistic missiles may appeal to the comparatively weak as one means of leverage against the conventional superiority of the strong (for example, as anti-access forces blocking U.S. rapid response to regional crises).[60] The staying power of nuclear weapons is underscored by the fact that some theorists still argue, mistakenly in my view, that the spread of nuclear weapons is not necessarily destabilizing or threatening to world peace.

APPENDIX 1.1: CHRONOLOGY OF U.S. NATIONAL MISSILE DEFENSE PROGRAMS, 1945–1989

- July 4, 1945: Despite conclusions by U.S. industry that available technology precludes building an effective defense, the Army makes its first recommendation to begin a research and development effort to counter ballistic missiles.
- December 1945: Army Air Force Science Advisory Group broaches the idea of using an "energy beam" for defense against ballistic missiles.
- March 4, 1946: The Army Air Force begins two studies, Project Thumper and Project Wizard, focused on the possibility of developing anti-missile missiles capable of destroying incoming projectiles traveling at 4,000 mph and at altitudes reaching 500,000 feet.
- May 29, 1946: The Stilwell Board Report, noting that future advanced "guided missiles . . . would be incapable of interception with . . . fighter aircraft and antiaircraft fire," recommends development of "guided interceptor missiles."

The 1950s

- 1955: After 50,000 simulated ballistic missile intercepts on an analog computer, Bell Laboratory scientists conclude that "hitting a bullet with another bullet" is possible.
- October 4, 1957: Sputnik is launched into space, initiating the era of long-range ballistic missiles.

- January 16, 1958: The Army, which had been working on the Nike-Zeus anti-ballistic missile (ABM) system since 1955, is designated lead service for ballistic missile defense.
- 1958–1968: Project Defender, a wide-ranging research and development program that explores the use of a 400-foot-diameter web as a hit-to-kill system for boost-phase intercepts, is funded. No system is deployed.

The 1960s

- July 19, 1962: During a test over the Pacific Ocean, a Nike-Zeus comes within two kilometers of a dummy Atlas intercontinental ballistic missile (ICBM) warhead, close enough for an actual nuclear warhead on the interceptor to destroy the target.
- December 22, 1962: Another Nike-Zeus comes within 200 meters of a target reentry vehicle. Nike-Zeus is replaced by the Nike-X program, which employs two types of nuclear tipped interceptors and the new phased array radar.
- November 10, 1966: Secretary of Defense McNamara publicly confirms that the USSR is deploying its Galosh anti-ballistic missile (ABM) system.
- September 18, 1967: The Pentagon announces the decision to deploy the two-layer Sentinel ABM system (which succeeded Nike-X) consisting of the nuclear tipped Spartan (long-range) and Sprint (short-range) interceptors in order to protect the United States from the "Nth country threat" of simple ICBMs such as those deployed by China.
- July 1, 1968: President Johnson announces that the United States and USSR will discuss limits on both strategic nuclear arsenals and ballistic missile defenses. Talks are canceled when Moscow invades Czechoslovakia in September.
- February 6, 1969: The Nixon administration halts Sentinel deployment pending a full review of U.S. strategic programs.
- March 14, 1969: President Nixon announces resumption of the deployment of the renamed ABM system—now called Safeguard—but with its initial focus to be on protecting U.S. ICBM sites. An "expansion option" allows for the system to cover population centers against the "Nth country threat."
- August 1969: The Senate votes for deployment of the Sentinel system with Vice President Spiro Agnew casting the tie-breaking vote.

The 1970s

- May 26, 1972: President Nixon and Soviet General Secretary Brezhnev sign the ABM Treaty that prohibits a nation-wide missile defense while permitting each side two deployment sites limited to 100 interceptors at each location.
- July 3, 1974: The ABM Treaty is amended to permit only one defensive missile site for each party.
- October 1, 1975: The Nekoma, North Dakota (Grand Forks) Safeguard ABM site becomes operational.

- October 2, 1975: The House of Representatives votes to close the Grand Forks site because the new Soviet multiple independent reentry vehicle (MIRV) program would easily overwhelm Safeguard. Vulnerability to direct attack and technical problems such as radar blinding by electromagnetic pulse from exploding nuclear warheads made the system unreliable, and even actually threatened Minuteman forces it was assigned to protect.
- November 18, 1975: The Senate follows the lead of the House in voting to terminate Safeguard.
- February 1976: The Grand Forks site goes into "caretaker status."
- 1978: Except for its supporting radar, which is incorporated into the North American Air Defense Command's (NORAD) warning and assessment network, Safeguard is closed completely.

The 1980s

- January 8, 1982: A private group of advisors recommends to President Reagan that he launch a crash program to develop missile defenses.
- February 11, 1983: The Joint Chiefs of Staff advise President Reagan of the need to emphasize strategic defensive systems.
- March 23, 1983: President Reagan delivers a national television address in which he calls for research into defenses that would make "nuclear weapons impotent and obsolete."
- March 24, 1983: Opponents in Congress label President Reagan's vision of a defensive umbrella "Star Wars."
- March 25, 1983: The administration's ABM policy on missile defense is formalized in National Security Decision Directive 85.
- April 18, 1983: Two evaluations are begun: the first to look at the state of ABM technology and recommend a way forward (Defense Technologies Study or the Fletcher Report), and the second to assess strategy and policy ramifications of the ABM effort (Future Security Strategy Study or Hoffman Report).
- October 1983: The Hoffman Report is completed. It states that missile defenses could enhance deterrence and development of tactical missile defenses could contribute toward development of a NMD system. The initial draft of the Fletcher Report is completed. It recommends two research options, one funded at $20.9 billion between fiscal years 1984–1989 and a less preferred, more fiscally restrained alternative.
- April 24, 1984: Secretary of Defense Weinberger signs the Stragegic Defense Initiative Organization's (SDIO's) charter.
- 1984: SDIO's master plan concentrates directed energy research on five technologies: space-based chemical weapons; ground-based laser weapons; space-based particle beam weapons; nuclear (X-ray) directed energy; and support subsystems for these weapons.
- June 10, 1984: After two earlier but only partially successful attempts, a Minuteman missile with a "web-like" hit-to-kill interceptor package guided by infrared sensors and a computer destroys a target missile over the Pacific.

(However, the General Accounting Office in a 1994 report notes that the target had been artificially heated to increase its infrared signature.)

- April 1985: The controversy over narrow vs. broad interpretation of the 1972 ABM Treaty gets underway.

- September 6, 1985: A Titan rocket simulating the conditions of a rocket booster is destroyed by an infrared advanced chemical laser.

- December 1985: Two reviews of SDIO are completed. The first finds SDIO is undermanned to fulfill its charter and needs to be reorganized. The second finds that developing computing and battle management software are "the paramount strategic problem[s]" facing SDIO.

- July 30, 1986: SDIO is reorganized to give greater weight to resolving system architecture problems.

- August 1986: A National Test Bed is established to help resolve problems associated with integrating battle management requirements.

- September 11, 1986: The Delta 180 experiment, the first "equivalent" of boost phase intercept, is completed.

- October 11–12, 1986: President Reagan declines to agree to limitations on SDI proposed by Soviet President Gorbachev.

- November 1986: The idea of employing "brilliant technologies"—miniature sensors and computers that would reduce size, cost, and vulnerability of SDI space-based components—is championed.

- May 13, 1987: A legal review of the 1972 ABM Treaty concludes that the Treaty does not prevent testing space-based missile defenses, including directed energy weapons.

- June/July 1987: As a result of a Defense Acquisition Board review of the SDI program, the baseline architecture for Phase I is approved and the program begins the demonstration and validation phase of the DoD acquisition process.

- January 19, 1988: Senator Sam Nunn (D-GA) proposes focusing SDI on development of a "limited system for protecting against accidental and unauthorized launches" with a subsequent goal of making the system more comprehensive.

- February 9, 1989: SDIO chief General Abrahamson, in his end-of-tour report, says that a space-based defensive architecture employing the "Brilliant Pebbles" concept could be ready in five years at a cost of $25 billion or less. Brilliant Pebbles consists of thousands of interceptors each capable of independent operations against whatever comes within its field of vision.

- June 14, 1989: Based on a general review of U.S. national security strategy, President Bush decides to continue the SDI program emphasizing development of space-based boost phase interceptor technologies such as Brilliant Pebbles.

Source: Colonel Daniel Smith, USA (Ret.), Center for Defense Information, December 1, 2000. Reprinted by permission.

NOTES

1. On the development of nuclear strategy, see Lawrence Freedman, *The Evolution of Nuclear Strategy* (New York: St. Martin's Press, 1981); Colin S. Gray, *Strategic Studies and Public Policy: The American Experience* (Lexington: University Press of Kentucky, 1982); Scott D. Sagan, *Moving Targets: Nuclear Strategy and National Security* (Princeton, N.J.: Princeton University Press, 1989); and Robert Jervis, *The Meaning of the Nuclear Revolution: Statecraft and the Prospect of Armageddon* (Ithaca, N.Y.: Cornell University Press, 1989). On the early years of U.S. strategic theorizing, see Marc Trachtenberg, *History and Strategy* (Princeton, N.J.: Princeton University Press, 1991), pp. 3–46. The logic of deterrence and deterrence rationality receives especially insightful treatment in Patrick M. Morgan, *Deterrence: A Conceptual Analysis* (Beverly Hills, Calif.: Sage Publications, 1977) and in Phil Williams, "Nuclear Deterrence," in John Baylis, Ken Booth, John Garnett and Phil Williams, *Contemporary Strategy, vol. I: Theories and Concepts* (New York: Holmes and Meier, 1987), pp. 113–139. The nuclear revolution is put into historical context in Michael Mandelbaum, *The Nuclear Revolution: International Politics before and after Hiroshima* (Cambridge: Cambridge University Press, 1981). Prenuclear examples of deterrence thinking and deterrent strategy are assessed in George H. Quester, *Deterrence before Hiroshima: The Airpower Background of Modern Strategy*, 2nd ed. (New Brunswick, N.J.: Transaction Books, 1986).

2. Major periods in the nuclear arms race and their relationship to U.S. military thinking are clarified in George H. Quester, "Relating Nuclear Weapons to American Power," in Stephen J. Cimbala, ed., *Deterrence and Nuclear Proliferation in the Twenty-First Century* (Westport, Conn.: Praeger Publishers, 2000), ch. 1.

3. David Alan Rosenberg, "U.S. Nuclear War Planning, 1945–1960," in Desmond Ball and Jeffrey Richelson, eds., *Strategic Nuclear Targeting* (Ithaca, N.Y.: Cornell University Press, 1986), pp. 35–56, esp. pp. 53–55.

4. Graham T. Allison, *Essence of Decision: Explaining the Cuban Missile Crisis* (Boston: Little, Brown, 1971) remains a landmark study. For more recent analyses, see Raymond L. Garthoff, *Reflections on the Cuban Missile Crisis*, rev. ed. (Washington, D.C.: Brookings Institution, 1989); James G. Blight and David A. Welch, *On the Brink: Americans and Soviets Examine the Cuban Missile Crisis* (New York: Hill and Wang, 1989); and McGeorge Bundy, *Danger and Survival: Choices about the Bomb in the First Fifty Years* (New York: Random House, 1988), pp. 391–462.

5. Alexander L. George, David K. Hall and William E. Simons, *The Limits of Coercive Diplomacy: Laos, Cuba, Vietnam* (Boston: Little, Brown, 1971) outlines and applies the concept of coercive diplomacy. Especially pertinent is George's chapter on Cuba.

6. On Kennedy administration nuclear war planning and strategic doctrine, see Janne E. Nolan, *Guardians of the Arsenal: The Politics of Nuclear Strategy* (New York: Basic Books, 1989), pp. 74–88, and Desmond Ball, "The Development of the SIOP, 1960–1983," in Desmond Ball and Jeffrey Richelson, eds., *Strategic Nuclear Targeting* (Ithaca, N.Y.: Cornell University Press, 1986), pp. 57–83, esp. pp. 62–70.

7. Important U.S. works during this period included Bernard Brodie, ed., *The Absolute Weapon* (New York: Harcourt, Brace, 1946); William W. Kaufmann, ed., *Military Policy and National Security* (Princeton, N.J.: Princeton University Press, 1956); Henry A. Kissinger, *Nuclear Weapons and Foreign Policy* (New York: Houghton Mifflin, 1957); Brodie, *Strategy in the Missile Age* (Princeton, N.J.: Princeton University Press, 1959); Thomas C. Schelling, *The Strategy of Conflict* (Cambridge, Mass.: Harvard University Press, 1960); Kaufmann, *The McNamara Strategy* (New York: Harper and Row, 1964); Schelling, *Arms and Influence* (New Haven, Conn.: Yale University Press, 1966); Brodie, *Escalation and the Nuclear Option* (Princeton, N.J.: Princeton University Press, 1966); and Klaus Knorr, *On the Uses of Military Power in the Nuclear Age* (Princeton, N.J.: Princeton University Press, 1966). A significant non-U.S. literature, especially that published in Britain and France during this time, tended to be more philosophical and historical in its cast, compared to the Americans. British works included Sir John Slessor, *Strategy for the West* (London: Cassell, 1954); P.M.S. Blackett, *Atomic Energy and East-West Relations* (Cambridge: Cambridge University Press, 1956); Alastair Buchan, *NATO in the 1960s* (London: Chatto and Windus, 1960); and B.H. Liddell Hart, *Deterrent or Defence* (London: Stevens, 1960). Important French theorists were Pierre Gallois and André Beaufre. See in particular Gallois, *The Balance of Terror: Strategy for the Nuclear Age* (Boston: Houghton Mifflin, 1961) and Beaufre, *Deterrence and Strategy* (London: Faber and Faber, 1965). See also Marc Trachtenberg, "Strategic Thought in America, 1952–1966," in Trachtenberg, *History and Strategy*, pp. 3–46, and Michael Howard, *Studies in War and Peace* (New York: The Viking Press, 1971), pp. 154–183.

8. Edward A. Kolodziej, *French International Policy under De Gaulle and Pompidou: The Politics of Grandeur* (Ithaca, N.Y.: Cornell University Press, 1974), esp. pp. 128–130.

9. Alain C. Enthoven and K. Wayne Smith, *How Much Is Enough? Shaping the Defense Program, 1961–1969* (New York: Harper and Row, 1971), pp. 207–208.

10. Raymond L. Garthoff, *Deterrence and the Revolution in Soviet Military Doctrine* (Washington, D.C.: The Brookings Institution, 1990), esp. ch. 2, p. 34 and passim. On the significance of diversity in national styles for nuclear strategy and policy making see Colin S. Gray, *Nuclear Strategy and National Style* (Lanham, Md.: Hamilton Press, 1986). On the development of Soviet nuclear strategy see David Holloway, *The Soviet Union and the Arms Race* (New Haven, Conn.: Yale University Press, 1983), chs. 2 and 3.

11. Prominent Soviet military theorists of the early 1970s noted that nuclear weapons provided strategic parity between the United States and the Soviet Union, making possible the limitation of any war to the conventional level and preventing Western blackmail of the Soviet Union or its allies through nuclear superiority. See Dale R. Herspring, *The Soviet High Command, 1967–1989: Personalities and Politics* (Princeton, N.J.: Princeton University Press, 1990), pp. 84–85. In the 1970s and subsequently the acceptance of parity allowed a great deal of room for disagreement, as between former Chief of the Soviet General Staff N.V. Ogarkov and his superiors in the early 1980s, on the value of detente and arms control compared to military buildup of Soviet forces. See ibid., pp. 202ff.

12. Desmond Ball, "U.S. Strategic Forces: How Would They Be Used?" *International Security*, No. 3 (Winter 1982/1983), reprinted in Steven E. Miller, ed.,

Strategy and Nuclear Deterrence (Princeton, N.J.: Princeton University Press, 1984), pp. 215–244, provides ample evidence of this tendency.

13. Walter Slocombe, "The Countervailing Strategy," in Miller, ed., *Strategy and Nuclear Deterrence*, pp. 245–254, esp. pp. 246–249.

14. Steven Kull, *Minds at War: Nuclear Reality and the Inner Conflicts of Defense Policymakers* (New York: Basic Books, 1988). Of course, the Soviets had little interest either before SALT or subsequently in nuclear flexibility, if nuclear flexibility meant deliberately created pauses in between volleys of nuclear exchanges into Soviet and U.S. territory. Soviet views on the desirability of various nuclear options for deterrence are more complex, and not monolithic even among military commentators. For perspective, see Garthoff, *Deterrence and the Revolution in Soviet Military Doctrine*, p. 41, and Maj. Gen. Engr-Tech Serv I.I. Anureev, "Determining the Correlation of Forces in Terms of Nuclear Weapons," *Voennaya mysl'*, No. 6 (1967), reprinted in Joseph D. Douglass, Jr. and Amoretta M. Hoeber, eds., *Selected Readings from Military Thought, 1963–1973* (Washington, D.C.: U.S. Government Printing Office, n.d.), pp. 161–172.

15. According to Scott Sagan, U.S. arguments for second-strike counterforce have usually fallen into one of three general categories: damage limitation; support extended deterrence or deny Soviet war aims. See his discussion in *Moving Targets*, pp. 72–82. Sagan's discussion notes the arguments in favor of second-strike counterforce but also acknowledges the difficulty of keeping first- and second-strike counterforce distinct in the minds of potential adversaries.

16. On escalation dominance, see Robert Jervis, *The Illogic of American Nuclear Strategy* (Ithaca, N.Y.: Cornell University Press, 1984), pp. 126–146.

17. Robert Powell, *Nuclear Deterrence Theory: The Search for Credibility* (Cambridge: Cambridge University Press, 1990), chs. 2–3 explains the difference between strategies based on limited nuclear retaliation and on manipulation of risk.

18. On manipulation of risk, see Thomas C. Schelling, *Arms and Influence* (New Haven, Conn.: Yale University Press, 1966), pp. 92–125.

19. On accidental or inadvertent war, see Sagan, *Moving Targets*, pp. 135–175.

20. Thomas C. Schelling, *The Strategy of Conflict* (Cambridge, Mass.: Harvard University Press, 1960), pp. 187–204.

21. On Soviet strategy as of the middle 1980s in the cases of unexpected strategic surprise attack in peacetime, and of anticipated strategic surprise attack during crisis, see Stephen M. Meyer, "Soviet Nuclear Operations," in Ashton B. Carter, John D. Steinbruner and Charles A. Zraket, eds., *Managing Nuclear Operations* (Washington, D.C.: Brookings Institution, 1987), pp. 470–534, esp. pp. 476–497 and 497–512. See also Lt. Gen. A.I. Yevseev, "O nekotorykh tendentsiyakh v izmenii soderzhaniya i kharaktera nachal'nogo perioda voiny," *Voenno-istoricheskii zhurnal*, No. 11 (November 1985): 10–20; Stephen M. Meyer, "Soviet Perspectives on the Paths to Nuclear War," in Graham T. Allison, Albert Carnesale and Joseph S. Nye, Jr., eds., *Hawks, Doves and Owls* (New York: W.W. Norton, 1985), pp. 167–205; William T. Lee, "Soviet Nuclear Targeting," in Ball and Richelson, eds., *Strategic Nuclear Targeting*, pp. 84–108; Edward L. Warner III, *Soviet Concepts and Capabilities for Limited Nuclear War: What We Know and How We Know It* (Santa Monica, Calif.: RAND, February 1989); Marshal N.V. Ogarkov, *Vsegda v gotovnosti k zashchite otechestva* (Moscow: Voyenizdat, 1982), p. 16; Ogarkov, *Istoriya uchit bditel'nosti* (Moscow: Voyenizdat, 1985), pp. 89–90; and M.A.

Gareev, *M.V. Frunze: Voennyi teoretik* (Moscow: Voyenizdat, 1985), translated and published by Pergamon-Brassey's in English (New York, 1988), esp. pp. 213–214. It would be superfluous to note that all of this underwent significant restructuring under Gorbachev, even prior to the abortive coup of August 18–21, 1991 and the official decommunization of the armed forces.

22. For recent evidence of Soviet views on controlling and possibly terminating a major war, see Garthoff, *Deterrence and the Revolution in Soviet Military Doctrine*, ch. 5, and Garthoff, "New Soviet Thinking on Conflict Initiation, Control and Termination," in Stephen J. Cimbala and Sidney R. Waldman, eds., *Controlling and Ending Conflict* (Westport, Conn.: Greenwood Press, 1992), pp. 65–94.

23. Nicolai N. Petro and Alvin Z. Rubinstein, *Russian Foreign Policy: From Empire to Nation-State* (New York: Addison-Wesley, 1997), pp. 135–136 and 140–143.

24. William J. Perry, Secretary of Defense, *Annual Report to the President and the Congress* (Washington, D.C.: U.S. Government Printing Office, March 1996), pp. 63–70.

25. Freedman, *The Evolution of Nuclear Strategy*, p. 290.

26. See P.H. Vigor, *Soviet Blitzkrieg Theory* (New York: St. Martin's Press, 1983), ch. 1 on the Soviet need to win a war in Europe quickly.

27. Alain C. Enthoven and K. Wayne Smith, *How Much Is Enough? Shaping the Defense Program, 1961–1969* (New York: Harper and Row, 1971), also cited in Freedman, *The Evolution of Nuclear Strategy*, p. 299.

28. Adam B. Ulam, *Dangerous Relations: The Soviet Union in World Politics, 1970–1982* (New York: Oxford University Press, 1984), p. 67.

29. Paul Bracken, *The Command and Control of Nuclear Forces* (New Haven, Conn.: Yale University Press, 1983), p. 164.

30. Although former Secretary of State Dean Acheson scored Eisenhower for being too dependent on nuclear threat in his handling of the 1958–1959 Berlin crisis, Acheson favored increased U.S. and allied capability to respond to renewed Soviet pressure with conventional means. See Bundy, *Danger and Survival*, p. 372. Kennedy administration contingency planning during the Berlin crisis of 1961 called for flexible and graduated options, including limited nuclear options. See Richard K. Betts, *Nuclear Blackmail and Nuclear Balance* (Washington, D.C.: Brookings Institution, 1987), pp. 96–97.

31. For an overview of this topic see Gordon A. Craig and Alexander L. George, *Force and Statecraft: Diplomatic Problems of Our Time* (New York: Oxford University Press, 1983), pp. 205–219 and Ole R. Holsti, "Crisis Decision Making," in Philip E. Tetlock, Jo L. Husbands, Robert Jervis, Paul C. Stern and Charles Tilly, eds., *Behavior, Society and Nuclear War*, Vol. I (New York: Oxford University Press, 1989), pp. 8–84.

32. For an argument that the outbreak of World War I was not a result of inadvertent war caused by crisis instability, see Trachtenberg, *History and Strategy*, pp. 47–99. For counterarguments see Bracken, *The Command and Control of Nuclear Forces*, p. 65 and Richard Ned Lebow, *Nuclear Crisis Management: A Dangerous Illusion* (Ithaca, N.Y.: Cornell University Press, 1987), passim. The most comprehensive investigation of the origins of World War I is Luigi Albertini, *The Origins of the War of 1914*, a three-volume study (London: Oxford University Press, 1952–1957). Also indispensable is Gerhard Ritter, *The Schlieffen Plan: Cri-*

tique of a Myth (London: Oswald Wolff, 1958), including the text of Schlieffen's "great memorandum" of December 1905 (pp. 134–147). Some of the useful historical and political science literature on this topic is reviewed in connection with modern strategic decision dilemmas in my *U.S. Nuclear Strategy in the New World Order* (New York: Paragon House, 1993), ch. 1.

33. The latter 1980s and early 1990s saw the publication of a large literature on the Cuban missile crisis, partly as a result of a series of conferences between U.S. and Soviet academics with crisis participants from both sides. See Garthoff, *Reflections on the Cuban Missile Crisis*; Garthoff, "The Havana Conference on the Cuban Missile Crisis," *Cold War International History Project Bulletin*, No. 1 (Washington, D.C.: Woodrow Wilson Center, Spring 1992): 2–4; Blight and Welch, *On the Brink*; and Gen. Anatoli I. Gribkov and Gen. William Y. Smith, *Operation ANADYR: U.S. and Soviet Generals Recount the Cuban Missile Crisis* (Chicago: Edition Q Publishers, 1994), pp. 62–63, and Appendix 1, Documents 1–3. See also Mark Kramer, "Tactical Nuclear Weapons, Soviet Command Authority, and the Cuban Missile Crisis," *Cold War International History Project Bulletin*, No. 3 (Fall 1993): 40, 42–46, and James G. Blight, Bruce J. Allyn and David A. Welch, "Kramer vs. Kramer: Or, How Can You Have Revisionism in the Absence of Orthodoxy?" *Cold War International History Project Bulletin*, No. 3 (Fall 1993): 41, 47–50.

34. Stephen M. Walt has shown that this can be a problem for potential participants in a revolutionary movement as well as for competitors in an international bargaining relationship. See Walt, *Revolution and War* (Ithaca, N.Y.: Cornell University Press, 1996), pp. 22–24 and passim.

35. Robert McNamara, "The Military Role of Nuclear Weapons," *Foreign Affairs*, vol. 62 (Fall 1983): 68. For counterarguments, see Jervis, *The Meaning of the Nuclear Revolution*, pp. 80–81.

36. Betts, *Nuclear Blackmail and Nuclear Balance*, passim.

37. Richard Ned Lebow and Janice Gross Stein, *We All Lost the Cold War* (Princeton, N.J.: Princeton University Press, 1994), ch. 2.

38. According to Scott Sagan, "despite Khrushchev's claims to the contrary, Soviet strategic nuclear forces had *not*, in fact, been placed on a high-alert status." Sagan, *Moving Targets*, p. 148. According to David Holloway and Condoleeza Rice, the Soviet Union as of 1988 "has never raised the alert status of its nuclear forces during a crisis." See Kurt Gottfried and Bruce G. Blair, *Crisis Stability and Nuclear War* (New York: Oxford University Press, 1988), p. 144. Khrushchev, on the other hand, contended in December 1962 that "the whole army of the Soviet Union and above all the Soviet intercontinental and strategic rocket forces, the anti-air missile defense and fighter aviation of the PVO (Air Defense Forces), strategic aviation and the Navy" had been ordered by the Soviet government to assume a state of full combat readiness. Khrushchev even noted that "Our submarine fleet, including the atomic (fleet), occupied its appointed positions." *Pravda*, December 13, 1962, p. 1 and October 24, 1962, cited in Holloway and Rice, "Soviet Forces, Strategy and Command," in Gottfried and Blair, *Crisis Stability and Nuclear War*, p. 152, n. 19. See also Bruce G. Blair, *The Logic of Accidental Nuclear War* (Washington, D.C.: Brookings Institution, 1993), pp. 22–26.

39. Craig and George, *Force and Statecraft*, p. 190. See also Alexander L. George, "Strategies for Crisis Management," in George, ed., *Avoiding War: Problems of Crisis Management* (Boulder, Colo.: Westview Press, 1991), p. 385.

40. Alexander L. George, "Coercive Diplomacy: Definition and Characteristics," in George and William E. Simons, eds., *The Limits of Coercive Diplomacy*, 2nd ed. (Boulder, Colo.: Westview Press, 1994), pp. 7–11, esp. p. 9.

41. Barry M. Blechman and Stephen S. Kaplan, *Force without War: U.S. Armed Forces as a Political Instrument* (Washington, D.C.: Brookings Institution, 1976).

42. Betts, *Nuclear Blackmail and Nuclear Balance*, p. 181.

43. Blechman and Kaplan, *Force without War*, p. 49.

44. Ibid., p. 48. The Blechman-Kaplan tabulations probably overstate the incidence of nuclear force–related signals, if we are to infer from those intended signals an actual likelihood, however slight it may have been, to employ nuclear weapons or nuclear-capable delivery vehicles (e.g., Uruguayan inaugural).

45. Richard Ned Lebow, "Windows of Opportunity: Do States Jump through Them?" *International Security*, Vol. 9 (Summer 1984): 147–186.

46. Richard Ned Lebow and Janice Gross Stein, *When Does Deterrence Succeed and How Do We Know?* (Ottawa, Ontario: Canadian Institute for International Peace and Security, 1990), pp. 64–65.

47. For example, Robert Jervis notes that one or both sides in a crisis can misperceive the motives of the other, practicing deterrence against a state which in fact does not want to upset the status quo. Jervis, *Perception and Misperception in International Politics* (Princeton, N.J.: Princeton University Press, 1976), ch. 3. See also Lebow and Stein, *When Does Deterrence Succeed?*, p. 85.

48. Lewis A. Dunn, *Controlling the Bomb: Nuclear Proliferation in the 1980s* (New Haven, Conn.: Yale University Press, 1982), esp. pp. 44–68. For more recent assessments see Leonard S. Spector and Virginia Foran, *Preventing Weapons Proliferation: Should the Regimes Be Combined?* (Warrenton, Va.: Stanley Foundation, October 1992); George H. Quester, *The Multilateral Management of International Security: The Nuclear Proliferation Model* (College Park, Md.: Center for International and Security Studies at Maryland, March 1993); and John Hawes, *Nuclear Proliferation: Down to the Hard Cases* (College Park, Md.: Center for International and Security Studies at Maryland, June 1993).

49. William C. Martel and William T. Pendley, *Nuclear Coexistence: Rethinking U.S. Policy to Promote Stability in an Era of Proliferation* (Montgomery, Ala.: Air War College, April 1994), pp. 105–106.

50. Louis Rene Beres, *Apocalypse: Nuclear Catastrophe in World Politics* (Chicago: University of Chicago Press, 1980), p. 82.

51. Alexander L. George, "The Tension between 'Military Logic' and Requirements of Diplomacy in Crisis Management," in George, ed., *Avoiding War: Problems of Crisis Management* (Boulder, Colo.: Westview Press, 1991), p. 18.

52. Sidney Bradshaw Fay, *The Origins of the First World War*, Vol. II, 2nd ed., rev. (New York: The Free Press, 1966), pp. 446–481.

53. Peter D. Feaver, *Guarding the Guardians: Civilian Control of Nuclear Weapons in the United States* (Ithaca, N.Y.: Cornell University Press, 1992), pp. 12–21.

54. Kenneth N. Waltz, "More May Be Better," in Scott D. Sagan and Kenneth N. Waltz, *The Spread of Nuclear Weapons: A Debate* (New York: W.W. Norton, 1995), pp. 1–46, citation p. 20.

55. Louis Rene Beres, *Apocalypse: Nuclear Catastrophe in World Politics* (Chicago: University of Chicago Press, 1980), p. 82.

56. Martel and Pendley, *Nuclear Coexistence*, p. 105. Apparently Israel has is-

sued at least one oblique threat from a high military source that was interpreted by Iran as a threat to strike at its nuclear facilities. Ibid., p. 103.

57. On the credibility of small nuclear forces, see Waltz, "More May Be Better," pp. 23–26.

58. Jeffrey Cooper, "Dominant Battlespace Awareness and Future Warfare," in Stuart E. Johnson and Martin C. Libicki, eds., *Dominant Battlespace Knowledge: The Winning Edge* (Washington, D.C.: National Defense University Press, 1995), p. 104.

59. Roger C. Molander, Andrew S. Biddle and Peter A. Wilson, *Strategic Information Warfare: A New Face of War* (Santa Monica, Calif.: RAND, 1996).

60. See Andrew Krepinevich, "Transforming the American Military," in H.W. Brands, ed., *The Use of Force after the Cold War* (College Station: Texas A&M University Press, 2000), pp. 201–216.

Chapter 2

Nuclear Weapons and Soviet Cold War Strategy: Adapting to MADness

INTRODUCTION

This chapter explains how nuclear weapons influenced Soviet views of war, of politics related to war and of military doctrine and strategy in the years from the end of World War II to the collapse of the Soviet Union. The discussion of the impact of nuclear weapons on Soviet military strategy flows naturally from the preceding chapter in which we traced the American nuclear journey. As in the American case, so here also, we are not providing a chronology of nuclear inventions or crises, nor a hermeneutics of military doctrinal debates within staff colleges and closed journals. Our focus is to elicit the main themes of the Soviet struggle to reconcile the unavoidable (existence of nuclear weapons in the hands of potential Soviet enemies) with the necessary (finding a way to use nuclear weapons for political dissuasion short of combat). Soviet generals and politicians, no less than Americans but from different historical and cultural traditions, were thrust into a revolutionary military-technical world after 1945 to go along with their revolutionary political pretentions.[1]

In this chapter, we emphasize two aspects of the Soviet adjustment to a nuclear armed world between 1945 and 1989: (1) the impact of nuclear weapons on Soviet thinking and planning for fighting or deterring a world war (and, logically enough, for fighting or deterring a major war in Europe that might possibly, although not inevitably, become a world war) and (2) the implications of nuclear weapons, and of the emergence of nuclear-strategic parity, for the likelihood of conventional war in Europe and for the way in which such a war might have been fought, if

deterrence had failed. The combination of acknowledged nuclear stalemate and increased activeness of conventional defenses made possible a
variety of East-West arms limitation agreements that helped to bring the
Cold War to an end.[2]

NUCLEAR WEAPONS AND SOVIET STRATEGY

In this section of the chapter, the development of Soviet military thinking about nuclear weapons, deterrence and war is described very generally. Three generalizations about the Soviet view of deterrence set it
apart from the standard American and NATO perspective of the Cold
War years. First, Soviet thinking was less centered on the military balance per se than it was conditioned by the idea of "correlation of forces"
(*sootnoshenie sil*), a more inclusive construct that took into account political, social, economic, and moral-psychological factors of the competing
systems. Second, the Soviet view of deterrence was not as specifically
oriented to nuclear weapons and nuclear war as was the American. Soviet leaders were equally as concerned to avoid a conventional war in
Europe on unfavorable terms, among other reasons because such a conflict might go nuclear under some conditions. Third, the Soviet political
leadership inherited a "defense of Mother Russia" or "Barbarossa" complex from Russia's history of invasions from Poles, Swedes, French, Germans and others who ravaged across her extended and vulnerable
borders. This explains why, despite the crudity of available technology
and in the face of American arms control biases against defenses, Russians took anti-missile defense of the homeland quite seriously.[3]

Stalin publicly deprecated the value of atomic weapons so long as the
United States maintained a nuclear monopoly: privately, he urged on his
own scientists and feared U.S. nuclear intimidation.[4] As Soviet military
thinkers adapted to the availability of plentiful nuclear weapons and
long-range delivery systems, they developed concepts of deterrence and
of crisis management considerably different in emphasis from those familiar to Americans. The facts of Russian and Soviet historical experience, the role of the professional armed forces in setting down the
"military science" aspects of military doctrine and the geopolitical setting
for Soviet postwar foreign policy making all implied a uniquely Russian
context for thinking about the role of nuclear forces and of nuclear dissuasion in defense policy.[5]

Stalin's successors in the party leadership and their military advisors
acknowledged after 1953 that nuclear weapons had brought about a revolution in military affairs. This acknowledgment came in stages and arrived in full force only after Khrushchev had finally disposed of serious
rivals for the party leadership in 1957. Between the time of Stalin's death
and his assumption of undisputed power in Moscow, Khrushchev

played a clever game against his most important rivals for leadership in the party and government: Georgiy Malenkov and Vyacheslav Molotov. Khrushchev first set up Malenkov. In March 1954, Malenkov, then chairman of the Council of Ministers of the USSR, averred that any war between the United States and the Soviet Union "considering the modern means of warfare, would mean the end of civilization."[6] Malenkov's initiative had been prompted in part by a classified report prepared the same month by four prominent physicists associated with the Soviet nuclear weapons program. The scientists noted that within a few years, the stockpiles of atomic explosives would be sufficient to "create conditions under which the existence of life over the whole globe will be impossible" and added that "we cannot but admit that mankind faces an enormous threat of the termination of all life on Earth."[7]

Malenkov's expression of pessimism about the outcome of modern war was in contradiction to then prevalent party and ideological orthodoxy. Khrushchev used Malenkov's alleged heresy against him to winkle the latter from his leadership posts. Khrushchev then turned against Molotov, pushing him out of the foreign ministry and into eventual political obscurity. One of Khrushchev's arguments against Molotov was the latter's obduracy in the face of the new situation created by nuclear weapons. In 1956, the Twentieth Party Congress of the CPSU rejected the previously avowed thesis of the inevitability of world war between capitalism and socialism. In place of inevitable world war, party doctrine (as guided by Khrushchev) endorsed the thesis of "peaceful coexistence" between different social systems.[8]

Khrushchev adopted no proposal or line of thinking without excessive enthusiasm. Having deposed his principal rivals from the early post-Stalin years, and having survived a later attempt to oust him from power by the "anti-party group," Khrushchev danced again on the question of nuclear weapons and military strategy. In the latter 1950s, he fully embraced the idea of nuclear missile warfare as the centerpiece of Soviet military planning guidance.[9] He was left with the problem of explaining how socialism would survive and triumph in the aftermath of a global nuclear war with the Americans and their NATO allies. After Khrushchev's departure from the top posts in party and government in 1964, party guidance continued to insist that socialism would prevail even in nuclear war.[10] But, under Brezhnev and his successors, military doctrine was adjusted to allow the problem of nuclear escalation to be considered as a variable instead of a constant.

Soviet military literature in the early 1960s emphasized that war would probably begin with a massive nuclear surprise attack and involve the Soviet Union and its allies against the West in a major coalition war. The military thinking that appeared in these studies was no mere theoretical exercise. War plans of the early 1960s also made similar assumptions about the early use of nuclear missiles within the European theater of military actions and between the American and Soviet homelands. For example, the 1964 Warsaw Pact plan for war in Europe, prepared and approved by the Soviet General Staff, discounted NATO's declared strategy of fighting a defensive war on its own soil as a hoax. Instead, Soviet commanders were told to anticipate that NATO would follow an offensive war plan, including early nuclear fire strikes against vital targets in Eastern Europe and in the Soviet Union.[11] In order to fight and prevail under the extreme conditions of a war including nuclear weapons, it would be necessary for Soviet political leaders to anticipate the outbreak of a war and to authorize military commanders to engage in prompt offensives that employed theater and, if necessary, strategic nuclear weapons. As Professor Vojtech Mastny has explained:

The Soviet generals, however, were no fools. They knew well enough that NATO was preparing for a defense against them. But they were so mesmerized by their still vivid memories of the very nearly successful German surprise attack on their country in 1941 that they could not imagine any other reliable strategy than that of striking at the enemy before he could strike at them.[12]

If Soviet generals were no fools, neither were their atomic scientists and more astute field commanders. It might be an article of faith for the High Command, reflecting Communist Party oversight, that nuclear combat in Europe or globally could be sustained at a high intensity and to an acceptable outcome. But it was also apparent to anyone with a slide rule that even in a "limited" nuclear war the amount of destruction that would take place in a short time would be unprecedented and complicate the planning of military offensive and defensive operations. In an authoritative account of current military doctrine prepared in August 1964 by the then chief of Soviet military intelligence, Col. Gen. P. Ivashutin, for the Head of the Military Academy of the General Staff, the author struggles to reconcile the political imperative for victory in combat with the nontraditional reality of nuclear weapons:

As a result of the mutual exchanges of nuclear strikes, an exceptionally difficult situation would emerge in the theater of military action. Numerous fires, destruction, flooding, and high radiation levels will most likely slow or completely stop any kind of movement of the troops that survived nuclear strikes on a number of directions, especially immediately after the nuclear strikes. However, one would suppose that the situation would not be the same everywhere . . . It is quite probable that there would be a sufficient number of directions in the theater where the troops, which preserved their combat capability, could conduct forward operations at least some time after the nuclear strikes, and we should be able to use such directions.[13]

Following Khrushchev's ouster in 1964 and changes in U.S. and allied NATO strategy toward "flexible response" in the second half of the 1960s, Soviet military strategists showed increased interest in scenarios other than massive retaliation and global conflict.[14] As the decade progressed there was, on the part of a variety of authoritative political and military thinkers, greater acknowledgment that even large-scale war could be waged with conventional weapons only. In addition, the potential payoff from Soviet support for wars of "national liberation" against pro-Western states outside of Europe directed additional military thinking toward local and limited wars. The development of Soviet military thinking in the 1950s and 1960s can be summarized by enumerating the five types of war conceived by leading theoreticians and military strategists during that time:

- a massive nuclear, but relatively short, war in which strategic nuclear weapons played the major role in deciding the outcome;
- a more protracted war including nuclear strikes but also involving all of the armed forces;
- a major war in which nuclear weapons are used in a restricted or limited manner in one or several theaters of military action;
- a major war limited to the use of conventional weapons;
- a local war involving conventional weapons.[15]

The willingness of Soviet military analysts to entertain multiple scenarios as equally valid possibilities increased in the 1970s as a result of detente between the United States and the Soviet Union. New threat assessments were also mandated by the geopolitical repositioning of China, hitherto included in the Soviet camp but henceforth treated as an ally of the United States and NATO.[16]

The period of threat preceding war, as explained by lecturers at the Soviet General Staff Academy during the 1970s, was a time in which the Soviet armed forces were in great danger of being caught by surprise.[17] In a nuclear war the ability to seize the strategic initiative in the first minutes would have, according to these estimates, a decisive impact on the development of military action and on the duration and outcome of the conflict. Soviet forces must be prepared for transition from conventional to nuclear operations at any moment. The first volume of the lecture materials from the General Staff Academy discussed the "forms of initiation of war by the aggressor" and, with regard to NATO, specified the following possibilities:

- surprise strikes with unlimited use of nuclear weapons;
- a strike with initially limited use of nuclear weapons and subsequently going over to full use of the complete nuclear arsenal;

- strikes by groupings of armed forces deployed in the TSMAs (TVDs) without the use of nuclear weapons;
- initiation of war by gradual expansion of local wars.[18]

Initiation of war by the United States and its NATO allies through a general nuclear attack was studied in the 1970s as "the basic form of initiating war, with respect to American doctrine."[19] This form of initiating war was the most dangerous and could have had the greatest consequences if unexpected and not reacted to promptly. The Soviet lecturers described at some length how the United States would have orchestrated a nuclear surprise attack.[20] Although the most dangerous from the Soviet standpoint, this course of action *was not* judged to be the most likely, according to the Voroshilov lecture materials. More likely was the limited use of nuclear weapons, followed by the unlimited use of the U.S. and NATO complete arsenals.[21]

On the threshold of nuclear first use, the moment at which NATO had taken the decision for nuclear escalation was of vital importance for Soviet intelligence to establish. Subsequent reactive movements of troops, command posts, logistics, and other assets and the preparation of counterstrikes would have to take place during the time between detection of NATO's decision to go nuclear and the launching of the first salvos. Otherwise the Soviet and allied forces thrusting into Central Europe would be confronted with a Barbarossa on the move, leading to a disruption of their attack plans, tempo of operations and combat stability.

Soviet sensitivity to these possibilities was apparently acute in the early 1980s. During NATO command post exercise Able Archer conducted in November 1983, Warsaw Pact intelligence monitored the flow of events according to tasking laid down by experience and precedent. The exercise included practice with NATO nuclear release procedures.[22] British and American listening posts detected unusual Soviet sensitivity to unfolding events, with a significant increase in the volume and sense of urgency in Warsaw Pact message traffic.[23] On November 8–9, according to Soviet defector Oleg Gordievsky, an "Operation RYAN" message was sent from Moscow Center to KGB residencies abroad. Operation RYAN (for *"raketno yadernoye napadeniye,* or rocket nuclear attack) had been established in 1981 for intelligence gathering and strategic warning with regard to the possibility of nuclear surprise against the Soviet Union and its East European allies.[24]

The danger of reciprocal alerting of nuclear forces leading to crisis instability was not hypothetical, for several reasons. First, the Soviet concept of an alerted or generated force might have been entirely different from the U.S. concept. The Soviet conceptual framework for military planning emphasized mobilization, readiness and concentration of all force components, regarding the generation of nuclear forces as one part of that process.[25] Second, Soviet political leaders and military planners were disinclined to use nuclear alerts as political signaling devices during a crisis. The Soviet view of crisis was that crisis was an objective condition or period of threat during which states actually prepare for war.[26] (Soviet, compared to U.S., views of crisis avoidance or management receive more specific treatment in the next chapter.)

Third, the skewing of intelligence and warning toward the extreme case of "bolt from the blue" attacks may have been less pronounced in Soviet nuclear planning compared to American. Although Soviet historical experience emphasized the importance of avoiding strategic military surprise, the totally unexpected and massive, surprise nuclear strike was not judged as the most probable of events by Soviet military thinkers of the 1970s and subsequently. Not only the previously cited Voroshilov materials confirm this, but so too do Soviet force deployments and crisis management behaviors.[27] Soviet perceptions of strategic nuclear inferiority in the 1950s and early 1960s eventually gave way in the face of improved U.S.-Soviet political relations and more diverse and survivable Soviet force deployments. The political leadership would have expected to receive from various intelligence sources at least some advance warning of any hostile intent to attack, and this warning would allow some time to prepare a response. Moreover, attainment of strategic nuclear parity with the United States provided to the Soviet leadership the options of preemption, launch under attack/launch on tactical warning, or second-strike ride-out.[28]

Strategic warning indicators provided by various Soviet intelligence agencies would have been derived from monitoring of Western communications traffic, troop movements, diplomatic initiatives and any other apparent preparations for higher levels of military alert or for war.[29] The Soviet view of combat readiness recognized that not all forces can be alerted at the same rate, or need be. Strategic retaliatory forces, air defense troops, and ground and air forces deployed in the first operational echelon had to be maintained "at full wartime strength and should be able to advance themselves to a level of full combat readiness in the shortest time for the accomplishment of assigned missions."[30] The decision for strategic deployment (*strategicheskoye razvertyvaniye*) and for the transition of the Soviet armed forces from a peacetime to a wartime standing was one to be made by the highest political leadership.[31] One of the most important aspects of strategic deployment of forces, according to authoritative Soviet sources, was continuous control of the armed forces by use of military communications networks and other links.[32] The reasons for this included not only the avoidance of enemy surprise, but also, the possibility of communications and command system breakdowns, and of the subsequent fragmentation of the command system into uncoordinated parts:

The complex situation in which strategic deployment of the Armed Forces is conducted requires centralized control. At the same time, considering the limited capabilities of control elements to furnish a wide range of timely information and taking into account the possible interruption of control, particularly in a nuclear war, special importance is given to the initiative of commanders at all levels on the basis of overall concepts and plans.[33]

There is little evidence in published Soviet military doctrine to suggest that their armed forces or political leadership would have been interested in fighting a strategic or theater nuclear war (strategic for them) in the controlled and selective manner sometimes envisioned in U.S. academic literature.[34] In the event of nuclear war, Soviet strategic forces "would be used massively rather than sequentially, and against a wide range of nuclear and conventional military targets, command-and-control facilities, centers of political and administrative leadership, economic and industrial facilities, power supplies, etc., rather than more selectively."[35] Urban areas would not have been attacked gratuitously or in pursuit of some arbitrary number of fatalities, but "neither would they be avoided if they were near military, political or industrial targets."[36]

Soviet long-range ballistic missile forces (land-based and submarine-launched) would have been hard pressed to satisfy the targeting requirements of a cautious Soviet war planner for most of the Cold War. Target arrays in the Transoceanic TVD (Theater of Military Action), essentially North America, would have included both "hard" and "soft" targets. Hard targets are those that are heavily protected and must be attacked by the most accurately delivered warheads: such targets include missile silos and launch control centers, nuclear weapons storage depots, and other reinforced command, control, communications and intelligence (C3I) facilities. Soft targets of interest to Soviet planners were presumably those related to the destruction of U.S. conventional military power or the disabling of U.S. war related economy: airfields, ports, bases, depots, electric power plants, petroleum refineries, chemical plants related to military use, and other facilities not specially protected against the effects of nuclear blast. A comparison of Soviet targeting requirements for selected years with strategic missile warheads available in the same years against hard and soft targets is provided in Table 2.1.

It became as self-evident to the Soviet political leadership as to their NATO opponents, especially subsequent to the Cuban missile crisis, that nuclear weapons were not really "usable" in battle, although the same weapons might be useful in deterrence.[37] This acceptance of mutual deterrence and its underlying arms control construct, strategic nuclear parity, became canonical during the SALT I negotiating period in the late 1960s and early 1970s. Mutual deterrence was a fact of life from the Soviet standpoint, although not a preferred condition: it did not preclude

Table 2.1
Soviet Cold War Nuclear Targeting Requirements and Available Weapons,
Transoceanic TVD

Year	Targets	Warheads Required (WHR)	Warheads Available (WHA)	Net, WHA – WHR
Soft Targets				
1960	1,000–1,200	2,000–2,400	10	(–)1,990–2,390
1965	1,000–1,200	2,000–2,400	415	(–)1,585–1,985
1970	1,000–1,200	2,000–2,400	1,440	(–)560–960
1980	1,000–1,200	2,000–2,400	2,780	380–780
1985	1,000–1,200	2,000–2,400	3,520	1,120–1,520
Hard Targets				
1960	—	—	—	—
1965	1,200	2,400	220*	– 2,180
1970	1,200	2,400	230	– 2,170
1980	1,200	3,600	4,200**	600
1985	1,200	3,600	4,900	1,300

*Soviet SS-7 and SS-8 ICBMs would not have been effective against hard targets such as
Minuteman silos, but they could have been targeted against the softer Atlas and Titan
launchers still in the U.S. inventory.
**The 1980 versions of SS-18 and SS-19 Soviet ICBMs would not have been effective against
upgraded U.S. Minuteman ICBM silos rated at about 2,000 psi. Thus Soviet countersilo
attacks in 1980 would have required much more than three-on-one targeting that the
later SS-18 Mod 4 and the SS-19 Mod 3 made feasible by the mid-1980s.

Source: Adapted from estimates by William T. Lee. See William T. Lee and Richard F. Staar,
Soviet Military Policy since World War II (Stanford, Calif.: Stanford University/Hoover
Institution Press, 1986), p. 160.

the possibility of nuclear war entirely.[38] Another marker of the Soviet
view of deterrence was Brezhnev's speech at Tula in January 1977 in
which the Soviet leader renounced the aim of nuclear superiority as an
objective of Soviet policy. Subsequent to Brezhnev's Tula speech, both
political and military leaders consistently acknowledged that Soviet policy was defensive and designed to prevent attacks on the USSR, not for
superiority over the United States or for fighting and winning a nuclear
war.[39]

The acceptance of nuclear parity and the inadmissibility of nuclear war
as deliberate policy were not acts of charity on the part of Moscow.
Soviet military analysts on the General Staff told their political leaders

in the Kremlin that the realities of modern war precluded victory in a large-scale conventional war, such as might occur in Europe, as well as in any nuclear war. The conventional forces of the Soviet empire and of NATO, were they to clash on the northern and central European fronts and somehow avoid escalation to nuclear attack, would nevertheless destroy the very social values the two sides were thought to be defending. A repeat of the Second World War to an acceptable, although costly, outcome was simply not feasible by any measure of military planning. The superfluity of large-scale conventional warfare was even more threatening to the Soviet state psyche than was the recognition, commonplace among elites by the late 1960s and by scientists even earlier, that a nuclear war would have no winners. The cult of the Great Patriotic War in Russia bolstered the regime against its many failures in economics and in public rectitude. If the Red Army was in fact no longer a usable instrument against the main enemy as defined by Moscow and at an acceptable cost, why should Soviet citizens continue to tolerate empty stores and shelves in order to devote 15 percent of their GNP to defense? (Table 2.2 summarizes indicators of U.S. and Soviet nuclear and conventional military power for selected years of the Cold War.)

During the Gorbachev era after 1985, theorists from civilian research institutes were encouraged to develop concepts of arms control and "reasonable sufficiency" in defense more in keeping with Gorbachev's desire to reduce defense expenditures and to stabilize the arms race.[40] Other defense intellectuals argued that numerical parity in nuclear arms even at lower levels was insufficient to guarantee stability: managing the problem of inadvertent war or escalation was equally significant.[41] Some authors contended that nuclear war stood apart from any relationship between war and politics as previously posited by Clausewitz or Lenin.[42] The agreement to entirely eliminate so-called long-range, intermediate nuclear forces (LRINF) in Europe, reached by Presidents Reagan and Gorbachev, testified not only to the shared recognition of the absurdity of nuclear war, but also to the changed perceptions of the two sides' intentions that had taken root between Reagan's first and second terms in office.

The insistence of Russia's post-Soviet leadership on adherence to the ABM Treaty of 1972 showed that the concept of nuclear forbearance by mutual deterrence had carried forward from the Cold War into an uncertain future. Post–Cold War U.S.-Russian cooperation on CIS denuclearization, on nonproliferation and on a Comprehensive Test Ban (CTB) agreement opened for signature in 1996 suggested continuing recognition that nuclear weapons were simply different, and excess numbers of them suitable for discard.[43]

Table 2.2
U.S. and Soviet Force Levels, Selected Years

| System | 1964 | | 1968 | | 1972 | | 1976 | | Change, 1964–1976 | | | | 1980 | |
| | | | | | | | | | Amount | | Percent | | | |
	U.S.	USSR	U.S.	USSR	U.S.	USSR	U.S.	USSR	U.S.	USSR	U.S.	USSR	U.S.	USSR
ICBMs	654	200	1,054	700	1,054	1,118	1,054	1,527	400	1,327	(61)	(664)	1,054	1,398
SLBMs	336	20	656	50	656	450	656	845	320	825	(95)	(4,125)	656	950
Bombers	630	190	650	250	569	140	387	140	−243	−50	(−39)	(−26)	348	150
Major surface combatant ships	300	200	325	200	250	225	175	225	−125	25	(−42)	(13)	175	260
Tactical aircraft	5,700	3,500	5,700	3,500	5,000	4,500	5,000	6,000	−700	2,500	(−12)	(71)	5,000	6,500
Division equivalents[a]	19	7	20	10	16	25	16	25	−3	18	(−16)	(257)	16	27

[a]U.S. and Soviet divisions are not directly comparable. Soviet divisions are made equivalent to those of the United States in this comparison.

Source: Lawrence J. Korb, "Where Did All the Money Go? The 1980s U.S. Defense Buildup and the End of the Cold War," in Stephen J. Cimbala, ed., Mysteries of the Cold War (Aldershot, U.K.: Ashgate Publishing Co., 1999), pp. 3–18.

CONVENTIONAL DETERRENCE AND DEFENSIVE
MILITARY STRATEGY

The great Russian commander and military theorist Aleksandr Suvorov was not enamored of defensive actions. "The very name defense,"
he once wrote, "already proves weakness, and so it incites timidity."[44]
But a Suvorov in command of Soviet forces in the 1970s and 1980s would
have recognized that new weapons and command/control systems made
possible more activeness in offensive and defensive battle, below the
nuclear threshold. In addition to new technologies, Soviet revisitation of
their own World War II history, and influential thinking about operational art by prominent commanders, called forth new appreciations of
the defensive as a necessary or expedient form of war. Prior to 1985 these
modern views of the defensive carried no implication of disjunction between the politico-military and military-technical levels of Soviet military
doctrine; after Gorbachev, reconciliation of the two levels became more
problematical.[45]

As early as 1982, Marshal N.V. Ogarkov (then Chief of the Soviet General Staff) had noted that "the previous forms of employment of combined units and formations have in large measure ceased to correspond
to present conditions."[46] A new U.S. military strategy, according to Ogarkov, called for "preparing the armed forces to wage a war with the employment of solely conventional weaponry."[47] This contention was
repeated by Ogarkov in a 1985 publication. After discussing the nuclear
strategy of the Reagan administration as one which was offensively oriented and designed to make possible a preemptive first strike, Ogarkov
noted that the U.S. military strategy "also envisions training its armed
forces to wage a war with the use of only conventional means of destruction."[48] What this might imply for the concept of the offensive engagement was noted in an authoritative study of tactics published in 1984
under the editorship of Lt. Gen. V.G. Reznichenko:

The offensive engagement today is more dynamic than in the last war. Being
fully motorized and amply equipped with tanks, forces can attack with smaller
densities of personnel and equipment than before, and yet in considerably greater
depth and with greater momentum.[49]

In the offensive engagement using only conventional weapons, the
enemy's first and second echelons and reserves were to be attacked sequentially while moving rifle and tank subunits into the depth of his
defense. The employment of modern weaponry "increases the decisiveness of an offensive engagement."[50] Decisiveness resulted from the continuous increase in troop capabilities and their ability to defeat the
enemy without having overall superiority in forces and equipment.[51] Al-

though decisiveness was important in offensive operations in past wars, in modern conditions of the 1980s offensive operations were thought to be even more decisive. According to Soviet tactical assessments, modern rifle and tank subunits with highly effective combat equipment and weapons were capable of quickly breaching a deeply echeloned defense even if the defenders were well equipped with nuclear weapons and high technology conventional forces, including ground-launched anti-tank weapons, artillery, reconnaissance-strike complexes, airborne and amphibious assault units, and helicopters.[52]

Note that this mid-1980s assessment of Soviet capabilities was offered for conducting offensive engagements using conventional weapons only. Its apparent optimism concealed a concern on the part of Soviet planners that these objectives might not be attainable in the event of actual war, as opposed to the conduct of military exercises. Much depended on the correct timing and coordination of efforts. Although total surprise against NATO was not probable during any crisis or period of tension, partial surprise was not precluded. And partial surprise was necessary if the Soviet Union were to have had any hope of breaching a fully prepared defense in depth, which NATO was increasingly more capable of presenting.[53] After the dramatic political events of 1989 in which the fall of communist governments in Eastern Europe disestablished the Warsaw Pact as a cohesive military alliance, the prospects for a short warning, unreinforced attack against NATO seemed to have dropped from improbable to impossible. Henceforth the Soviet Union might have to assume the defensive, not the offensive, in the initial period of war.

Colonel-General M.A. Gareev, then Deputy Chief of the Soviet General Staff, wrote in 1985 that Soviet military theory and operational plans on the eve of World War II gave insufficient attention to the proper conduct of the operational and strategic defensive. He noted that the "idea of the continuous shifting of war at its very outset to enemy territory (and the idea was unsound both scientifically and backed up neither by an analysis of the actual situation or by operational calculations) had so beguiled certain leading military workers that the possibility of conducting military operations on our own territory was virtually excluded."[54] This same assessment was offered by Andrei Kokoshin and Valentin Larionov in their discussion of the battle of Kursk as a model for the implementation of the doctrine of defensive sufficiency.[55] The authors did not dwell on the fact that Kursk was an example of very active defense nor that it was based on the acquisition of very precise intelligence about the opponent's intentions. Kursk was also a case of an operational counteroffensive planned and conducted after war had been declared and fought for several years. Thus it provided little in the way of guidance for harried Soviet planners who might be tasked to defend expansive borders on the basis of force posture and military doctrine which excluded preemption or even defensive activeness as an option.

However, the problem of military stability has always been two sided: the prevention of accidental/inadvertent war was as important as the deterrence of deliberate aggression. According to prominent Soviet military theorists of the 1980s, previous military planning did not always take into account all aspects of the complex relationship between mobilization and deterrence. In a departure from the precedent set by V.D. Sokolovskiy's *Voennaya strategiya* (Military Strategy) in the 1960s, Gareev in his *M.V. Frunze—voennyi teoretik* (M.V. Frunze—Military Theorist) doubted whether mobilization of all essential forces and means prior to war was either necessary or desirable.[56] The Sokolovskiy volume reflected the shared conviction by the Soviet military leadership in the 1960s that any war between East and West would shortly become nuclear and all-out. By the time of Gareev's *M.V. Frunze* (the mid-1980s), Soviet planning guidance and military theory had changed considerably, beginning with a major shift in 1966 toward a priority for the prevention of world war and the nuclear destruction of the USSR.[57]

Prevention of the nuclear destruction of the Soviet Union could not be guaranteed once fighting had expanded to include strikes against the territorial homelands of the superpowers. Even the limited use of nuclear weapons in Europe carried incalculable risks of expansion into total war. Therefore, to the extent possible, escalation to the level of nuclear warfare would have to be forestalled, and the Soviet ground and tactical air forces in Europe would have to fight below the nuclear threshold. Soviet theater and strategic nuclear forces would assume the roles of counterdeterrents to NATO's theater and strategic nuclear deterrents, opening the highway for a conventional test of strength.[58]

Even without nuclear escalation, the problem of military stability and the possibility of first strike fears leading to war demanded further attention. Gareev referred to mobilization as "tantamount to war" in the sense that mobilization sends signals to the other side, raising its level of awareness and raising its sensitivity to any indicators of planning for surprise attack.[59] The Soviet General Staff would have preferred to have authorization for prewar mobilization which was proof even against worst-case surprises, but the likelihood is that the post-1985 political leadership would have denied them this.[60] Therefore, the armed forces had to plan for war under disadvantageous conditions and allow for the possibility of enemy preemption with conventional deep strike. According to the guidelines provided by Soviet political leadership (Gorbachev) in the latter 1980s, military doctrine emphasized the prevention (*predotvrashchat'*) of war, and for this purpose the political leadership had to avoid provocative mobilizations inviting enemy preemption.[61] For some Soviet military planners of the latter 1980s, the problem of optimizing preparedness while avoiding unnecessary provocation of potential enemies was a reminder of the months immediately preceding Barbarossa:

The Soviet leadership did not want to provoke hostilities at a time of complex secrecy in the Soviet system, so that there was a fundamental dysfunction—a cybernetic dysfunction—between two Soviet systems of information. One was among the initiated, and that included a good portion of the General Staff and certainly the political leadership who thought that war was coming, although how close they could not say. The second was an attitude among the rank-and-file that war was not close and therefore should not be anticipated.[62]

For both prospective attackers and defenders using large and technologically well-equipped forces in the last two decades of the Cold War, the capability for rapid mobilization, concentration and deployment of combat and combat support elements, once war was judged likely, became an important deterrent. This importance was emphasized in lecture materials from the Soviet General Staff Academy during the 1970s.[63] The capabilities of modern reconnaissance systems, weapons and control made possible as never before the seizure of initiative by the defense. It was precisely this possibility, of NATO seizing the initiative from an initially defensive posture and inflicting deep strikes on Soviet reinforcements and logistics, which worried Soviet planners in the 1980s.

In short, current and future weapons technology could make it possible to overturn the enemy's plans, to attack enemy forces at great depth, and to inflict decisive losses *whether fighting from the offensive or the defensive*. The complexity of even small high technology conventional forces, let alone larger ones, made the struggle for information even more important for the defender who must seize the initiative as soon as the prospective attacker's plans are successfully gleaned. However, in an era of nuclear and highly destructive conventional weapons, provocation of an attack which was not actually being planned had to be avoided. The line between deterrence and provocation could be maintained by prospective defenders only if their command and control systems were intact and functioning with high effectiveness.

Under the relentless pressure of modern battle, command and control systems and other aspects of defensive combat stability (*zhivuchest'*) were almost certain to be stressed to the ultimate, even if nuclear escalation could have been avoided. Authoritative Soviet assessments of NATO potential to conduct an "air-land operation" in the latter 1980s warned that the objective of such an operation would be "destroying the enemy throughout the entire depth of his army's operational formation."[64] In these conditions of uninterrupted battle emphasizing combined arms and three dimensional combat:

Defensive combat within the framework of an air-land operation is a combination of static and dynamic actions by combined-arms formations and units, coupled with growing fire pressure upon the advancing, deploying and attacking enemy. It presupposes integrated application of the principles of positional and mobile defense with the purpose of halting an offense and seizing the initiative. In this case *defense is conducted no less decisively than offense.*[65]

The increased activeness of offensive and defensive combat, should deterrence fail, posed a problem for those who sought in the latter 1980s to revise Soviet military theory in a direction more declaredly defensive. In an article in the December 1989 issue of *Kommunist*, Soviet defense minister Dmitri Yazov outlined his view of a change in the relationship between the political or socio-political and military-technical levels of Soviet military doctrine.[66] Yazov acknowledged that a contradiction had marked the past development of Soviet military doctrine, between its political and military-technical aspects. If, in its political aspects, military doctrine was always defensive, stipulating the rejection of military attack on anyone at all, on the military-technical plane reliance was placed on "decisive offensive actions" if war was unleashed against the Soviet Union and its allies. It was also assumed that, the higher the capability of the Soviet armed forces for such actions, the more solid the defense, and the less likely an attack by the enemy. Eventually this resulted in a contradiction which had to be acknowledged and resolved; the defensive thrust of the political aspect of military doctrine was in contradiction, according to Yazov, to its military-technical emphasis on offensive action. Therefore, "in the contemporary contents of our doctrine, brought into action in 1987, this contradiction is completely eliminated."[67] The contradiction was resolved, according to Yazov and in conformity with authoritative party guidance at the time, by movement toward a posture of reasonable sufficiency for defense which would become evident through changes in Soviet defense budgets and in force structure.

Gorbachev's effort to impose defensiveness to Soviet military doctrine was, as we now know, only successful in part.[68] The parlous state of the Soviet economy in the latter 1980s drove Gorbachev toward decisions favoring nuclear and conventional arms reductions and toward redefinition of the East-West competition along the lines of common European security.[69] The rapid collapse of the Warsaw Treaty Organization and Soviet control over their former military satellites in East Central Europe resulted in premature closure of the debate over "defensive sufficiency" in favor of matters more urgent. In February 1988, Gorbachev announced that the Limited Contingent of Soviet Forces in Afghanistan would be completely withdrawn within one year. In one sense the Soviet military, rid of Afghanistan, breathed a sigh of relief: from another standpoint, it was a serious blow to professional military self-esteem. The Soviet army had "lost" a war for the first time and the setbacks could not be blamed on "third world" clients.[70] Military participation in the attempted overthrow of Gorbachev in August 1991 provided additional evidence that some members of the Soviet officer corps had become more politicized in favor of "Soviet" military doctrine than had their nominal party and government civilian superiors.[71] The collapse of the Soviet Union in December 1991 brought a halt to the further development of a uniquely "Soviet" military theory, strategy and doctrine, but much of it would obviously be carried forward into the armed forces of newly democratic Russia.

CONCLUSION

Faced with a bipolar, nuclear world for more than four decades, the Soviet political and military leadership adjusted authoritative views on the nature of a future war, on the relationship between technology and military power, and on other sociopolitical and military-technical aspects of doctrine. Eventually recognizing that victory in a general nuclear war was impossible and that the limitation of any nuclear war to a particular theater of operations was unlikely, Soviet military thinkers accepted the fact of mutual deterrence based on survivable retaliatory forces. However, in the Soviet view, an essentially equivalent balance of nuclear forces between Russia and its enemies could not guarantee peace and security. War could break out for reasons having little or nothing to do with rational calculation or with the prewar correlation of military and other forces. Therefore authoritative and expert Soviet views on the prevention of war, by deterrence or by other means, had to take into account the possible outbreak of crisis leading to war.

The results of Soviet military adaptation to Cold War demands were successful in the short run, although at dizzying cost to an already stagnant economic system in the longer term. Soviet military adaptation created the image of a superpower equivalent in power and potential to the United States and its NATO allies. But this putative military equivalency was, in the Russian tradition, mostly Potemkinism. Behind the facade of Russia's superpower status lay its dormant economy, its dissident nationalities and its sclerotic party and military leadership. When it all crashed between 1989 and 1991, the Russian core of Soviet military power was forced to reinvent itself with truncated conventional military forces and residual nuclear weapons of uncertain purpose.

NOTES

I am grateful to David Glantz and Jacob Kipp for encouraging me to undertake this research, portions of which appear in my article, "The Cold War and Soviet

Military Strategy," *The Journal of Slavic Military Studies*, Vol. 10, No. 3 (September 1997): 25–55.

1. On Soviet military innovation during the Cold War years see Kimberly Marten Zisk, *Engaging the Enemy: Organization Theory and Soviet Military Innovation, 1955–1991* (Princeton, N.J.: Princeton University Press, 1993). For theoretical explanations for military innovation and pertinent cases see Stephen Peter Rosen, *Winning the Next War: Innovation and the Modern Military* (Ithaca, N.Y.: Cornell University Press, 1991).

2. Raymond L. Garthoff, *The Great Transition: American-Soviet Relations and the End of the Cold War* (Washington, D.C.: Brookings Institution, 1994), esp. pp. 551–598.

3. Garthoff, *Deterrence and the Revolution in Soviet Military Doctrine* (Washington, D.C.: Brookings Institution, 1990), pp. 6–28 is especially helpful on these points. Other sources pertinent to Soviet deterrence concepts are cited in notes that follow.

4. David Holloway, *Stalin and the Bomb: The Soviet Union and Atomic Energy, 1939–1956* (New Haven, Conn.: Yale University Press, 1994), p. 253. Although Stalin emphasized the development of delivery vehicles for Soviet atomic weapons and defense against atomic attack, he did not regard the atomic bomb as a decisive weapon. Ibid., p. 250.

5. Harriet Fast Scott and William F. Scott, *Soviet Military Doctrine: Continuity, Formulation, and Dissemination* (Boulder, Colo.: Westview Press, 1988), passim.

6. Speech of Comrade G.M. Malenkov, *Pravda*, March 13, 1954, cited in Yuri Smirnov and Vladislav Zubok, "Nuclear Weapons after Stalin's Death: Moscow Enters the H-Bomb Age," *Cold War International History Project*, http://cwihp.si.edu/cwihplib.nst/, November 6, 2000.

7. Smirnov and Zubok, "Nuclear Weapons after Stalin's Death."

8. Ibid.

9. See V.D. Sokolovskiy, ed., *Voennaya Strategiya* (Military Strategy) (Moscow: Voenizdat, 1962) illustrates the impact of Khrushchev's views of the priority of nuclear-missile war on officially approved military doctrine. Later editions of this work were published in 1963 and 1968. See also Harriet Fast Scott and William F. Scott, *Soviet Military Doctrine: Continuity, Formulation and Dissemination* (Boulder, Colo.: Westview Press, 1988), pp. 34–41.

10. Evolution of the Soviet definition of victory in the Cold War years is traced in A.A. Kokoshin, V.M. Sergeev and V.L. Tsymbursky, "Evolution of the Concept of 'Victory' in Soviet Military-Political Thought after World War II," paper presented at workshop sponsored by the Committee on Contributions of Behavioral and Social Science to the Prevention of Nuclear War, Commission on Behavioral and Social Sciences and Education, National Research Council (Talinn, Estonia, January 1999).

11. The 1964 Warsaw Pact plan was brought to light by the Parallel History Project under the direction of Professor Vojtech Mastny. For his commentary on the plan, see the PHP web site at http://www.isn.ethz.ch/php/documents/introvm.htm.

12. Vojtech Mastny, "Taking Lyon on the Ninth Day? The 1964 Warsaw Pact Plan for a Nuclear War in Europe and Related Documents," Introduction, p. 2, http://www.isn.ethz.ch/php/documents/introvm.htm.

13. Col. Gen. Pyotr Ivashutin, "Strategic Operations of the Nuclear Forces," August 28, 1964, p. 9, http://www.isn.ethz.ch/php/documents/1/ivashutin-engl.htm.

14. Andrei A. Kokoshin, *Soviet Strategic Thought, 1917–1991* (Cambridge, Mass.: MIT Press, 1998), p. 124. See also Zisk, *Engaging the Enemy*, pp. 47–81 on Soviet reactions to NATO flexible response strategy.

15. Kokoshin, *Soviet Strategic Thought*, p. 126.

16. Ibid., p. 127.

17. Ghulam Dastagir Wardak, comp., and Graham Hall Turbiville, Jr., gen. ed., *The Voroshilov Lectures: Materials from the Soviet General Staff Academy*, Vol. I (Washington, D.C.: National Defense University Press, 1989), pp. 233–254.

18. Ibid., pp. 244–245.

19. Ibid., p. 245.

20. Ibid., pp. 245–246.

21. Ibid., p. 247. This is one clue to apparent Soviet unwillingness to accept U.S. versions of controlled nuclear escalation, as for example in National Security Decision Memorandum (NSDM) 242 later referred to as the "Schlesinger doctrine."

22. Ben B. Fischer, *A Cold War Conundrum: The 1983 Soviet War Scare* (Washington, D.C.: U.S. Central Intelligence Agency, Center for the Study of Intelligence, September 1997), pp. 24–26 provides an informative account of Able Archer and its presumed relationship to Soviet fears of war.

23. Gordon Brook-Shepherd, *The Storm Birds: Soviet Postwar Defectors* (New York: Wiedenfeld and Nicolson, 1989), p. 329.

24. Ibid., pp. 330–331.

25. See Graham H. Turbiville, Jr., "Strategic Deployment: Mobilizing and Moving the Force," *Military Review*, Vol. 68 (December 1988): 41–49. According to the first volume of the Voroshilov Military Academy of the General Staff lecture materials of the 1970s, "the notification by alert given to bring the strategic nuclear forces to full combat readiness, is only some minutes, while, for the units, large units and operational formations of the various Services of the Armed Forces, such notification will be longer to a greater extent." *Voroshilov Lectures*, Vol. I, p. 181. On the levels of combat readiness (*boevoy gotovnost'*) and the process of bringing the Soviet armed forces to full combat readiness, see ibid., ch. 4. Although the process of bringing the armed forces to the highest level of combat readiness "should be conducted under all conditions in close consideration of the employment of nuclear weapons by the enemy" and "control should ensure centralized and simultaneous communication of signals and instructions" according to measures developed by the General Staff and made known to the troops (ibid., pp. 193–194).

26. Stephen Shenfield, "Crisis Management: The Soviet Approach," in Carl Jacobsen, ed., *Strategic Power: USA/USSR* (New York: Macmillan, 1990), pp. 198–205, citation p. 200. See also the discussion in the next chapter on Soviet versus American views of crisis management.

27. Bruce G. Blair, *The Logic of Accidental Nuclear War* (Washington, D.C.: Brookings Institution, 1993), esp. pp. 25–26.

28. Stephen M. Meyer, "Soviet Nuclear Operations," in Ashton B. Carter, John

D. Steinbruner and Charles A. Zraket, eds., *Managing Nuclear Operations* (Washington, D.C.: Brookings Institution, 1987), pp. 470–534.

29. Ibid., pp. 513–516.

30. *Voroshilov Lectures*, Vol. I, p. 181.

31. Ibid., p. 229. Soviet military writers also use the term "strategic leadership" (*stratigicheskaya rukovodstva*) to refer to the highest political and military leaders as a group. Prior to 1987 this was assumed to be the Defense Council, a smaller body within the Politburo, and it was supposed that in wartime the Defense Council assumed the same functions and authority as had the GKO (State Committee for Defense) in World War II. Under Gorbachev, realignments of power among party, government and armed forces after 1987, there was more guesswork involved in extrapolating from Soviet peacetime to wartime command arrangements. For pertinent background, see Harriet Fast Scott and William F. Scott, *The Soviet Control Structure: Capabilities for Wartime Survival* (New York: Crane, Russak/National Strategy Information Center, 1983), pp. 45–58.

32. *Voroshilov Lectures*, Vol. I, p. 229.

33. Ibid., p. 231.

34. Soviet General Staff discussion and debate over the issue of limited strategic nuclear war is considered in Zisk, *Engaging the Enemy*, pp. 98–119. For additional discussion of limited nuclear war, see Edward L. Warner III, *Soviet Concepts and Capabilities for Limited Nuclear War: What We Know and How We Know It* (Santa Monica, Calif.: RAND, February 1989). This study contains many important primary source references. See also Lt. Gen. A.I. Yevseev, "O nekotorykh tendentsiyakh v izmenenii soderzhaniya i kharaktera nachal'nogo perioda voiny" *Voenno-istoricheskii zhurnal*, No. 11 (November 1985): 10–20. Writing of the impact of a massive nuclear strike at the outset of a war, Yevseev notes that "the initial period of a future nuclear-rocket war may be the fundamental and decisive period which in large measure predetermines the further development of armed conflict, and in certain conditions the outcome of war" (Yevseyev, "O nekorotykh tendentsiyakh . . . ," p. 17).

35. Desmond Ball, *Soviet Strategic Planning and the Control of Nuclear War* (Canberra: Strategic and Defence Studies Centre, Australian National University, November 1983), p. 5. See also p. 8 for his notional RISOP table.

36. Ibid., p. 5.

37. Garthoff, *Deterrence and the Revolution in Soviet Military Doctrine*, esp. p. 52 and passim, and David Holloway, *The Soviet Union and the Arms Race*, 2nd ed. (New Haven, Conn.: Yale University Press, 1983), esp. pp. 43–52.

38. See the opening Soviet statement at the SALT I negotiations, as quoted in Holloway, *The Soviet Union and the Arms Race*, p. 46.

39. For example, Marshal of the Soviet Union N.V. Ogarkov, *Istoriya uchit bditel'nosti* (Moscow: Voenizdat, 1985), pp. 75–77. See esp. p. 77 for Ogarkov's emphasis on Soviet "no first use" policy with regard to nuclear weapons and his pejorative reference to U.S. nomenclature of strategic "offensive" forces. See also p. 68 for his discussion of U.S. plans for limited nuclear war in Europe and for building up U.S. strategic forces under Reagan.

40. See, for example, Andrei Kokoshin, "Nuclear Arms Reduction and Strategic Stability," *SShA: Ekonomika, politika, ideologiya*, No. 2 (February 1988): 3–12, FBIS-SOV-88-051, March 16, 1988; Alexei Arbatov, "Parity and Reasonable Suf-

ficiency," *International Affairs* (in English), No. 10 (October 1988): 75–87; Arbatov, "How Much Defence is Sufficient?" *International Affairs* (in English), No. 4 (1989): 31–44; Lev Semeiko, "Razumnaya dostatochnost'—put' k nadezhnomy miry" (Reasonable Sufficiency—Path to Reliable Peace), *Kommunist*, No. 7 (May 1989): 112–121;

41. Vitaliy Zhurkin, Sergei Karaganov and Andrei Kortunov, "Security Challenges: Old and New," *Kommunist*, No. 1 (January 1988): 42–50, JPRS-UKO-88-006, March 24, 1988.

42. Daniil Proektor, "Politics, Clausewitz and Victory in Nuclear War," *International Affairs* (in English), No. 5 (1988): 74–80. A large debate about politics and nuclear war had been stimulated by an earlier article in the same journal: see Boris Kanevsky and Pyotr Shabardin, "The Correlation of Politics, War and a Nuclear Catastrophe," *International Affairs* (in English), No. 2 (1988): 95–104.

43. Graham Allison, Ashton B. Carter, Steven E. Miller and Philip Zelikow, *Cooperative Denuclearization: From Pledges to Deeds* (Cambridge, Mass.: Center for Science and International Affairs, Harvard University, January 1993). See also William C. Martel and William T. Pendley, *Nuclear Coexistence: Rethinking U.S. Policy to Promote Stability in an Era of Proliferation* (Montgomery, Ala.: Air War College, April 1994), esp. pp. 49–66.

44. Suvorov, quoted in V.Ye. Savkin, *Osnovnye printsipy operativnogo iskusstva i taktiki* (Moscow: Voenizdat, 1972), translated in U.S. Air Force Soviet Military Thought Series as *The Basic Principles of Operational Art and Tactics* (Washington, D.C.: U.S. Government Printing Office, n.d.), p. 244.

45. See, in particular, Scott and Scott, *Soviet Military Doctrine*, pp. 110–115.

46. Marshal N.V. Ogarkov, *Vsegda v gotovnosti k zashchite Otechestva* (Moscow: Voenizdat, 1982), p. 34.

47. Ibid., p. 16.

48. Ogarkov, *Istoriya uchit bditel'nosti*, pp. 68–69.

49. V.G. Reznichenko et al., *Taktika* (Tactics) (Moscow: Voenizdat, 1984), translated by CIS Multilingual Section, National Defense Headquarters, Ottawa, Canada, p. 69.

50. Ibid., p. 67.

51. Ibid.

52. Ibid.

53. On partial surprise, see Vigor, *Soviet Blitzkrieg Theory*, pp. 156–157 and passim.

54. M.A. Gareev, *M.V. Frunze—Voennyi teoretik* (M.V. Frunze: Military Theorist) (New York: Pergamon-Brassey's, 1988, in English), p. 208.

55. Andrey Kokoshin and Valentin Larionov, "Kurskaya bitva v svete sovremennoye oboronitel'noye doctriny," *Mirovaya ekonomika i mezhdunarodnyye otnosheniya*, No. 8 (1987): 32–40.

56. Gareev, *M.V. Frunze*, p. 216. Gareyev cites V.D. Sokolovskiy, ed., *Voennaya strategiya* (Moscow: Voenizdat, 1963), p. 22.

57. Michael McGwire, *Military Objectives in Soviet Foreign Policy* (Washington, D.C.: Brookings Institution, 1987), chs. 2 and 3.

58. See John G. Hines and Phillip A. Petersen, "The Changing Soviet System of Control for Theater War," *International Defense Review*, No. 3 (1986), revised in Stephen J. Cimbala, ed., *Soviet C3* (Washington, D.C.: AFCEA International Press,

1987): 191–219; Hines, Petersen and Notra Trulock III, "Soviet Military Theory from 1945–2000: Implications for NATO," *The Washington Quarterly*, No. 4 (1986): 117–137; and Raymond L. Garthoff, "Mutual Deterrence, Parity and Strategic Arms Limitation in Soviet Policy," in Derek Leebaert, ed., *Soviet Military Thinking* (London: Allen and Unwin, 1981), pp. 92–124.

59. Gareev, *M.V. Frunze*, p. 216.

60. Ibid.

61. See Marshal of the Soviet Union and former Defense Minster Sergei Akhromeyev, "Doktrina predotvrashcheniya voiny, zashchity mira i sotsializma" (Doctrine for the Prevention of War, the Defense of Peace and Socialism), *Problemy mira i sotsializma*, 12 (1987): 23–28.

62. Kipp, "Soviet War Planning," in Glantz, ed., *The Initial Period of War on the Eastern Front*, pp. 40–50, citation p. 49.

63. *Voroshilov Lectures*, Vol. I, pp. 205–232.

64. Reznichenko et al., *Taktika*, p. 20.

65. Ibid., p. 21.

66. D.T. Yazov, "Novaya model' bezopasnosti i vooruzhennyye sily" (A New Model of Security and the Armed Forces), *Kommunist*, Vol. 18 (December 1989): 61–72.

67. Ibid., p. 66.

68. Dale R. Herspring, *The Soviet High Command, 1967–1989: Personalities and Politics* (Princeton, N.J.: Princeton University Press, 1990), pp. 265–276. See also Garthoff, *The Great Transition*, pp. 528–530.

69. Nicolai N. Petro and Alvin Z. Rubinstein, *Russian Foreign Policy: From Empire to Nation-State* (New York: Longman, 1997), p. 151.

70. George M. Mellinger, "Survey: The Military Year 1989 in Review," in Mellinger, ed., *Soviet Armed Forces Review Annual*, 1989, Vol. 13 (Gulf Breeze, Fla.: Academic International Press, 1995), p. 2.

71. Thomas M. Nichols, *The Sacred Cause: Civil-Military Conflict over Soviet National Security 1917–1992* (Ithaca, N.Y.: Cornell University Press, 1993). On the failed coup of August 1991 see John B. Dunlop, *The Rise of Russia and the Fall of the Soviet Empire* (Princeton, N.J.: Princeton University Press, 1993), pp. 186–255, esp. pp. 247–250.

Chapter 3

Friction and Nuclear Deterrence

Nuclear weapons were thought by many to contradict much that had been taught previously about military strategy. Nuclear weapons would keep the peace by means of deterrence: the threat of using means of destruction so absolute in their consequences would suffice to replace war, and friction along with it. Generations of nuclear strategic thinkers in the United States and some policy makers treated the end of the Cold War as confirmation of this logic. Both the peaceful withdrawal of Soviet military power from East Central Europe, and the demise of the Soviet Union itself without war, provided for some observers the proof that nuclear deterrence worked by freezing the frame of war until communism collapsed in Europe. Political leaders such as Mikhail Gorbachev, the last president of the Soviet Union, and eminent scholars asserted that nuclear weapons had severed the necessary relationship between war and politics that the Prussian philosopher of war, Karl von Clausewitz, had placed at the center of his military thought.

The reasons why the Cold War ended peacefully and in favor of the West are more complicated than the singular role of nuclear weapons or nuclear deterrence alone.[1] The expectation that nuclear deterrence has invalidated great power wars and thereby circumvented Clausewitz is even more mistaken than the assumption that nuclear weapons gave the West victory in the Cold War. Nuclear and other deterrence as practiced during the Cold War was marked by a dangerous and unavoidable component of what Clausewitz referred to as friction, and so too will it be in the future. Friction (defined below) is not determined by the size of arsenals nor by the devastation that weapons can inflict if fired, but by the human relationships that must be engaged in order to deter or, if need be, to fight with weapons of mass destruction, including nuclear ones.[2]

A great deal was assumed about human behavior by deterrence theory, and the theory has been subjected to numerous critiques that will not be repeated here, including my own. Instead, this chapter asks about the impact on deterrence of friction as Clausewitz understood the term and as further elaborated in this study: friction is the difference between expected outcomes and actual results. The first part of the chapter discusses Clausewitz's concept of friction, albeit very briefly and in general terms. In the second part of the chapter we consider different kinds of deterrence and the difference between deterrence and coercive diplomacy. In the third section, we discuss the operational aspects of friction as it might affect nuclear offenses and anti-missile defenses.

CLAUSEWITZ AND THE CONCEPT OF FRICTION

One of Clausewitz's more interesting and thought-provoking ideas about military art was the concept of *friction*. This seminal concept has been cited repeatedly by writers on military art and strategy as a pivotal notion that must be comprehended by all great captains and students of military history. As Colin Gray has noted: "If Clausewitz had written only about friction in war, his place among the heroes in the Valhalla of strategic theory would be secure."[3] Despite this acknowledgment by military theorists and historians of the significance of friction for Clausewitzian (or other) interpretations of war, the concept has received comparatively little attention from modern social scientists.

This fact is regrettable, and no one would be more disappointed than Clausewitz. He was not writing a museum piece for display among historical curiosities. Unfinished in Clausewitz's lifetime and organized for publication by his wife after his death in 1831, *On War* is a living and breathing treatise on the nature of war and its attributes for commanders and for policy makers. If only warriors and not policy makers understand what Clausewitz has to say about war eternal as well as about war in particular, much of the intended value of Clausewitz's insights will be lost. Related to the requirement for policy makers as well as military leaders to comprehend the major insights of *On War* is the recognition that Clausewitz did not intend a static theory resembling his bust at Carlisle Barracks. A late-twentieth-century Clausewitz would insist on taking into account what has been learned since the initial publication of *On War* from military history, from politics and from other social science research applicable to war. If Clausewitz was anything he was one of the first, and most durable, examples of a behavioral scientist in the study of war. In that spirit, the present study takes that concept of friction from its originator and applies it to help understand aspects of international security in the recent past and present. Having done so, we should be better prepared to understand the future too.

The subject of friction in war is most explicit in Book One, Chapter Seven of Clausewitz's widely read and highly regarded work, *On War*.[4] The Prussian military philosopher begins by pointing out that a person who has not experienced war cannot comprehend why the conduct of battle is so difficult. The tasks that have to be accomplished in war seem very simple, but that semblance is deceptive: "Everything in war is very simple, but the simplest thing is difficult. The difficulties accumulate and end by producing a kind of friction that is inconceivable unless one has experienced war."[5] So far, it might be thought that Clausewitz was expressing an idea related to the physics of motion or the mechanics of machine breakdown. Far from it. Friction affects the material components of a war plan, to be sure. But its most unpredictable aspect is the relationship of friction to people: the troops who fight and the commanders who command them. Of the military machine, Clausewitz notes that "none of its components is of one piece: each part is composed of individuals, every one of whom retains his potential for friction."[6] In theory, discipline keeps the behavior of individuals fully consistent with the expectations of commanding officers. In practice, as Clausewitz explains: "A battalion is made up of individuals, the least important of whom may chance to delay things or somehow make them go wrong."[7]

Friction is not alone a cause of disparity between the aim of commanders and the unfolding of events in battle. Friction is compounded by other factors and forces, including the environment of danger that characterizes war and the physical exertions required in battle. The most unpredictable element is introduced by the relationship between friction and *chance* in war.[8] Chance in contact with friction "brings about effects that cannot be measured, just because they are largely due to chance."[9] One example given by Clausewitz of friction related to chance is the weather and its effects on the outcome of battle. He then offers a simile that is as memorable as it is appropriate: "Action in war is like movement in a resistant element. Just as the simplest and most natural of movements, walking, cannot easily be performed in water, so in war it is difficult for normal efforts to achieve even moderate results."[10] In the same passage, Clausewitz disparages the views of theorists "who have never swum."

Clausewitz did not limit his discussion of friction to the happenings of battle. In a letter to his future wife, editor and publisher Marie von Bruhl in September 1806, Clausewitz expressed his frustration with the decision-making process within the Prussian high command. As he explained, the Prussian army at the time had "three commanders-in-chief and two chiefs of staff." His mentor Gerhard von Scharnhorst was frustrated in this situation because "he is constantly confronted by obstacles of convenience and tradition, when he is paralyzed by constant *friction* (*Friktion*, in German) with the opinions of others."[11] The three commanders-in-chief were the Duke Karl of Brunswick, nominally in command of the army; King Frederick William III, who decided to accompany the army in the field; and Prince Hohenlohe-Ingelfingen, who was given command of one-half the army.[12] The concerns of Clausewitz were justified: less than three weeks later France defeated Prussia at the battles of Jena and Auerstadt, thus destroying the Prussian army created by Frederick the Great. After France later defeated what remained of Prussia's armies in the battle of Friedland in June 1807, she knocked Prussia temporarily out of the ranks of the powers and reduced her to a satellite within the French empire.[13]

In a later elaboration of the concept of friction, Clausewitz in 1812 wrote to the Prussian crown prince (later Frederick William IV), whom he had been tutoring while also teaching at the Prussian war academy. In this correspondence Clausewitz listed eight sources of "tremendous friction" that make even the simplest plans difficult to realize in war:

1. insufficient knowledge of the enemy;
2. rumors (information gained by remote observation or spies);
3. uncertainty about one's own strength and position;
4. the uncertainties that cause friendly troops to tend to exaggerate their own difficulties;
5. differences between expectations and reality;
6. the fact that one's own army is never as strong as it appears on paper;
7. the difficulties in keeping an army supplied;
8. the tendency to change or abandon well-thought-out plans when confronted with the vivid physical images and perceptions of the battlefield.[14]

In addition, in his discussion on danger in war in Book One, Chapter Four of *On War*, Clausewitz notes that "danger is part of the friction of war. Without an accurate conception of danger we cannot understand war."[15] Clausewitz's concluding observations on Book One include the following summation on the topic of friction:

We have identified danger, physical exertion, intelligence, and friction as the elements that coalesce to form the atmosphere of war, and turn it into a medium that impedes activity. In their restrictive effects they can be grouped into a single concept of friction.[16]

The preceding discussion shows that, in his earlier thinking as well as that later appearing in his posthumously published *On War*, Clausewitz was viewing friction as a multidimensional concept, fundamental both to the art of war *and* to the relationship between war and policy. Were Clausewitz alive and writing about friction today, he would also be aware of the research developments in social and behavioral science since the 1840s (when *On War* was published by his widow) and of the additional military history written since then. We should do as he would: build on his foundation laid down in the first half of the nineteenth century, but not rest there.

TYPES OF DETERRENCE

Deterrence is used in academic and policy-making circles to refer both to a process and to a condition or situation (i.e., a state party to a dispute may be practicing deterrence, or not; or a disputant may be deterred, or not). Deterrence is a psychological process by which an actor influences one or more other actors to behave in accord with the desires of the first actor. In military affairs that are usually conducted by governments or "state actors," deterrence is thought to rest on the ability of the influencer (or deterrer) to manipulate both threats and reassurances in a way that maximizes its influence over the behavior of the party being threatened. As Alexander L. George has noted:

Deterrence, which relies on threats, is better conceived as part of a broader influence theory that combines threats with positive inducements and diplomatic efforts to explore the desirability and feasibility of working out a mutually acceptable accommodation of conflicting interests.[17]

George emphasizes that the successful practice of deterrence is not necessarily guaranteed by careful study of the theory. In state-to-state behavior, one is dealing with an opponent whose very aim is to confound one's own military or diplomatic strategy. Therefore, the most skillful combination of threats and reassurances may fall short if it assumes on the part of the adversary a set of motives and expectations that are not present. One must comprehend the "otherness" of the opponent, and this requires some understanding of his cultural and social parameters as well as his politics and military art. In addition, deterrence cannot substitute for, or be practiced in ignorance of, the hard realities of national interest and geopolitics. A state's threat to defend a vital interest is simply more credible, other things being equal, than its willingness to defend an interest of secondary importance to its security. As George has indicated:

Early deterrence theory was defective in that it placed too much emphasis on various gimmicks for enhancing the credibility of commitment—such as the "threat that leaves something to chance," playing the game of "chicken," etc.—

and failed to recognize that credibility is based on the magnitude and nature of the national interests at stake.[18]

Deterrence is related to, but distinct from, coercive diplomacy. Coercive diplomacy, or compellence, is the use of force or threats of force to persuade an opponent to stop an action already begun or undo that action and its effects.[19] During the Cuban missile crisis of 1962, for example, President Kennedy used coercive diplomacy in order to get Soviet Premier Khrushchev initially to halt further shipments of nuclear-capable missiles to Cuba and eventually to remove the missiles from Cuba and return them to the Soviet Union. Coercive diplomacy, when skillfully practiced, employs only the amount of force, or the degree of threat of force, necessary to demonstrate resolve to the opponent and to make credible one's threat to employ a military strategy. As Gordon A. Craig and George have explained:

Coercive diplomacy needs to be distinguished from pure coercion. It seeks to *persuade* the opponent to cease his aggression rather than bludgeon him into stopping. In contrast to the crude use of force to repel the opponent, coercive diplomacy emphasizes the use of threats and the exemplary use of limited force to persuade him to back down.[20]

It has been established that deterrence relies for its success either on threats of denial (physically or otherwise preventing the opponent from accomplishing his military object) or of punishment. Nuclear deterrence rests mainly on the threat of punishment and that threat has two parts: capability and credibility.[21] Capability implies the means to retaliate once having been attacked or in the expectation of an attack (more on that below). Credibility implies that the deterree understands the threat being made and believes that if the specified behavior is engaged in, the deterrer will actually carry out the threat. Capability is easier to show than credibility, on the evidence. It seemed relatively simple for the Cold War superpowers to demonstrate that they could not only blow themselves up simultaneously or sequentially, but much of the exterior world besides. But this capability endured for most of the Cold War as a constant. It did not necessarily follow that, in the variable circumstances of a specific crisis or attack, deterrence would work as expected to.

There is some controversy over whether deterrence is truly a strategy or an experiment in applied psychology. Successful deterrence means that a war does not have to be fought, but success is defined in a very short-term manner. In the Agadir crisis several years before the start of World War I, the outbreak of war among the major powers was avoided, so Germany was presumably deterred by the denouement of that crisis. However, Germany (at least the Kaiser) was also frustrated and enraged and resolved not to yield the next time around. So being deterred in the short term can light the fuse for failed deterrence later.

Deterrence in history also suffers from a lack of evidence of its effects. One cannot prove that deterrence "worked" when one state failed to attack another: there are many reasons why a state contemplating an attack might stay its hand. Deterrence is also latent as well as manifest. A *latent* deterrence system exists among all states dependent on self-help for military security: the possibility of war in general is ever present, although the specific causes for war and the lineup of enemies may vary. *Manifest* deterrence takes place when a state or other actor has issued a specific threat against another, has defined conditions for compliance, and has explained what will happen if compliance is not forthcoming. It follows that states that cannot or will not communicate, cannot play at deterrence: they can engage in other mischief though, including aggression.[22]

During the Cold War it was assumed by most Western policy makers and military analysts that technology favored the offense over the defense in the case of nuclear weapons. The defender's task was judged as especially problematic if it aspired to defend cities instead of retaliatory forces. The ABM Treaty of 1972 was regarded by U.S. arms control advocates, but apparently not by Soviet military or political leaders, as an acknowledgment that this state of affairs could never be changed. Soviet leaders continued to work on the development of anti-nuclear strategic defenses and deployed an ABM system around Moscow subject to treaty constraints. In 1983 President Ronald Reagan called on the U.S. defense technology community to produce a multitiered missile defense system that could protect the American homeland even against large scale Soviet attacks. After the Cold War, the U.S. research and development program was scaled back to one favoring a smaller defense system for limited strikes by rogue states or accidental launches.

This rejection of defense and embrace of offensive retaliation as a necessary evil, or as a desirable condition, simplified arms control negotiations but also nullified much of traditional military strategy. Traditional strategy for conventional deterrence or for prevailing in war regarded offenses and defenses as competitive and interactive war forms. Historically, a temporarily superior form of attack had eventually produced its antithesis: a countervailing form of defense. Nuclear weapons seemed to exist apart from this action–reaction dynamic, although it was possible that the years between 1945 and 1990 offered too short a time interval to tell. Some argued in the 1980s that eventually space and terrestrially-based non-nuclear weapons, based on new physical principles, would unlock the deadlock of deterrence based on assured retaliation. This futuristic technology remained out of reach at century's end, and Congressional advocates of limited national missile defense (NMD) for the

Table 3.1
First-Strike Stability and Central Deterrence in Three Environments

	Offense Dominant	Defense Dominant	Offense-Defense Competitive
Central deterrence	STRONG	STRONG	UNCERTAIN
	Assured retaliation by offenses	Replaced by denial of attack objectives	Retaliatory threats may not be credible
First-strike stability	STRONG	STRONG	UNCERTAIN
	No advantage to going first— both destroyed	No advantage to going first— both survive	Survival may be dependent upon first strike

Source: Adapted from Glenn A. Kent and David E. Thaler, *First Strike Stability and Strategic Defenses* (Santa Monica, Calif.: RAND, 1990), p. 4. I have reworded some cell entries in keeping with my purposes but not changed the thrust of the Kent-Thaler model.

U.S. homeland advocated ground-based, kinetic kill interceptor and other technologies closer to hand.

The potential for first-strike stability and for central deterrence is partly related to the prevailing technology environment: offense dominant, defense dominant, or mixed. Central deterrence exists if, in a two-sided relationship, neither side can calculate "in cold blood" that a first strike would pay. First-strike stability requires, in addition to the standards for central deterrence, that neither side be tempted to launch its forces preemptively on the assumption that it is under attack or about to be attacked. Table 3.1 summarizes possible relationships between technology environments and optimism or pessimism about central deterrence and first-strike stability.

Some prominent military thinkers now hold that nuclear weapons may give pride of place to a "revolution in military affairs" led by improved electronics, information and communications technologies.[23] Nuclear weapons would not be defeated so much as circumvented. The United States and other high technology societies that were first to exploit advanced information technologies for military purposes would, in this view, have a rich deterrent in the form of "dominant battlespace awareness." This meant being able to see and interpret the entire battlefield and to deny the opponent a clear vision of it, perhaps by confusing or distorting the opponent's own information systems themselves. Some visionaries foresaw techniques for cyberwar that could bypass the actual destruction of armies and missile silos by holding hostage or incapacitating enemy communications, computers, electric power grids, banking records or other social and economic necessities for modern life. Cyberwar might make possible both "counterforce" and "countervalue" attacks against nuclear command and control systems and against civilian infrastructure without firing a single shot in anger.

In summary thus far, both conventional and nuclear deterrence can rely on punishment or denial, on offensive or defensive technology, and on offensively or defensively oriented military doctrines. We will ignore for purposes of this discussion the fact that politicians and others use the terms "offensive" and "defensive" for pejorative and approbative references to the strategies of their enemies and allies. The terms have familiar meaning to readers of this study. The preceding considerations are a necessary prologue to the more specific arguments that follow. They establish that friction in war or deterrence depends upon the specifics of strategy and force structure as well as upon the generalities to which theorists are naturally attracted. What kind of friction relative to nuclear deterrence might be of interest to theorists and to military operators in the next century, based on experience?

FRICTION IN OPERATIONS

In the discussion that follows, I consider friction in offensive and defensive force operations. Models will be used in order to try to pin down some of the more abstract, but policy-relevant, aspects of offensive or defensive force operations. There is an obvious asymmetry here. We know a great deal about the behavior of launchers and reentry vehicles for offensive forces, based on considerable testing during the Cold War and later. But the state of defensive technology is comparatively immature and extrapolations about defenses are, of necessity, less confident.

Offensive Force Operations

Accounts of U.S. or Soviet strategy for nuclear war published during the Cold War years had an antiseptic, unreal quality, something like Clausewitz's reference to "war by algebra." Statistical estimates of the outcomes of nuclear wars were necessary substitutes for the real thing. The danger was that models of nuclear war might distort probable outcomes by ignoring friction and assuming best-case performances for missiles, bombers and command systems never tested in combat conditions. Contributors to the academic literature on nuclear strategy and arms control during the Cold War tended to assume away the significance of operational issues. The large and redundant force structures of the nuclear superpowers, it was presumed, would make irrelevant any comparisons among post-attack states of affairs.

The assumption of nuclear operations' irrelevancy was not necessarily correct even for the years of the Cold War. It becomes even more important to consider offensive and defensive operational issues, including those related to friction, when American and Russian forces are greatly reduced from their Cold War levels. Both governments ratified START II, establishing overall ceilings on deployed strategic nuclear warheads between 3,000 and 3,500. START II was never implemented, and negotiations moved on to START III. Presidents George W. Bush and Vladimir Putin met in November 2001 and declared their intent to reduce their states' deployed strategic nuclear warheads to limits well below START II and III.

These promising hopes for reducing the sizes of deployed forces are dependent on the confidence that both Washington and Moscow can have in the capabilities of their remaining forces. Even if their respective launchers and warheads are no longer aimed at one another's territory (nowadays a matter of several minutes to adjust), neither the United States nor Russia wants to doubt its retaliatory capability even after absorbing a surprise attack. Planners will continue to use their survivability against one another's arsenals as the "worst-case" test case. How would friction in offensive force operations reduce the numbers of surviving and retaliating U.S. or Russian forces under various post–Cold War arms control regimes, compared to a baseline Cold War force (1991)?

Friction can be said to affect offensive force operations as a gradient between the maximum number of weapons originally deployed, on one end of the scale, and the minimum number of weapons actually fired back at enemy targets. Between these high and low extremes are intervening variables. Some deployed weapons are not on line at the time of attack. Some weapons deployed and on line are not yet alerted. Among weapons deployed, on line and alerted, not all will survive attack. Finally, some fraction of weapons deployed, on line, alert and surviving a first strike will fail to arrive at their intended targets due to a variety of technical malfunctions or errors (gravitational anomalies, incorrect navigation fixes, unstable accelerometers, and so forth).

Let us make use of a model for estimating how many actual surviving and retaliating warhead and equivalent megatons (EMT) would be available to the United States or to Russia after absorbing a first strike under plausible conditions of attack (the attack takes place after a political crisis has begun so that forces are alerted above normal peacetime operating tempos, but variation exists in the extent to which force components require prompt launch for survivability). Table 3.2 summarizes the ex-

Table 3.2
Outcomes of Nuclear Exchanges at Various START Levels

	START I	START II	START III (2,500)	START III (1,500)
Russian Survivable, Deliverable Warheads	1,639	1,141	675	539
U.S. Survivable, Deliverable Warheads	1,938	1,063	805	497
Russian Survivable, Deliverable Equivalent Megatons	520	318	193	173
U.S. Survivable, Deliverable Equivalent Megatons	327	292	226	144

Source: Author, based on Steve's Nuclear Assessment Matrix (SNAM), a statistical model for calculating the results of nuclear exchanges originally developed by Dr. James J. Tritten. He is not responsible for its application here.

pected numbers of surviving and retaliating warheads and EMT for Russian and for U.S. START I, START II and START III compliant forces at two levels: 2,500 and 1,500 ceilings.

The results of Table 3.2 suggest the following inferences. First, at START I and START II levels, enough redundancy existed in force structure that the numbers of surviving and retaliating warheads for each side would suffice to fulfill both countervalue (attacks on economic and social value) and some counterforce missions. At START III levels, and especially if the two sides eventually agree to limit those forces to 1,500 warheads per country, the smaller number of survivors makes the possibility of friction in alertness, survivability and reliability more significant. In other words, when you have a great deal of overkill you do not have to worry as much about the Clausewitzian friction that may constrain force operations, by creating pressures for prompt retaliatory launch or by imposing limits on targeting.

In addition, there is the possibility of friction in the divergent expectations imposed by U.S. arms control policy, on one hand, and presidential guidance for the development of actual nuclear war plans. Clinton administration policy guidance laid down in 1997 requires that the United States maintain a number of deployed and survivable warheads sufficient to destroy some 2,260 highly valued targets in Russia. Approximately 1,100 of these targets are thought to be nuclear forces or installations that support nuclear forces. In order to guarantee that the

Table 3.3
U.S. Strategic Nuclear Targeting, 1997 Presidential Guidance

Requirement	Number
Total Targets (Russia, China, other)	3,000
High Value Targets	2,560
Russia	2,260
—Nuclear Forces and Sites	1,100
—OMT (Other Military Targets, or conventional forces and their bases and installations)	500
—Leadership (Major military command centers, communications and supporting infrastructure)	160
—War-Supporting Industry (factories for arms production, equipment storage facilities, etc.)	500
China	
Limited nuclear options for attacking nuclear forces, leadership and major war-supporting industry	300
Secondary Targets	
Additional targets in China, plus Iran, Iraq and North Korea	450–500

Source: Author, based on Bruce Blair, "Going Backwards: Number of U.S. Nuclear Targets Has Grown since 1993," *Manchester Guardian*, June 16, 2000, http://www.cdi.org/ issues/proliferation/goingbckbb.html. This table extrapolates from Blair's article and includes some deductions not in the original; therefore, the author alone is responsible.

United States can retaliate after absorbing a first strike and meet destruction requirements (80% or more) against this target set, the survivability of at least 1,800 warheads must be guaranteed under all circumstances. In addition, military planners say they need to maintain 2,200 warheads on alert. A summary of the requirements inferred by target planners by current (1997) policy appears Table 3.3.

Clearly, policy guidance and targeting requirements will have to be "downsized" in order to mesh with the expectations of further arms reductions, especially if the United States and Russians prefer to reduce START III–accountable force ceilings to 1,500 deployed warheads instead of 2,500 (as the Russians may prefer, on account of economic constraints on their force modernization). Whether targeting guidance and arms control can be synchronized will also depend upon Russian and Chinese reactions to any U.S. decision to deploy national missile defenses (NMD) in this decade (see below, and also Chapter 5).

The larger context of these results, however, is more reassuring. Even friction-constrained retaliatory forces at START III levels will inflict destruction beyond historical precedent on either society. It remains as it did during the Cold War. The cost of being number one or number two in strategic nuclear forces is that the United States and Russia, absent friendly political relations, invite massive destruction on themselves in the name of making deterrence credible. There was no escape from this nuclear straitjacket during the Cold War. Will post–Cold War defenses get Houdini out of this jacket, and what part might friction play in their operations?

Defenses

Post–Cold War U.S. and Russian officials still have reason to worry about another kind of friction not noted in the preceding section: the possibility of accidental/inadvertent war or small attacks from third parties that might draw in the Americans and Russians. Some of these scenarios are rather far-fetched, including a Russia that implodes and allows its government to fall into the hands of a "Red-Brown" military dictatorship brandishing the nuclear sword. However, both Russian and U.S. political and military leaders have expressed serious concern about the possibility of rogue state attacks or accidental launches, and Boris Yeltsin on at least one occasion suggested that the United States and Russia might collaborate on joint defense deployments. In 2001 the George W. Bush administration indicated it would proceed unilaterally if necessary to deploy a limited National Missile Defense system (NMD) to protect U.S. territory against limited strikes.

Offensive technologies are mature compared to anti-nuclear missile defenses (hereafter, BMD for ballistic missile defenses). It was easier to identify possible points of friction in offensive force operations than it would be for defenses, since the latter are still in the stage of exploratory technologies. During the Cold War the Soviets deployed a limited, early generation ABM (anti-ballistic missile, early nomenclature for BMD) system around Moscow, causing some U.S. partisans of BMD to demand an arms race in defenses as well as in offenses. The United States deployed a one-site BMD system (Safeguard) to defend ICBM fields at Grand Forks, North Dakota, until 1974. Neither the Soviet nor the U.S. technologies of the Cold War years could have coped with a large-scale attack. The Soviets feared in the 1980s that President Ronald Reagan's "Strategic Defense Initiative" would produce a technological leap ahead in missile defense for the United States that would undermine the Soviet deterrent. But the technology to make the president's dream a Cold War reality was not at hand. Under Bush and Clinton, the United States reduced its research and development objectives for NMD to defense against limited strikes. The Clinton administration, goaded by the Rumsfeld Report issued in 1998 on ballistic missile threats, moved toward

Table 3.4
Phases in National Missile Defense (NMD)

NMD Program	Mission	Defense
Phase I (1987–1989)	Enhance deterrence of Soviet first strike	Thousands of interceptors, ground- and space-based
Global Protection Against Limited Strikes (GPALS) (1989–1992)	Protect against accidental or unauthorized launch	Hundreds of interceptors, ground- and space-based
Technology Readiness (1993–1995)	Prepare technology to reduce deployment time	Ground-based system— deployment not a consideration
Deployment Readiness—"3 + 3" (1996–1999)	Integrate systems; prepare for deployment three years after a future decision	Tens of interceptors, ground-based only
NMD Acquisition (1999–2005)	Prepare for initial deployment in 2005	Tens of interceptors, ground-based only

Source: Ballistic Missile Defense Organization, *Fact Sheet* No. Jn-00-04, January 2000, p. 1.

an all but certain commitment to begin to deploy a limited NMD system in 2005. A summary of the steps in the development of the U.S. national missile defense technology appears in Table 3.4.

A notional BMD system based on non-nuclear exoatmospheric intercept might involve different kinds of friction. First, space- and terrestrially-based radars would have to track incoming reentry vehicles and the warheads they dispensed. Second, interceptors would have to accelerate very rapidly in order to attain the velocities necessary for non-nuclear kill by impact with incoming warheads. Third, command, control and communications (C3) would have to synchronize threat detection with the appropriate pattern of response. C3 would be even more important if the defenses involved a preferential firing doctrine instead of one that was random subtractive. Also related to C3 is the necessity for political leadership to take a timely decision to fire. Fourth, offensive countermeasures to defeat the defense might include chaff or other devices to blind or to confuse radar tracking. Fifth, the "footprint" or area covered by the missile might not be as extensive as planners hoped: targets outside of the footprint would be vulnerable. Friction in any or all of these components of the defense might add to "leakage" or the overall rate at which attackers succeed in penetrating the defense. Table 3.5 summarizes some of the more important possible sources of friction in missile defenses by type and performance requirement.

Table 3.5
Possible Sources of Friction in Missile Defenses

Detection	Detection might not take place in time for response or mischaracterize innocent event as attack.
	Large-scale or sneak attack might overwhelm or confuse defenses.
Interception	Extreme accuracies and velocities required for exo-non-nuclear kill.
	Firing doctrine must be appropriate to the attack.
Command and control	Policy makers must react quickly and decisively to indications of attack, which might be ambiguous.
	C3 (command, control and communication) system must provide for feedback on intercept failures to correct follow-on forces.
Enemy countermeasures	Chaff, decoys and other devices might confuse detection and tracking.
	Enemy might use nonstandard methods of attack (e.g., low-trajectory ballistic or cruise missiles).
Footprint	Not all areas within the footprint of the defender are equally important in terms of military assets, population or other values.
	Enemy method of attack may outsmart defensive firing doctrine, making some areas within the footprint vulnerable.

Source: Author.

These illustrations do not cover the entire range of possible sources of friction in defenses any more successfully than the earlier short resume of problems in offenses. And we have the additional disadvantage of dealing in hypothetical technologies instead of actual forces deployed and (occasionally) alerted. Despite these handicaps in discussing defenses, some discussion of friction even in defenses based on very simple concepts, and tasked against very limited attacks only, might be useful now.

The question of most importance to Russian and to U.S. policy makers in this hypothetical situation is: will defenses be so competent as to negate or impose significant penalties on the *second* or retaliatory strike by either side? If so, that state would fear loss of its deterrent, and it is all the more motivated toward a decision for preemption or launch on warning in time of crisis.

Figures 3.1 and 3.2 summarize the results of playing hypothetical defenses against the second-strike warheads for U.S. and Russian forces at START III levels (both 2,500 and 1,500). Since the actual competency of future defense technology is unknown, we postulated a range of successful defense intercept probabilities: (1) terminal defenses only, with a 20 percent rate of successful intercept; (2) terminal plus midcourse intercept, with a 40 percent rate of success; (3) terminal, midcourse and post-boost intercept, with a 60 percent intercept rate; and (4) terminal, midcourse, post-boost and boost phase intercept, with an 80 percent success rate. We designed these defenses as Phase I for the least competent to Phase IV for the most successful. Figure 3.1 shows the surviving and penetrating warheads against each of these types of defenses for U.S. and Russian START III forces within a 2,500 warhead limit; Figure 3.2 gives the same information for forces reduced to a 1,500 deployment ceiling.

The data summarized and oversimplified in Figures 3.1 and 3.2 are based on models of hypothetical offense-defense exchanges, but they show something important. Even very competent defenses combined with first strikes cannot reduce the numbers of U.S. or Russian survivors to an acceptable level of retaliation. This is true for deployments with ceilings of 2,500 or 1,500 warheads, although defenses combined with first strikes could limit offensive retaliation to countersocietal attacks only. There is no overturning of mutual deterrence based on offensive retaliation evident here, but there could be friction attendant to the combining of offensive missile and defensive anti-missile technologies that we have not explored.

Of course, much remains uncertain about the evolution of U.S. or Russian missile defense technology. Missile defenses are part of the complex arms control negotiations that are ongoing between the two states. U.S. and Russian anti-nuclear strategic defenses would also have implications not only for one another's deterrents, but for those of other powers, including China, Britain and France. Thus friction characterizes not only the problem of defense technology development, but also the arms control and political relationships between the United States and Russia, between Russia and Europe, and between the United States and its NATO allies. Russian President Putin has already taken advantage of this friction-free fire zone by putting forward a proposal in June 2000 for a Euro-missile defense system, including Russia and NATO. We are in for an interesting decade on the politics and technology of missile defense.

Figure 3.1
START III, 2,500 Warhead Limit: Surviving Re-entry Vehicles vs. Defenses

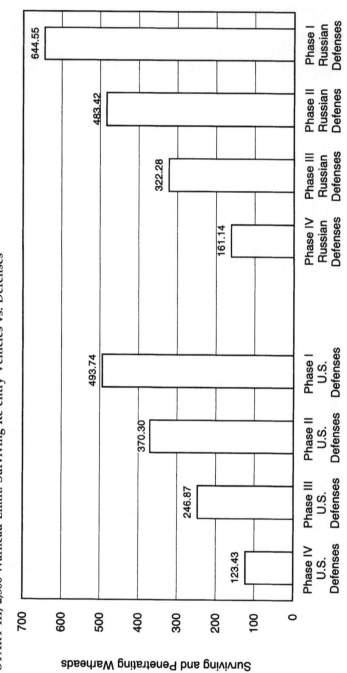

Source: Author.

Figure 3.2
START III, 1,500 Warhead Limit: Surviving Re-entry Vehicles vs. Defenses

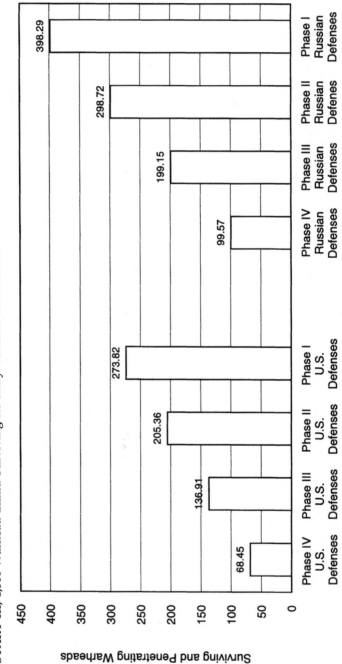

Source: Author.

CONCLUSIONS

Clausewitz is alive and well, and the concept of friction has not been repealed by nuclear weapons. Even if nuclear weapons are never again fired in anger, the practice of nuclear deterrence requires the making of credible threats based on both the capability and the willingness to engage in nuclear first use, first strike or retaliation. This existential decision by states to play nuclear deterrence opens the door to friction in policy making, in strategic planning, in crisis management and in the actual peacetime and crisis operations of nuclear forces. (Chapters 6 and 7 provide additional evidence and discussion on these points.)

Partisans of a passé Clausewitz might concede that he is still relevant to nuclear deterrence, but would still contend that he has been superseded by the nonexistent connection between nuclear war and any rational or sensible policy objective. This author would not quibble with the disconnection between nuclear war and policy, but this author is not seeking to acquire nuclear weapons and ballistic missiles for military purposes. Some of those who are investing in weapons of mass destruction and in long-range delivery systems for those weapons are not of a post-Clausewitzian mentality. Very much in the tradition of the great master, they see a very direct connection between the exploitation of nuclear fear in the West and the denial of U.S. and allied interventionary rights into troubled regions.

Nor is this all. The cost-benefit rationality assumed as the basis of the theory of deterrence by so many of its adherents has a decidedly Western accent. Non-Western audiences, including some heads of state seeking to acquire nuclear weapons in the near term, may reason differently than their Soviet, American or NATO predecessors did (see Chapter 8). They may decide to disconnect the "rationality" of U.S. deterrence theory by refusing to be deterred even under circumstances that would otherwise deter us. For example, Saddam Hussein, faced with an opposed coalition of overwhelming force poised to strike in January 1991, nevertheless was not compelled by threats alone to withdraw his forces from Kuwait.

APPENDIX 3.1: U.S. AND RUSSIAN START I, START II, AND START III FORCES

	START I Forces		
	Launchers	Warheads per Launcher	Total Warheads
Russian Forces			
SS-11/3	0	1	0
SS-13/2	0	1	0

APPENDIX 3.1 (continued)

| | START I Forces | | |
	Launchers	Warheads per Launcher	Total Warheads
Russian Forces			
SS-17/3	0	4	0
SS-18/4/5	154	10	1,540
SS-19/3	0	6	0
SS-24 (fixed)	60	10	600
subtotal fixed land	214		2,140
SS-24 (rail)	36	10	360
SS-25 (road)	715	1	715
subtotal mobile land	751		1,075
subtotal land-based	965		3,215
SS-N-6/3	0	1	0
SS-N-8/2	0	1	0
SS-N-18/2	96	7	672
SS-N-20	120	6	720
SS-N-23	160	4	640
subtotal sea-based	376		2,032
Tu-160 Blackjack bomb	70	8	560
Bear-H6 ALCM	130	8	1,040
Tu-160 Blackjack ALCM	70	16	1,120
subtotal air-breathing	270		2,720
Total Russian forces	**1,611**		**7,967**
U.S. Forces			
Minuteman II	0	1	0
Minuteman III	0	1	0
Minuteman IIIA	500	3	1,500
Peacekeeper MX	0	10	0
subtotal land-based	500		1,500
Trident C-4	192	8	1,536
Trident D-5/W-76	0	8	0
Trident D-5/W-88	144	8	1,152
subtotal sea-based	336		2,688
B-2	10	16	160
B-52G gravity/ALCM	0	0	0
B-52H gravity/ALCM	95	20	1,900
B-1	97	24	2,328
subtotal air-breathing	202		4,388
Total U.S. forces	**1,038**		**8,576**

APPENDIX 3.1 (continued)

START II Forces

	Launchers	Warheads per Launcher	Total Warheads
Russian Forces			
SS-11/3	0	1	0
SS-13/2	0	1	0
SS-17/3	0	4	0
SS-25 silo	90	1	90
SS-19/3	105	1	105
SS-25 silo	0	1	0
subtotal fixed land	195		195
SS-24 (rail)	0	10	0
SS-25/SS-27 (road)	605	1	605
subtotal mobile land	605		605
subtotal land-based	800		800
SS-N-6/3	0	1	0
SS-N-8/2	0	1	0
SS-N-18/2	176	3	528
SS-N-20	120	6	720
SS-N-23	112	4	448
subtotal sea-based	408		1,696
Tu-95 H6	20	6	120
Tu-95 H16	35	16	560
Blackjack	6	12	72
subtotal air-breathing	61		752
Total Russian forces	**1,269**		**3,248**
U.S. Forces			
Minuteman II	0	1	0
Minuteman III	0	1	0
Minuteman IIIA	500	1	500
Peacekeeper MX	0	10	0
subtotal land-based	500		500
Trident C-4	0	4	0
Trident D-5/W-76	0	4	0
Trident D-5/W-88	336	5	1,680
subtotal sea-based	336		1,680
B-52G gravity	0	0	0
B-52H/ALCM	32	20	640
B-52H/ALCM	30	12	360

APPENDIX 3.1 (continued)

START II Forces

	Launchers	Warheads per Launcher	Total Warheads
B-2	21	12	252
subtotal air-breathing	83		1,252
Total U.S. forces	**919**		**3,432**

START III Forces (2,500 Warhead Limit)

	Launchers	Warheads per Launcher	Total Warheads
Russian Forces			
SS-11/3	0	1	0
SS-13/2	0	1	0
SS-17/3	0	4	0
SS-18/4/5	0	10	0
SS-19/3	105	1	105
SS-24 (fixed)	0	10	0
subtotal fixed land	105		105
SS-24 (rail)	0	10	0
SS-25/SS-27 (road)	490	1	490
subtotal mobile land	490		490
subtotal land-based	595		595
SS-N-6/3	0	1	0
SS-N-8/2	0	1	0
SS-N-18/2	0	1	0
SS-N-20	120	5	600
SS-N-23	112	4	448
subtotal sea-based	232		1,048
Tu-95 H6/ALCM	10	6	60
Tu-95 H16	27	16	432
Tu-160 Blackjack	4	8	32
subtotal air-breathing	41		524
Total Russian forces	**868**		**2,167**
U.S. Forces			
Minuteman II	0	1	0
Minuteman III	0	1	0
Minuteman IIIA	300	1	300

APPENDIX 3.1 (continued)

START III Forces (2,500 Warhead Limit)

	Launchers	Warheads per Launcher	Total Warheads
Peacekeeper MX	0	10	0
subtotal land-based	300		300
Trident C-4	0	4	0
Trident D-5/W-76	0	4	0
Trident D-5/W-88	336	4	1,344
subtotal sea-based	336		1,344
B-52G gravity/ALCM	0	0	0
B-52H gravity/ALCM	40	12	480
B-2	21	12	252
subtotal air-breathing	61		732
Total U.S. forces	**697**		**2,376**

START III Forces (1,500 Warhead Limit)

	Launchers	Warheads per Launcher	Total Warheads
Russian Forces			
SS-11/3	0	1	0
SS-13/2	0	1	0
SS-17/3	0	4	0
SS-18/4/5	0	10	0
SS-19/3	0	1	0
SS-24 (fixed)	0	10	0
subtotal fixed land	0		0
SS-24 (rail)	0	10	0
SS-25/SS-27 (road)	490	1	490
subtotal mobile land	490		490
subtotal land-based	490		490
SS-N-6/3	0	1	0
SS-N-8/2	0	1	0
SS-N-18/2	0	1	0
SS-N-20	120	3	360
SS-N-23	112	3	336
subtotal sea-based	232		696
Tu-95 H6/ALCM	5	6	30
Tu-95 H16	16	16	256

APPENDIX 3.1 (continued)

START III Forces (1,500 Warhead Limit)

	Launchers	Warheads per Launcher	Total Warheads
Tu-160 Blackjack	3	8	24
subtotal air-breathing	24		310
Total Russian forces	**746**		**1,496**
U.S. Forces			
Minuteman II	0	1	0
Minuteman III	0	1	0
Minuteman IIIA	300	1	300
Peacekeeper MX	0	10	0
subtotal land-based	300		300
Trident C-4	0	4	0
Trident D-5/W-76	0	4	0
Trident D-5/W-88	288	3	864
subtotal sea-based	288		864
B-52G gravity/ALCM	0	0	0
B-52H gravity/ALCM	9	12	108
B-2	19	12	228
subtotal air-breathing	28		336
Total U.S. forces	**616**		**1,500**

NOTES

1. William E. Odom, *The Collapse of the Soviet Military* (New Haven, Conn.: Yale University Press, 1998), esp. pp. 388–404; Edward A. Kolodziej, "The Pursuit of Order, Welfare and Legitimacy: Explaining the End of the Soviet Union and the Cold War," in Stephen J. Cimbala, ed., *Mysteries of the Cold War* (Aldershot, U.K.: Ashgate Publishing Co., 1999), pp. 19–48, and in the same volume, Peter Rainow, "The Strange End of the Cold War: Views from the Former Superpower," pp. 49–69.

2. Carl von Clausewitz, *On War*, edited and translated by Michael Howard and Peter Paret (Princeton, N.J.: Princeton University Press, 1976), pp. 119–121.

3. Colin S. Gray, *Modern Strategy* (Oxford: Oxford University Press, 1999), p. 94.

4. Clausewitz, *On War*, pp. 119–121.

5. Ibid., p. 119.

6. Ibid.

7. Ibid.

8. For useful comments on the relationship between friction and chance in *On War*, see Gray, *Modern Strategy*, p. 41.

9. Ibid., p. 120.

10. Ibid.

11. Clausewitz to Marie von Bruhl, September 29, 1806, cited in Peter Paret, *Clausewitz and the State: The Man, His Theories and His Times* (Princeton, N.J.: Princeton University Press, 1976), p. 124. I am grateful to Barry D. Watts for calling this reference to my attention. See Watts, *Clausewitzian Friction and Future War* (Washington, D.C.: Institute for National Strategic Studies, National Defense University, McNair Paper 52, October 1996), pp. 7–8.

12. Watts, *Clausewitzian Friction and Future War*, p. 8. See also Carl Von Clausewitz, "From Observations on Prussia in Her Great Catastrophe," in *Historical and Political Writings*, edited and translated by Peter Paret and Daniel Moran (Princeton, N.J.: Princeton University Press, 1992).

13. Watts, *Clausewitzian Friction and Future War*, p. 8.

14. Paret, *Clausewitz and the State*, pp. 197–198, cited also in Watts, *Clausewitzian Friction and Future War*, p. 10.

15. Clausewitz, *On War*, p. 114.

16. Ibid., p. 122.

17. Alexander L. George, "The Role of Force in Diplomacy: A Continuing Dilemma for U.S. Foreign Policy," in H.W. Brands with Darren J. Pierson and Reynolds S. Kiefer, eds., *The Use of Force after the Cold War* (College Station: Texas A&M University Press, 2000), pp. 59–92, esp. pp. 73–79.

18. Ibid., p. 76.

19. Compellence is explained in Thomas C. Schelling, *Arms and Influence* (New Haven, Conn.: Yale University Press, 1966), passim.

20. Gordon A. Craig and Alexander L. George, *Force and Statecraft: Diplomatic Problems of Our Time* (New York: Oxford University Press, 1983), p. 189.

21. Gray, *Modern Strategy*, ch. 11, esp. p. 309, offers some interesting retrospective and contemporary appraisals of U.S. nuclear strategy and strategy debates.

22. My distinction parallels that drawn by Patrick M. Morgan between *general* and *immediate* deterrence. See Morgan, *Deterrence: A Conceptual Analysis*, 2nd ed. (Beverly Hills, Calif.: Sage Publications, 1983), pp. 27–48. A related distinction of significance is made by Alexander L. George, with regard to the type of peace that deterrence is intended to help achieve: precarious peace, conditional peace or stable peace. *Precarious peace* implies an acute conflict relationship between parties in which general deterrence must be reinforced by frequent and timely resort to immediate deterrence (i.e., specific threats and/or reassurances). *Conditional peace*, on the other hand, points to a less intense conflict relationship in which general deterrence plays the predominant and usually effective part in discouraging crises. In contrast to either, a *stable peace* is a relationship between parties in which neither considers threatening or using force to resolve disagreements. See George, "The Role of Force in Diplomacy," pp. 73–74.

23. For views on the RMA and information-based warfare see John Arquilla and David Ronfeldt, "A New Epoch—and Spectrum—of Conflict," in Arquilla and Ronfeldt, eds., *In Athena's Camp: Preparing for Conflict in the Information Age* (Santa Monica, Calif.: RAND, 1997), pp. 1–22. See also, on definitions and con-

cepts of information warfare, Martin Libicki, *What Is Information Warfare?* (Washington, D.C.: National Defense University, ACIS Paper 3, August 1995); Libicki, *Defending Cyberspace and other Metaphors* (Washington, D.C.: National Defense University, Directorate of Advanced Concepts, Technologies and Information Strategies, February 1997); Alvin Toffler and Heidi Toffler, *War and Anti-War: Making Sense of Today's Global Chaos* (Boston: Little, Brown, 1993), pp. 163–207; Arquilla and Ronfeldt, *Cyberwar Is Coming!* (Santa Monica, Calif.: RAND, 1992); and David S. Alberts, *The Unintended Consequences of Information Age Technologies: Avoiding the Pitfalls, Seizing the Initiative* (Washington, D.C.: National Defense University, Institute for National Strategic Studies, Center for Advanced Concepts and Technology, April 1996).

Chapter 4

A Near Escape? The 1983
"War Scare" and Nuclear Danger

INTRODUCTION

The Cuban missile crisis was arguably the most dangerous single moment of the Cold War years. But 1962 may not have been the most dangerous year in the 45-year span from 1946 through 1991. Some evidence suggests that a series of apparently unrelated events from 1979 through 1983 may have culminated in a "war scare" that brought U.S. and Soviet political relations near to the point of violent conflict.

This study reviews some of the available evidence in support of the "war scare" thesis. In order to evaluate the war scare arguments, it is necessary but insufficient to consider the historical or anecdotal evidence. One must also ask: what difference would it have made, given the fact of mutual deterrence that existed between the two nuclear superpowers for decades of Cold War? Accordingly, we also consider quantitative evidence on nuclear force structure and operations pertinent to the political atmosphere between Washington and Moscow in 1983. Together the anecdotal and quantitative evidence shed light on why a crisis might have turned to war in 1983 despite the apparent irrationality of any such conflict by any policy standard.

OPERATION RYAN

In May 1981, Soviet KGB Chairman and future Communist Party Chairman Yuri Andropov addressed a KGB conference in Moscow. He told his startled listeners that the new American administration of President Ronald Reagan was actively preparing for nuclear war. The possibility of a nuclear first strike by the United States was a real one. Andropov announced that, for the first time ever, the KGB and GRU (main intelligence directorate of the Soviet armed forces general staff) were ordered to work together in a global intelligence operation named *Raketno Yadernoye Napadeniye*—Nuclear Missile Attack.[1] During the next three years or so, the Soviet intelligence services were tasked to collect a variety of indicators, including political, military and economic information, suggestive of any U.S. and NATO intent to launch a nuclear first strike. RYAN was, according to some sources, the largest intelligence operation conducted in time of peace in Soviet history.[2] Collection of indicators continued well into 1984 and was contributory to partial Soviet leadership paranoia that outran even the normal suspicions of intelligence professionals in Moscow Center.

In an attachment to a Center directive to KGB Residents in NATO capitals in February 1983 it was stated that the threat of an immediate nuclear attack has acquired "an especial degree of urgency."[3] KGB were tasked to detect and assess signs of preparation for RYAN in political, military, economic and other sectors. The attachment noted that the United States maintained a large portion of its strategic retaliatory forces in a state of operational readiness. Soviet intelligence estimated that all American ICBMs, 70 percent of U.S. "naval nuclear facilities" and 30 percent of the American strategic bomber force were alerted and capable of rapid response. Thus, according to the instructions in the attachment, it was imperative to detect U.S. or NATO decisions or preparations for war as far ahead of D-day as possible. The authors go into considerable detail summarizing U.S. and NATO systems for military alert, including the aspects related to nuclear weapons.[4] Information about the U.S. Single Integrated Operational Plan (SIOP) for nuclear war, and about NATO's general defense and nuclear support plans, was specifically emphasized in the tasking from Center to the various residencies. Uncovering of the process leading to a decision for war by the United States and its NATO allies, and of the related measures by those countries to prepare for war, was imperative: it would enable Soviet leaders "to increase the so-called period of anticipation essential for the Soviet Union to take retaliatory measures."[5]

What had brought the Soviet Union to this brink of pessimism and near fatalism about U.S. intentions and, in the case of Andropov, nearly apocalyptic doomsaying? A series of events treated in isolation by political actors at the time apparently combined, in unexpected and potentially dysfunctional ways, to produce a mentality among some members of the Soviet high command that shifted policy expectations in Moscow tectonically from 1979 through 1984. If so, the sequence of events and their impact on Soviet decision makers fulfill the law of unanticipated consequences that often appears in social and political decision making.

This "law" is well known to social scientists and everyday practitioners of the art of politics. It says that some of the effects of any decision or action will be unexpected and unpredicted, and that some of these unexpected and unpredicted effects may be contrary to the policy intent of the original decision makers. This problem of unanticipated consequences certainly applies to the possibility of a U.S.-Soviet crisis slide in 1983, since the last thing that either intended was an actual outbreak of war.

THE INF DECISION

In December 1979, NATO took a decision to modernize its intermediate nuclear missile force (INF) by deploying 572 new cruise and ballistic missiles in five European countries beginning in November 1983. This "dual track" decision also called for negotiations with the Soviet Union with the objective of limiting or eliminating its SS-20 intermediate range, mobile ballistic missiles first deployed in 1977. The Soviets were strongly opposed to the NATO INF modernization: the connection between Soviets' SS-20 deployments and NATO's theater nuclear force modernization was one of challenge and response from NATO's perspective, but not in the Soviet view.[6] Moscow mounted an aggressive active measures campaign through a variety of European peace movements and in other ways in order to stop the scheduled NATO deployments. The Soviet campaign failed to divide the Western alliance or to dissuade it from beginning its deployments on the original timetable. U.S. ground-launched cruise missiles (GLCMs) first arrived in England in mid-November, and on November 23 Pershing II intermediate range ballistic missiles were first deployed in West Germany.[7]

The Soviet military establishment was most concerned about the Pershings. Pershing IIs deployed in West Germany could be launched across trajectories that Soviet early warning installations were poorly equipped to detect in good time. In addition, a Soviet intelligence appreciation in February 1983 estimated that the Pershings could strike at long-range targets in the Soviet Union within four to six minutes. This compared very unfavorably with the 20 minutes or so that Moscow assumed it would have to detect and react to missiles fired from the continental United States.[8]

The Pershings reestablished for NATO a credible threat of escalation dominance below the threshold of general (global) nuclear war. Moscow could not initiate the use of theater nuclear weapons in Europe with any confidence that it could establish local or regional military superiority while American and Soviet strategic nuclear forces remained uninvolved, and their respective homelands spared.

NATO and Soviet assessments of one another were complicated by the dual purpose character of each side's modernized theater missiles. The missiles served to enhance deterrence, but they would also increase nuclear war–fighting capabilities if deterrence failed. The missile deployments were a competition in political intimidation as much as they were an enhancement of deployed and usable military power. The competition in political intimidation was also an issue of alliance unity and management for the United States. NATO's steadfastness or weakening in the face of Soviet threats and blandishments would signal diminished U.S. influence within the Western alliance and a collapse of alliance unity on nuclear force modernization. Moscow's defeat, once NATO INF deployments began, was an affirmation of NATO solidarity and renewed U.S. leadership competency in alliance nuclear affairs. These political effects meant more to beleaguered Soviet military planners and political leaders than NATO's commitment to deploy additional firepower in Europe.

STAR WARS

On March 23, 1983, President Ronald Reagan surprised many of his own advisors as well as American listeners with his proposal for the Strategic Defense Initiative (SDI), rapidly dubbed "Star Wars" by media pundits and critics. Reagan also surprised allied NATO and Soviet audiences. The president shared with the U.S. public his vision of a peace shield that would protect the U.S. homeland from nuclear attack, even a large-scale attack of the kind that the Soviets could mount in the early 1980s. The reaction in Moscow was predictably negative, but unpredictably hysterical.

The Soviet leadership might have denounced the U.S. initiative as a potential abrogation of the ABM Treaty and a complication of the U.S.-Soviet relationship of mutual deterrence, while at the same time pointing out that no feasible near-term technology could accomplish what the president demanded. Instead, the Kremlin reacted with public diplomacy filled with venomous denunciations of the Reagan administration and privately concluded that SDI was part of a U.S. plan to develop an effective nuclear war–fighting strategy. Even if SDI were not a feasible technology within the present century, making sure that the United States could not deploy enough missile defense to neutralize Moscow's deterrent might cost a strapped Soviet economy more than it could bear. As Robert M. Gates has noted:

SDI was a Soviet nightmare come to life. America's industrial base, coupled with American technology, wealth, and managerial skill, all mobilized to build a wholly new and different military capability that might negate the Soviet offensive buildup of a quarter century. A radical new departure by the United States that would require an expensive Soviet response at a time of deep economic crisis.[9]

SDI therefore presented to the Soviet leadership a two-sided threat of military obsolescence and of economic stress. As in the case of INF, a Soviet propaganda campaign against SDI (in part by drawing upon well-informed U.S. critics who pointed to the gap between aspirations and available technology) failed to deter the Reagan administration from persisting in its research and development program on missile defense. This attempted great leap forward in defensive technology, combined with a U.S. strategic nuclear offensive force modernization and increased defense spending that began under President Carter and continued under Reagan, faced the Kremlin leadership with depressing possibilities far into Moscow nights. The Soviet economy would not permit matching of U.S. offensive and defensive force innovation and modernization. A future time of troubles might confront Soviet leaders by the end of the decade, faced with upgraded U.S. theater and intercontinental missile systems and early SDI technology for anti-missile defenses. Even a first generation SDI system might, according to Moscow pessimists, introduce enough uncertainty into the estimated effects of a Soviet second or retaliatory strike to weaken confidence in mutual deterrence and in strategic stability. A group of Soviet scientists issued a statement in May 1983 opposing the U.S. anti-missile system in language that also reflected the views of top Soviet political and military leaders:

In reality, an attempt to create a so-called "defensive weapon" against the nuclear strategic weapons of the other side, which the U.S. president has announced, would inevitably result in the emergence of another element strengthening the American "first strike" potential. . . . Such a "defensive weapon" would leave no hope for a country subjected to massive surprise attack since it (the weapon) is obviously not capable of protecting the vast majority of the population. Antimissile weapons are best suited for use by the attacking side to seek to lessen the power of the retaliatory strike.[10]

KAL 007

Another factor contributory to exacerbating U.S.-Soviet tensions in 1983 was the shootdown of Korean Air Lines flight 007 by Soviet air defenses on September 1, 1983. U.S. intelligence monitored and recorded the transmissions between the pilot of the Soviet fighter-interceptor that shot down the plane and his ground controllers. American policy makers, including President Reagan and Secretary of State George Shultz, referred to the contents of these intercepts as proof that the Soviet Union had deliberately and knowingly destroyed the civilian airliner in cold

blood. UN Ambassador Jeane Kirkpatrick, playing selected excerpts from
the pilot's transmissions for the benefit of UN and American media audiences, claimed that the Soviets "decided to shoot down a civilian airliner, shot it down, murdering the 269 people on board, and then lied
about it."[11] However, some U.S. Air Force assessments of communications intelligence and other data available shortly after the shootdown
disputed the claim that the Soviets must have known that KAL 007 was
a civilian plane. It was quite possible that Soviet air defenses had inadvertently confused the track of KAL 007 with that of a U.S. Cobra Ball
intelligence flight in the same general area on the evening of August 31.[12]

Moscow's reaction was anger and disbelief in U.S. characterizations of
the Korean airliner's reason for straying over Russian territory dotted
with secret military installations and noted on international aviation
maps as a forbidden zone for civilian overflight. The Soviet leadership
charged that the airliner had been on a U.S. intelligence mission. Besides
the Air Force, other U.S. intelligence sources later concluded that Soviet
air defenses might have confused the path of the Korean airliner with
the nearby track of the American RC-135 reconnaissance plane on a Cobra Ball mission. The CIA reported in the president's daily intelligence
briefing September 2 that, throughout most of the time interval when
Soviet air defenses were attempting to track the "intruder" and deciding
what to do about it, they may have thought they were tracking a U.S.
RC-135 reconnaissance plane monitoring a Soviet ICBM test.[13] This supposition was not an unlikely hypothesis, given the well-known
weaknesses of Soviet air defenses (painfully demonstrated several years
later in the Gorbachev era when a German civilian flew a Cessna through
Soviet air defenses and landed it in Red Square).

The Soviet leadership maintained the official position that KAL 007
was a deliberate intelligence provocation and that U.S. public denunciations of the Soviets for the shootdown were a deliberate escalation of
East-West tension.[14] One consequence of KAL 007 was to add to the high
priority already assigned to Operation RYAN. According to Christopher
Andrew and Oleg Gordievsky, Party Chairman Andropov spent the last
months of his life after the KAL 007 shootdown "as a morbidly suspicious invalid, brooding over the possible approach of a nuclear Armageddon."[15] After the collapse of the Soviet Union, the Russian
government made public transcripts of the September 2, 1983, Politburo
meeting to discuss the incident. Those high officials in attendance, especially Defense Minister Dmitri Ustinov, believed that Soviet actions
the previous day had been appropriate and resented U.S. depiction of
their actions as barbaric. Although the actual impact of the shootdown
on day-to-day U.S.-Soviet foreign relations was slight, the Soviet perception of anti-Soviet rhetoric in Washington, together with Soviet concerns
about SDI and INF modernization, raised the level of Kremlin anxiety

about American intentions in the autumn of 1983 to levels not seen for many years.

THE SEPTEMBER 1983 SATELLITE WARNING INCIDENT

On September 26, 1983, a false alarm occurred in a Soviet early warning installation that could have, given the previously described mood of the Politburo in 1983 and the tense atmospherics of U.S.-Soviet political relations, become more than a footnote in history books. The incident took place in a closed military facility south of Moscow designed to monitor Soviet early warning satellites over the United States. On September 26 at this installation, designated Serpukhov-15, a false alarm went off signaling a U.S. missile attack.[16]

According to Stanislav Petrov, a lieutenant colonel who observed and participated in the incident, one of the Soviet satellites sent a signal to his command bunker in the warning facility that a missile had been launched from the United States and was headed for Russia. Soon the satellite was reporting that five Minuteman ICBMs had been launched. The warning system was white hot with indicators of war. However, Colonel Petrov decided that the satellite alert was a false alarm less than five minutes after the first, erroneous reports came into his warning center. He based this decision partly on the fact that Soviet ground-based radar installations showed no confirming evidence of enemy missiles headed for the Soviet Union. Petrov also recalled military briefings he had received, stressing that any enemy attack on Russia would involve many missiles instead of a few.[17]

Under the circumstances, Colonel Petrov's decision was a courageous one. He was in a singular position of importance and vulnerability in the command structure. He oversaw the staff at his installation that monitored satellite signals and he reported to superiors at warning system headquarters who, in turn, reported to the Soviet General Staff. The immediate circumstances were especially stressful for him because reported missile launches were coming in so quickly that general staff headquarters had received direct, automatic notification. At the time, the Soviet version of the U.S. "football," or nuclear suitcase linking political leadership with nuclear commands, was still under development. This made prompt alert directly to the General Staff necessary.

Soviet investigators first praised and then tried to scapegoat Petrov for the system failures. The false alarm was actually caused when the satellite mistook the sun's reflection off the top of clouds for a missile launch. The computer program designed to prevent such confusion had to be rewritten.[18] The September warning incident took place weeks after the KAL 007 shootdown and shortly before the start of a NATO military exercise (see below) that may have been the single most dangerous incident contributing to the war scare atmosphere in 1983. The September satellite warning incident has another implication, carrying forward into post–Cold War Russia. The Russian satellite and early warning/command-control network is undoubtedly less reliable now (in 2002) than it was in 1983 under more resourceful Soviet support.

ABLE ARCHER

According to several accounts, the most dangerous single incident in 1983 related to military stability between the superpowers was the Soviet reaction to NATO command post exercise Able Archer. The exercise took place from November 2 through 11 and was designed to practice the alliance's procedures for nuclear release and alert. Unfortunately it took place within a context overshadowed by Soviet fears of U.S. and NATO plans for initiating a war in Europe and/or a nuclear war between the superpowers.[19]

As Able Archer got under way, Soviet and allied Warsaw Pact intelligence began routine monitoring of the exercise. NATO was, of course, observing and reacting to the Soviet monitoring of Able Archer. Soon the British and U.S. listening posts detected that "something was going badly wrong."[20] Intelligence traffic from the other side suggested that the Soviets might be interpreting Able Archer not as an exercise but as a real prelude to a decision for war. Soviet "paranoia" at Moscow Center during this time might have been fueled by the awareness that Moscow's own contingency plans for surprise attack against NATO used training exercises to conceal an actual offensive.[21]

According to Christopher Andrew and Oleg Gordievsky, there were two aspects of Able Archer that caused particular concern in Moscow. First, message formats and procedures used in previous exercises were different from the ones being used now. Second, the command post exercise simulated all phases of alert from normal day-to-day readiness to general alert.[22] Thus Able Archer seemed more realistic to Soviet monitors than earlier exercises had. In addition, thanks to Operation RYAN and the increasingly sensitive Soviet nose already out of joint and predisposed to find sinister meaning behind standard operating procedures, Able Archer rang unusual alarm bells in KGB and GRU intelligence channels. Thus KGB reports at one point during the exercise led the Center to believe that there was a real alert of NATO forces in progress, not just a training exercise.

Moscow Center on November 6 sent the London KGB residency a checklist of indicators of Western preparations for nuclear surprise attack. The checklist included requirements to observe key officials who might be involved in negotiations with the United States preparatory to a surprise attack, important military installations, NATO and other government offices, and communication and intelligence centers. Several days later, KGB and GRU residencies in Western Europe received "flash" (priority) telegrams that reported a nonexistent alert at U.S. bases. The telegrams suggested two probable reasons for the "alert": concerns about U.S. military base security following a terrorist attack against a U.S. Marine barracks in Lebanon; and U.S. army maneuvers planned for later in the year. But the telegrams also implied that there might be another reason for the putative U.S. "alert" at these bases: the beginning of plans for a nuclear surprise first strike.[23]

Soviet reactions to Able Archer apparently had gone beyond warnings and communications within intelligence bureaucracies. During the NATO exercise, some important activity took place in Soviet and Warsaw Pact military forces. Elements of the air forces in the Group of Soviet Forces in Germany and in Poland, including nuclear capable aircraft, were placed on higher levels of alert on November 8–9.[24] Units of the Soviet Fourth Air Army went to increased levels of readiness and all of its combat flight operations from November 4 through 10 were suspended. Soviet reactions may have been excessive and driven by selective perception, but they were not posturing. According to then (1983) Deputy Director of Intelligence Robert M. Gates, writing in reflection after the end of the Cold War:

After going through the experience at the time, then through the postmortems, and now through the documents, I don't think the Soviets were crying wolf. They may not have believed a NATO attack was imminent in November, 1983, but they did seem to believe that the situation was very dangerous. And U.S. intelligence had failed to grasp the true extent of their anxiety.[25]

EAST GERMAN INTELLIGENCE

The Soviets may not have been crying wolf, but they were crying Wolf. Even prior to Able Archer, the KGB enlisted allied intelligence services, especially the highly regarded East German foreign intelligence directorate (HVA) of Colonel-General Markus Wolf, in its Operation RYAN intelligence gathering and reporting. According to Ben B. Fischer of the CIA's History Staff, Wolf created an entire early warning system that included required reports keyed to a KGB catalogue of indicators of U.S. or NATO preparations for war; a large situation center for monitoring global military operations with a special link to the KGB headquarters; a HVA headquarters staff dedicated to RYAN; and special alert drills, annual exercises and military training for HVA officers that simulated a surprise attack by NATO.[26]

Of special interest is that East German wariness about a possible nuclear attack continued after the war scare atmosphere had apparently calmed down in Moscow. Acting in his capacity as head of foreign intelligence and deputy director of the East German Ministry for State Security, Wolf tasked the entire ministry in June 1985 to conduct an aggressive search for indicators of planning for a nuclear missile attack. His Implementation Regulation of June 5 directed that the operational and operational-technical service units of the ministry engage in "goal oriented operational penetration of enemy decisionmaking centers." Top priority, he stated in the same message, are "signs of imminent preparations of a strategic nuclear-missile attack (KWA)" as well as other imperialist state plans for military surprise.[27] In addition, the East German political leadership had built a large complex of bunkers (*Führungskomplex*, or leadership complex) near Berlin designed to save the military, political and intelligence elites from nuclear war.[28]

Markus Wolf was more skeptical than alarmists in Moscow about the urgency for RYAN. But he carried out orders to increase surveillance and collect indicators pertinent to a possible surprise attack for reasons of alliance solidarity, fraternal intelligence sharing and bureaucratic self-protection. Although the foreign intelligence services of East Germany and the Soviet Union often cooperated for obvious reasons, their specific reactions to Cold War situations of threat were by no means always identical. Wolf's reputation as an intelligence icon (allegedly the model for John Le Carre's fictional spymaster Karla, although Le Carre denies it) and his tenacious competency at intelligence (respected by friends and enemies alike) made him the least likely intelligence officer in the entire Soviet bloc to overreact to indicators of crisis or possible war. Wolf's reputation, to the contrary, was that of an intelligence supervisor who was careful, methodical and politically astute in his judgments about allies and adversaries.[29] Wolf contends, in fact, that his service eventually provided a definitive estimate that no threat of war was imminent, based in part on NATO documents obtained by one of his agents who worked at the alliance's Brussels headquarters.[30] He was careful not to dispute any of Moscow Center's pessimistic assumptions about NATO intentions in real time, however.

THE SOVIET NUCLEAR DETERRENT

Nuclear forces have quantitative and qualitative attributes. Numbers of warheads and launchers matter, but so too do the operational characteristics of forces and the military-strategic assumptions on which they are deployed. By 1983, the Soviet Union had long since attained parity in numbers of deployed systems and the capability for assured retaliation after surviving a first strike. On the other hand, there were important qualitative differences between U.S. and Soviet force structures, related to assumptions made by American and by Soviet political and military leaderships about the requirements for deterrence and for war if necessary.

Speaking broadly, the Soviet view of deterrence was different from the American one, and involved some additional subtleties. Soviet military writers distinguished between deterrence as *sderzhivanie* (forestalling or avoiding) and deterrence as *ustrashenie* (intimidation).[31] Deterrence in the Soviet view was not a deterministic outcome of force balances. It was as dependent on political as it was on military factors.[32] Thus military-strategic parity, or an essential equivalence in deployed force structures, was not in itself a sufficient condition for military stability. The imperialist camp led by the United States and NATO was a political threat by virtue of its existence and regardless of particular fluctuations in its patterns of military spending. Therefore, Soviet survival in the nuclear age could not be trusted to force balances alone. How the forces would operate in time of crisis or threat of war had to be taken into account.

This stance on the part of many Soviet military thinkers was quite logical from their perspective. One must remember that, notwithstanding their disclaimers about the historical inevitability of socialist victory, some Soviet leaders by the 1980s recognized that their economy had failed. As dedicated Marxists they knew what might follow from that: if the economy could not be saved, then neither could national defense and the communist grip on Soviet power. Somehow resources had to be freed up for economic growth and renewal, but this required a favorable threat assessment. This combination of a reduced threat assessment and economic restructuring was not attempted seriously by the Kremlin leadership until Gorbachev became party chairman in 1985.

In the early 1980s the Soviet leadership was in a bind. The need for reduced defense expenditures and for economic restructuring was obvious. But the perceived threat from the West was not judged to have been diminished compared to previous decades; quite the contrary. The Carter-projected defense buildup, followed by Reagan's even larger increases and hostile rhetoric, convinced the Soviet leadership that there were no immediate prospects for U.S.-Soviet detente. The explicitness of Carter military doctrine (PD-59) on the requirement for protracted nuclear war fighting (for deterrence) had resonated in Moscow in the same way as the INF deployment decision a year earlier had. For present purposes, the point is not whether any of these U.S. or NATO decisions was correct or incorrect in itself. It is the cumulative effect of these decisions as seen from Moscow and in the context of Soviet threat perception that is pertinent to our discussion.

Soviet force structure in 1983 also affected its view of the requirements of deterrence and of nuclear crisis management. The makeweight of Soviet strategic retaliatory forces was its ICBM force: all of these in 1983 were deployed in underground silos. In order to guarantee their survival against a U.S. first strike (which might, in the view of Soviet military planners, come as a "bolt from the blue" or from escalation after conventional war fighting in Europe), these land-based missiles would have to be launched before U.S. warheads exploded against their assigned targets.[33] This meant, in American military jargon, that Soviet ICBMs would have to be launched "on warning" or "under attack."[34] Only launch on warning could guarantee that sufficient numbers of Soviet ICBMs would survive a well-orchestrated U.S. first strike. Soviet leaders could not rely upon retaliation after ride-out to do so. According to some expert analysts, neither did the United States plan to rely mainly on retaliation after ride-out in order to fulfill the requirements of its retaliatory strike plans.[35]

According to Western experts, the Soviet armed forces were eventually tasked to prepare for a continuum of retaliatory options from preemption to retaliation after ride-out. However, leaders' decisions about a preferred option in actual crisis or wartime would have been constrained by capabilities available at the time. During the latter 1960s and early 1970s, improved capabilities for rapid launch and better warning communication and control systems made it possible for Soviet leaders to place more reliance upon launch on warning (LOW) and to be less dependent on preemption.[36] The option of preemption was not discarded. The variety of accidental or deliberate paths by which a nuclear war might be initiated left the Soviet leadership no choice, in their view, but contingent preparedness for a spectrum of possibilities.

Differences between U.S. and Soviet force structures would also have implications for the willingness of either side to rely upon LOW as its principal retaliatory option. U.S. retaliatory capabilities in 1983 were spread more evenly among three components of a strategic triad: intercontinental ballistic missiles (ICBMs); submarine-launched ballistic missiles (SLBMs); and long-range bombers, compared to Soviet forces. The most survivable part of the U.S. deterrent was its fleet ballistic missile submarine (SSBNs) force, virtually invulnerable to first-strike preemption. The U.S. bomber-delivered weapons, including air-launched cruise missiles (ALCMs), gravity bombs and short-range attack missiles (SRAMs), were slow flyers compared to the fast flying ICBMs and SLBMs. Nevertheless, the highly capable U.S. bomber force, compared to its Soviet counterpart, forced the Soviets to expend considerable resources on air defense and complicated their estimates of time on target arrivals for U.S. retaliatory forces.

The effects of force structure and doctrine combined created some significant pressures for Soviet reliance upon prompt launch to save the ICBM component of their deterrent. Doctrine suggested that crises were mainly political in their origin and were to be avoided, not managed. The onset of a serious crisis was a threat of war. The U.S. view that brinkmanship could be manipulated to unilateral advantage during a crisis struck most Soviet leaders before and after Khrushchev as a highly risk acceptant strategy. The Soviet leadership, after Khrushchev's enforced retirement, did engage in rapid nuclear force building in order to eliminate American strategic nuclear superiority, but they also eschewed "adventurism" in the forward deployments of nuclear weapons and in the use of nuclear forces as backdrops. Because they were pessimistic about "managing" a crisis once confrontation was forced upon them (in their view), Soviet leaders would have to include in crisis preparedness a capability for, and perhaps a bias toward, prompt launch to save the Strategic Rocket Forces. Pessimism about crisis management combined with an ICBM-heavy deterrent constrained Soviet leaders' choices once general deterrence (the basic Hobbesian condition of threat created by the international system of plural sovereignty and the security dilemma) turned to immediate deterrence (a situation in which one state has made an explicit military threat against another or others).

ANALYSIS

How might the strategic nuclear deterrent relationship between the Soviet Union and the United States in 1983 have been influenced by expected war outcomes if deterrence failed, given the factors discussed above? In order to answer this question, we first consider how stable the 1983 relationship was by comparing the outcomes that would have resulted from any breakdown of deterrence. Table 4.1 summarizes and compares the numbers of U.S. and Soviet retaliatory warheads and equivalent megatonnage (EMT) expected to survive a first strike in 1983.

The results of Table 4.1 show that neither side could have launched a first strike without receiving a retaliatory blow that inflicted socially unacceptable and economically catastrophic damage. In addition, despite very different force structures, the two states' overall retaliatory capabilities are very similar. The degree of similarity is emphasized in the summary provided in Table 4.2.

The ratio of U.S. to Soviet survivors is one possible measure of the stability of their nuclear deterrent relationship in 1983, but not the only one. Another possible measure compares the metastability of that relationship. A metastable relationship is one that simultaneously reduces the incentive for both sides to strike first. To measure this, we will calculate a Soviet first-strike advantage, a U.S. first-strike advantage, and the ratio between the two advantages (see Table 4.3). The "advantage" for each state is the difference between the number of warheads available for striking first, compared to the number available for retaliation after accepting a first strike.

A metastability index of 1.0 is a best case: the two sides' first-strike

Table 4.1
1983 Force Outcomes

	Russia	United States
Surviving Warheads	1,831	1,947
Surviving Equivalent Megatonnage	894	436
Reserve Warheads	668	1,064
Reserve Equivalent Megatonnage	216	234

Source: Author.

Table 4.2
Ratio of U.S. to Soviet Survivors, 1983

Deliverable Warheads	1.06
Deliverable Equivalent Megatonnage	0.49
Reserve Warheads	1.59
Reserve Equivalent Megatonnage	1.08

Note: A ratio of unity (1.0) means the two sides are equal. Ratios higher or lower than 1.0 indicate results favorable to the United States or to the USSR, respectively.

Source: Author.

advantages are equal and cancel one another out. The closer to 1.0 the metastability index, the greater the degree of first-strike stability. The more the index deviates from 1.0 (either higher or lower), the lesser the degree of stability. A metastability index of 1.17 says that, in 1983, the U.S. and Soviet "first strike advantages" were very similar; therefore, there was little incentive to strike first in order to obtain a relatively preferred outcome. Of course, this is a very static measure and does not capture some of the true differences between the basic concept of *first-strike stability* and the more nuanced concept of *crisis stability*. Crisis stability involves issues that go beyond first-strike stability, including the perceptions and expectations of policy makers and their principal military advisors. The next section offers a proposal for comparing the 1983 war scare crisis with other possible "war scares" of the Cold War in order to develop some comparative historical perspective on the problem of crisis stability.

Table 4.3
Comparative First-Strike Advantages, 1983

Soviet First-Strike Advantage	9,507.25
U.S. First-Strike Advantage	8,134.89
Metastability Index	1.17

Note: Metastability Index is the ratio of Soviet to U.S. first-strike advantage.

Source: Author.

OTHER WAR SCARES?

Do the preceding conclusions apply only to the situation in 1983? Undoubtedly the situation at the top of the Soviet leadership was unsettled, feeding expectations that if not paranoid, were certainly suspicious with regard to U.S. intentions. Comparison with other periods of tension and crisis might help to establish whether the analytic part of our methodology has applicability across different cases, before and after the Cold War. Let us, for example, take 1962, 1991 and 1995 as candidate benchmark "war scare" years.

The reasons for these choices are as follows. The Cuban missile crisis of 1962 is self evidently the most dangerous single 13 days of the Cold War. The failed coup of August 1991 led to the demise of the Soviet Union and solidified the end of the Cold War. From August 19 through 21, the world waited nervously for the outcome of the power struggle between Boris Yeltsin and the coup forces in Moscow. During the crisis, the exact chain of command by which Kremlin leaders would authorize nuclear release was uncertain and fogged from outside observers, including the U.S. president and NATO. Gorbachev was a temporary prisoner in his dacha in Foros in the Crimea, and the other two nuclear briefcases or "footballs" used by leaders to authorize nuclear retaliatory launch were in the possession of the defense minister and the chief of the General Staff. On August 19, Defense Minister Dmitri Yazov ordered the armed forces, including strategic nuclear forces, to Increased Combat Readiness. According to Peter Vincent Pry:

During the August 1991 coup, the United States was in grave danger without knowing it. A NATO or Strategic Air Command exercise, or the generation of U.S. forces to counter Moscow's escalation to Increased Combat Readiness, might have provoked the Committee (the coup plotters) to launch a preemptive nuclear strike.[37]

The situation in 1995 was somewhat different. There was no legitimacy crisis in Russia. But another kind of risk of accidental or inadvertent war presented itself. On January 25, 1995, a U.S.-Norwegian scientific experimental rocket launched from Andoya Island off the Norwegian coast was identified by Russian early warning as a possible threatening launch vehicle headed for Russia. The initial launching position and early trajectory of the meteorological rocket resembled, from the perspective of operators at the Russian missile attack warning system, a possible U.S. submarine-launched ballistic missile fired off the northern coast of Russia and arriving within 10 minutes or so over Russian territory. Russia's General Staff had in fact anticipated that a likely form of any U.S. surprise nuclear strike would begin with submarine-launched ballistic missiles (SLBMs) fired from the Norwegian and/or Barents Seas. The General Staff was especially concerned about the possibility of an SLBM electromagnetic pulse (EMP) precursor strike disabling radar warning systems, cutting off strategic communications, and disabling computers. Russian President Boris Yeltsin for the first time opened his "football" or briefcase with communications codes used to authorize a nuclear launch. After some minutes it was determined that the rocket's trajectory would not actually impact Russian territory and a mistaken prompt launch by Russian rocket forces was avoided.[38]

Each of these cases offers anecdotally interesting, and somewhat disconcerting, evidence of a higher than normal risk of accidental or inadvertent nuclear war. But each case has unique political and military aspects. Some method permitting comparison across cases is called for. To accomplish this, we will use various measures of the "trigger happiness" or degree of dependency of the United States and the Soviet Union or Russia on launch on warning, or on force generation, in the four cases: 1962 Cuban missile crisis; 1983 war scare; 1991 failed coup; and 1995 mistaken scientific rocket. Each of these situations will be interrogated for the numbers of surviving and retaliating (arriving) warheads in each of four conditions: generated forces/launch on warning; generated forces/ride out attack; day-to-day alerted forces/launch on warning; day-to-day alerted forces/ride out attack. Both the numbers of surviving warheads and the relative percentages of dependency on (sensitivity to) force generation or launch on warning are computed in Table 4.4.

All Soviet and post-Soviet Russian forces were more dependent than their U.S. contemporary/counterparts on launch on warning, whether the Soviet or Russian forces were on generated or day-to-day alert. And Soviet or Russian forces riding out the attack were more dependent on generated alert during these crises than U.S. forces were. On the other hand, Soviet or Russian forces launched on warning were less dependent on generated alert than their U.S. counterparts in three of four crisis

Table 4.4
Surviving and Arriving Re-entry Vehicles: Four Scenarios and Four Time Periods

	U.S. 1962	USSR 1962	U.S. 1983	USSR 1983	U.S. 1991	USSR 1991	U.S. 1995	Russia 1995
Generated Forces/Launch on Warning	2,630	412	8,011	9,504	9,375	9,228	6,726	5,786
Generated Forces/Ride Out Attack	2,517	344	6,273	4,425	7,390	4,373	5,511	3,329
Day-to-Day Alerted Forces/Launch on Warning	920	87	5,299	6,332	5,929	6,405	3,768	3,751
Day-to-Day Alerted Forces/Ride Out Attack	807	13	3,561	909	3,944	822	2,553	536
Percent Dependency on Generated Alert/Launch on Warning	186	373	51	50	58	44	78	54
Percent Dependency on Generated Alert/Ride Out Attack	212	2,471	76	387	87	432	116	521
Percent Dependency on Day-to-Day Alerted Forces/Launch on Warning	4	20	28	115	27	111	22	74
Percent Dependency on Day-to-Day Alerted Forces/Ride Out Attack	14	552	49	597	50	679	48	600

Source: NIE 11-5-58, *Soviet Capabilities in Guided Missiles and Space Vehicles*, pp. 65–70; NIE 11-8/1-61, *Strength and Deployment of Soviet Long Range Ballistic Missile Forces*, pp. 121–138; and NIE 11-3/8-82, *Soviet Capabilities for Strategic Nuclear Conflict, 1981–1991*, pp. 483–490, all in Donald P. Steury, ed., *Intentions and Capabilities: Estimates on Soviet Strategic Forces, 1950–1983* (Washington, D.C.: CIA History Staff, Center for the Study of Intelligence, 1996). See also NIE 11-3/8-91, *Soviet Forces and Capabilities for Strategic Nuclear Conflict Through the Year 2000*, in Benjamin B. Fischer, ed., *At Cold War's End: U.S. Intelligence on the Soviet Union and Eastern Europe, 1989–1991* (Washington, D.C.: Central Intelligence Agency, 1999), pp. 359–368. Author's results table involves calculations from model developed by Dr. James Scouras, Strategy Research Group. He is not responsible for its use here.

situations. Only in the Cuban missile crisis of 1962 were Soviet forces more dependent than those of the other side on generated alert.

The significance of these findings across various cases is as follows. The findings do *not* change the inescapable statistics of the Cold War nuclear balance. Neither the United States nor the Soviet Union (or later Russia) could launch a nuclear surprise attack without receiving historically unprecedented and socially unacceptable retaliation. But crisis behavior of leaders is conditioned not only by scientific facts, but also by subjective expectations about the likely behavior of the other side. In each of these situations, strategic warning of a tense situation that might, with unknown probability, lead to an actual outbreak of war was already on the table. What mattered next was the expected reaction by each side to tactical warning of an actual attack in progress, or to indicators considered tantamount to confirmation of an attack.

The results summarized in Table 4.4 and in other information presented in this study suggest that, at the cusp of decision about how hard or how soft tactical warning would have to be, Soviet and Russian leaders were far too dependent on early alerted nuclear forces and, even more so, on launch on warning in order to guarantee retaliatory strikes against desired target sets. It deserves reemphasis that it is in the unknown, but potentially deadly, conjunction of images of the enemy and actual capabilities that the difference between a war and a crisis can be found. Neither theorists nor policy makers can derive any complacency from the fortuitous escape from disaster repeated four times.

Another issue raised by these findings is the operational propensity of the Russian nuclear command and control system. There is considerable evidence from Russians that the strategic nuclear command and control system may be tilted toward the prevention of decapitation and loss of control by enemy first strikes. Less emphasis, if any, is given to the avoidance of accidental/inadvertent nuclear war or escalation. We are not speaking here of technical use control devices such as Permissive Action Links (electronic locks that must be unlocked by codes before launch vehicles or warheads can be activated). Instead, we are now addressing the military ethos in the minds of principal commanders who control the use of, or have custody of, nuclear forces. According to Peter Vincent Pry, although the president of the Russian Federation is the only person who can legally order the launch of nuclear weapons, the General Staff "controls all of the electronic, mechanical, and operational means for waging nuclear war."[39]

This situation by itself is not necessarily disquieting. The United States too has arranged means by which retaliation will still take place in the event that the top political leadership and even the major military commands are destroyed in surprise nuclear attacks. These kinds of arrangements are called delegation of authority and devolution of command.[40]

However, in the U.S. case, orderly political succession in peacetime or even during a crisis is ensured. In addition, the U.S. nuclear command and control system is designed to shift gradually from an emphasis on negative control (prevention of accidental or unauthorized nuclear release or launch) to positive control (guaranty that authorized alerting and launch commands will be readily obeyed).

The Russian nuclear command and control system apparently emphasizes positive compared to negative control even apart from times of crisis. Some Western experts believe that Russian officers charged with the day-to-day management of nuclear forces could, from the main General Staff underground command post at Chekov, initiate a nuclear attack even in the absence of authorized commands from President Putin or from senior officers.[41] Noted Russian analyst and nuclear arms control expert Alexei Arbatov warned in a 1992 article that the monopoly of the military in devising the control system and operational plan resulted "in a concept which guards not against an accidental strike due to a mistake, a nervous breakdown, or a technical problem, but against failure to respond to an attack promptly and on a massive scale. . . . This is a reflection of a typically militaristic mentality—the main goal is to crush the enemy; deterrence is just a sideline."[42]

The point of these citations is not to imply that Russians are, or ever were, war acceptant to an extent that Americans or others are not. Russians, above all others in the twentieth century, paid the costs of war. The issue raised here is the possible consequences of system design combined with crisis stimulation to produce the equivalent of a "normal accident."[43] As in other large and complex organizations, standard operating procedures and organizational routines built into the nuclear command and control system, as well as the operational habits and expectations of operators, create biases and predispositions that could be dysfunctional in a crisis.[44] If, in addition, leading Russian military theorists expect that any Western attack might be preceded by strategic information warfare against computers and communication systems, cyber-glitches could be mistaken for the first wave of enemy attacks during a period of tension. (See Chapter 5 for more on the problem of information warfare and its relationship to nuclear deterrence.)

CONCLUSIONS

Was the 1983 war scare real or imaginary, and how serious was it? These are important questions for students of Cold War history and of contemporary strategy and arms control. Not all aspects of the issue can be dealt with here. We can say this. Significant anecdotal evidence, combined with modeling of some aspects of U.S. and Soviet likely operational performance in 1983, supports the case that Soviet fears of an outbreak of war in 1983 were real, and in some cases, justified, given their political and military-strategic outlooks. U.S. intelligence needed to have done a better job of "seeing the other" and not for the first time in 1983. A series of apparently discrete events between 1979 (NATO's INF modernization decision) and November 1983 (Able Archer) cumulated unexpectedly into a "positive feedback loop" of negative expectations. Soviet foreign and military intelligence, tasked by their uptight political masters, reported back to Moscow Central those indicators and pessimistic appraisals that seemed to confirm initial suspicions that the West was up to something. And data analysis shows that this misperception by both sides could have been linked with a realistic concern on the part of Soviet military planners that their first strike might be their last. Nor are these patterns necessarily confined to 1983. Modeling of situations in 1962, 1991 and 1995 shows disturbingly similar Soviet and Russian dependencies on prompt launch and early force generation in a crisis.

The preceding discussion is not just an historical excursion. It offers some lessons for present and future arms control policy. The war scare episode does show the priority of politics over force balances in bringing nuclear armed states toward, or away from, the brink of war. But it also shows that the attributes of nuclear forces, including their launch readiness and firing doctrines, can contribute to an atmosphere of tension and mistrust. From a political standpoint, the relations between the United States and Russia are not now hostile, as they were between the Americans and the Soviets in the Cold War years. Every encouragement should be given the Russians and Americans, having decoupled the threat of war from their political relations, to reduce nuclear force sizes. Equally important, the two states should align their operational doctrines and crisis management expectations as far away from fast trigger dependency as possible, and toward relaxed expectations based on flexible and survivable, but nonprovocative, deployments and doctrines.

APPENDIX 4.1: SOVIET AND U.S. STRATEGIC NUCLEAR FORCES, 1983

	Launchers	Warheads per Launcher	Total Warheads
Soviet Forces			
SS-11/3	550	1	550
SS-13/2	60	1	60
SS-17/3	150	4	600
SS-18/4/5	308	10	3,080
SS-19/3	330	6	1,980
SS-24 (fixed)	0	10	0
subtotal fixed land	1,398		6,270

APPENDIX 4.1 (continued)

	Launchers	Warheads per Launcher	Total Warheads
Soviet Forces			
SS-24 (rail)	0	10	0
SS-25 (road)	0	1	0
subtotal mobile land	0	0	0
subtotal land-based	1,398		6,270
SS-N-6/3	384	1	384
SS-N-8/2	292	1	292
SS-N-18/3	224	7	1,568
SS-N-20	200	10	2,000
SS-N-17	12	1	12
SS-N-5	9	1	9
subtotal sea-based	1,121		4,265
Bison	43	4	172
Tu-95 Bear B/G ALCM	100	2	200
Tu-95 Bear B/G Bomb	100	2	200
subtotal air-breathing	243		572
Total Soviet forces	**2,762**		**11,107**
U.S. Forces			
Minuteman II	450	1	450
Minuteman III	250	3	750
Minuteman IIIA	300	3	900
Titan	45	1	45
subtotal land-based	1,045		2,145
Poseidon C-3	304	10	3,040
Poseidon C-4	192	8	1,536
Trident C-4	72	8	576
subtotal sea-based	568		5,152
B-52G gravity	41	4	164
SRAM	41	8	328
B-52G gravity	46	4	184
ALCM/SRAM	46	20	920
B-52H gravity	90	4	360
SRAM	90	8	720
B-52D	31	4	124
subtotal air-breathing	208		2,800
Total U.S. forces	**1,821**		**10,097**

NOTES

The author gratefully acknowledges Dr. Ben B. Fischer, Central Intelligence Agency, for sources pertinent to this study and for additional helpful suggestions; Dr. Raymond L. Garthoff, Brookings Institution, for important critical comments and corrections; and Dr. James Scouras, for assistance in developing historical data bases. None of these persons is responsible for any arguments or opinions.

1. Christopher Andrew and Oleg Gordievsky, *KGB: The Inside Story* (New York: HarperCollins, 1990), p. 583.

2. Andrew and Gordievsky, eds., *Comrade Kryuchkov's Instructions: Top Secret Files on KGB Foreign Operations, 1975–1985* (Stanford, Calif.: Stanford University Press, 1993), pp. 68–90, provides a full account of RYAN.

3. See Reference No. 373/PR/52, Attachment 2, *The Problem of Discovering Preparation for a Nuclear Missile Attack on the USSR*, in Andrew and Gordievsky, eds., *Comrade Kryuchkov's Instructions*, pp. 74–81, citation p. 74.

4. Ibid., pp. 77–81.

5. Ibid., p. 76.

6. My appreciation of the Soviet perspective here owes much to helpful comments from Raymond Garthoff. See Raymond L. Garthoff, *Detente and Confrontation: American-Soviet Relations from Nixon to Reagan* (Washington, D.C.: Brookings Institution, 1985), pp. 864–872.

7. Robert M. Gates, *From the Shadows: The Ultimate Insider's Story of Five Presidents and How They Won the Cold War* (New York: Simon and Schuster, 1996), p. 262.

8. Andrew and Gordievsky, *Comrade Kryuchkov's Instructions*, p. 76. Soviet fears of the preemptive value of Pershing II seemed excessive from the U.S. and NATO perspective. The range of the Pershing II given by U.S. official sources would not have permitted prompt attacks against main military command bunkers in or near Moscow. However, Soviet military planners might have feared that, once in place, Pershing II missiles could be enhanced and given extended ranges bringing Moscow and environs within their reach.

9. Gates, *From the Shadows*, p. 264.

10. Statement of Soviet scientists on SDI quoted in Andrei A. Kokoshin, *Soviet Strategic Thought, 1917–1991* (Cambridge, Mass.: MIT Press, 1998), p. 182.

11. Gates, *From the Shadows*, p. 268.

12. Seymour M. Hersh, *"The Target Is Destroyed": What Really Happened to Flight 007 and What America Knew about It* (New York: Vintage Books, 1987), esp. pp. 147–150 and 246–247.

13. Ibid., p. 267.

14. Andrew and Gordievsky, *KGB*, p. 597.

15. Ibid., p. 598.

16. My account of this episode is taken from David Hoffman, " 'I Had a Funny Feeling in My Gut': Soviet Officer Faced Nuclear Armageddon," *Washington Post*, February 10, 1999, p. A19.

17. Ibid.

18. Ibid.

19. Accounts of Able Archer appear in Andrew and Gordievsky, *KGB*, pp. 599–600; Gates, *From the Shadows*, pp. 270–273. See also Gordon Brook-Shepherd, *The Storm Birds: Soviet Postwar Defectors* (New York: Wiedenfeld and Nicolson, 1989), pp. 328–335.

20. Brook-Shepherd, *The Storm Birds*, p. 329.

21. Andrew and Gordievsky, *KGB*, p. 599.

22. Ibid.

23. Ibid., p. 600.

24. Peter Vincent Pry, *War Scare: Russia and America on the Nuclear Brink* (Westport, Conn.: Praeger Publishers, 1999), p. 41.

25. Gates, *From the Shadows*, p. 273.

26. Ben B. Fischer, "Intelligence and Disaster Avoidance: The Soviet War Scare and U.S.-Soviet Relations," in Stephen J. Cimbala, ed., *Mysteries of the Cold War* (Aldershot, U.K.: Ashgate Publishing Co., 1999), pp. 89–104, esp. p. 98. I gratefully acknowledge Ben Fischer for calling this important aspect of Operation RYAN to my attention.

27. Council of Ministers of the German Democratic Republic, Ministry for State Security, Deputy of the Minister, Implementation Regulation to Order Nr. 1/85 of 15.2.1985: *Comprehensive Use of Capabilities of the Service Units of the MfS for Early and Reliable Acquisition of Evidence of Imminent Enemy Plans, Preparations, and Actions for Aggression* (Berlin, June 5, 1985).

28. Fischer, "Intelligence and Disaster Avoidance," p. 98.

29. Markus Wolf, *Man without a Face: The Autobiography of Communism's Greatest Spymaster* (New York: Times Books, 1997) is a first person account of his amazing career.

30. Wolf, *Spionage Chef im geheimen Krieg: Erinnerungen* (Dusseldorf and Munich: List Verlag, 1997), p. 332, cited in Fischer, "Intelligence and Disaster Avoidance," p. 101.

31. Raymond L. Garthoff, *Deterrence and the Revolution in Soviet Military Doctrine* (Washington, D.C.: Brookings Institution, 1990), pp. 24–25.

32. William E. Odom, *The Collapse of the Soviet Military* (New Haven, Conn.: Yale University Press, 1998), pp. 1–15 is excellent on this point. See also Garthoff, *Deterrence and the Revolution in Soviet Military Doctrine*, pp. 16–22.

33. Ghulam Dastagir Wardak, comp., and Graham Hall Turbiville, Jr., gen. ed., *The Voroshilov Lectures: Materials from the Soviet General Staff Academy*, Vol. I (Washington, D.C.: National Defense University Press, 1989), pp. 69–75.

34. In theory according to some U.S. distinctions, launch "on warning" would take place in response to multiple indicators that an attack had been launched but prior to the actual detonations of warheads on U.S. soil. Launch "under attack" would be delayed until after actual dontations had occurred. Skeptics can be forgiven for assuming that launch "under attack" was a euphemism in declaratory policy for action policy that was likely to be launch "on warning." Launch on warning would be necessary to save the ICBM force from prompt destruction. The difference between LOW and LUA might, at most, affect some components of an already partly alerted U.S. bomber force.

35. Bruce G. Blair, *The Logic of Accidental Nuclear War* (Washington, D.C.: Brookings Institution, 1993), p. 177 and passim.

36. Garthoff, *Deterrence and the Revolution in Soviet Military Doctrine*, p. 78.

37. Pry, *War Scare*, p. 81.

38. The preceding summary of the January 1995 incident is taken from ibid., pp. 214–221.

39. Ibid., p. 152.

40. Paul Bracken, *The Command and Control of Nuclear Forces* (New Haven, Conn.: Yale University Press, 1983), passim.

41. Pry, *War Scare*, p. 152.

42. Alexei Arbatov, cited in Pry, *War Scare*, p. 155.

43. Charles Perrow, *Normal Accidents: Living with High-Risk Technologies* (New York: Basic Books, 1984) develops this concept.

44. This case is argued with regard to U.S. systems in Scott D. Sagan, *The Limits of Safety: Organizations, Accidents and Nuclear Weapons* (Princeton, N.J.: Princeton University Press, 1993). See especially his discussion of the U-2 "stray" into Soviet air space during the Cuban missile crisis (pp. 135–146).

Chapter 5

Nuclear Weapons and U.S.-Russian Arms Control

INTRODUCTION

In this chapter, we consider the future of Russia's nuclear deterrent and its relationship to U.S. and Russian arms control objectives. Russia's nuclear weapons are its remaining claim upon great power status as it enters the twenty-first century. This is a complete reversal from the Soviet position relative to that of NATO during most of the Cold War. Soviet forces had the conventional military power not only to defeat any invasion of Mother Russia but also to pose a substantial threat of territorial conquest without having to rely upon nuclear first use. Now nuclear first use is Russia's option out of necessity instead of choice. Putting nuclear weapons on the front end of Russia's deterrent only makes more urgent and important the question of U.S.-Russian strategic nuclear arms control.

In the early years of the twenty-first century, Russia faces some fundamental policy choices with regard to nuclear weapons and arms control. These choices bear upon Russia's relationship with the United States and with NATO. For example, Russia must decide whether to continue a U.S.-Russian deterrent relationship based exclusively on the capability for offensive retaliation, or to entertain the possibility of unilateral or joint deployments of missile defenses for U.S. or Russian national territory. In the following discussion, we first consider why nuclear weapons and deterrence remain important in Russian military strategy. Second, we provide an assessment of whether deterrence stability can be maintained at or below START III levels. Third, we consider the implications of missile defense technology and the likely impact of a U.S.-deployed national missile defense system on deterrence and arms race stability.

WHY NUCLEAR WEAPONS STILL MATTER

There are at least five reasons why nuclear weapons and nuclear arms control remain as important issues in the Russian security policy agenda, including its agenda for negotiations with the United States on nuclear force reductions.

First, Russia still has many thousands of nuclear weapons, including those of intercontinental range. Second, the other acknowledged nuclear powers, in addition to the United States and Russia, show no inclination to abandon nuclear weapons as ultimate deterrents. China is, in fact, by all accounts engaged in a significant modernization of its military technology base, including the base that supports improved delivery systems for nuclear weapons. A third reason for the continued importance of nuclear deterrence is the addition of India and Pakistan in 1998 to the club of acknowledged nuclear powers and the potential for additional non-nuclear states to acquire these and other weapons of mass destruction.

A fourth reason for the continuing significance of nuclear deterrence in the post–Cold War system is, somewhat paradoxically, Russia's military and economic weakness. There are two aspects of this weakness that might contribute to nuclear deterrence failure based on failed crisis management, mistaken preemption or accidental/inadvertent war. First, Russia's conventional military weakness makes it more reliant on nuclear weapons as weapons of first choice or first use, instead of last resort. Second, Russia's economic problems mean that it will have difficulty maintaining personnel morale and reliability.[1] In addition, Russia's military will also be lacking in funds to modernize and properly equip its early warning and nuclear command, control and communications systems. These weaknesses may encourage reliance on prompt launch doctrines for strategic nuclear retaliation or raise the odds in favor of a mistaken decision for preemption.

Fifth, Russia's new draft military doctrine of October 1999, as well as its national security concept of the year 2000, reaffirmed the significance of nuclear weapons in Russian military strategy by noting that nuclear arms are an "effective factor of deterrence, guaranteeing the military security of the Russian Federation and its allies, supporting international stability and peace."[2] And despite the dire financial straits in which Russia's conventional military forces found themselves at century's end, civilian and military leaders reaffirmed the priority of nuclear force modernization in the face of American and NATO assertiveness and possible U.S. deployments of ballistic missile defenses.[3] Nuclear weapons guarantee Russia a seat at the great power table and, thus, a claim to future status as one of the influential poles in a twenty-first century multipolar international system.

The draft military doctrine of 1999 was less significant for its military-technical aspects than for its political frame of reference. Compared to its 1993 predecessor, it was explicitly anti-Western and anti-U.S. Expressing the Kremlin's obvious pique at having to swallow NATO enlargement and Operation Allied Force against Yugoslavia in 1999, the draft doctrine contrasted two opposing trends. The first trend was unipolar, meaning U.S. superpower domination; the second, multipolar, meaning many centers of influence, including Russia.[4] The Russian National Security Concept signed into law in April 2000 coincides with the thrust of the 1999 military doctrine. It elevates the significance of external compared to internal threats to Russia, deplores U.S. and NATO unilateralism outside of the UN Charter, and replaces language in the 1997 security concept by "partnership" with the West based on acceptance of Russia as a great power.[5] According to Stephen J. Blank:

Russian military apprehensions have grown with the collapse of Russian power, the augmentation of power of the United States and NATO, Kosovo, the Anglo-American bombing campaign against Iraq, the Revolution in Military Affairs (RMA), and the onset of information warfare and operations (IW and IO respectively). Kosovo was the last straw since it united many of the most feared military and political elements of threat.[6]

One of the most problematical aspects of Russia's military doctrine and national security policy is the apparent willingness to turn to nuclear weapons in conflicts short of world war or even major regional war growing out of an invasion of Russian state territory. The possibility is not excluded that tactical nuclear weapons might be used with the intention of de-escalating a local war that Russians feared was getting out of hand and not controllable by available conventional forces. In addition, ranking Russian military commentators link their concerns about separatism and secession with external sources of actual or potential aggression against Russia. Thus, for example, Russia is especially sensitive to political upheavals in the Caucasus and the possibility of external Islamic or NATO support for those outbreaks of revolt. As the then Prime Minister and later President Vladimir Putin noted in November 1999:

What happened this summer should not be seen as some particular, local occurrence. Combine in a single whole Dagestan, the incursions of the gang elements from Afghanistan and Tajikistan, and the events in Kyrgyzstan. What was happening—we will call a spade a spade—was an attempt at the military and political assimilation of part of the territory of the former Soviet Union . . . A rebellious self-proclaimed state supported by extremist circles of a number of

Islamic countries . . . A self-proclaimed state which, in the intentions of these extremist circles, was to have become Greater Ichkeria from the Caspian to the
Black Sea, that is to have seized all of the Caucasus, cut Russia off from the
Transcaucasus, and closed the route into Central Asia. Dagestan was, after all,
to have been merely the first step.[7]

Western readers would consider these statements to have embodied a
great deal of nationalist hyperbole, not to say hysteria. But Russia's
decade-long decline in conventional military power has increased its fear
of encirclement, penetration and rebellion even apart from its somewhat
frenetic reaction to NATO's war against Yugoslavia in 1999.

Russian sensitivity over Kosovo is somewhat misplaced and based on
some false optimism about U.S. technology and the coercive military
influence that can be derived from it. Some U.S. strategists have described Operation Allied Force as less than a triumph, either of technology or of policy. The United States and NATO ruled out a ground
operation at the outset of the bombing campaign, destroyed far fewer
Serbian tanks and other high value targets than was expected or initially
claimed, and in the last analysis required Russian diplomatic mediation
in order to terminate the bombing and pave the way for a peace settlement acceptable both to Serbia and to NATO. Some Russian pessimists
about Allied Force appear to share the perspective of U.S. Air Force
optimists: that air power alone or virtually by itself can win wars. Russians may see a progressive increase in U.S. capability for long-range,
precision strike, automated command and control systems, stealth and
the military exploitation of space that could turn a future version of
Allied Force against territory adjacent to, or even within, the Russian
Federation itself.

A more sober assessment of Allied Force calls for more humility on
the part of U.S. air officers and NATO planners. NATO's air war against
Yugoslavia was not fought on a level playing field. NATO's military and
economic assets are second to none. Second, the early phases of the
bombing were corrupted by intelligence leaks to Serbia, attributed by
some to Russian sources within NATO's three newly admitted members
(Poland, the Czech Republic and Hungary). Third, NATO's reluctance
to use ground forces suggested a potential weakness that others might
exploit in future cases of humanitarian intervention. Fourth, Slobodan
Milosevic was still in power at the end of the day and in command and
control of his government and armed forces.

In sum, Russia in 1999 had some additional reasons to worry about
its perceived or actual military strength. But the drift of its security policy
and military doctrine throughout Yeltsin's second term as president was
decidedly pessimistic about threat assessments on all azimuths. Within
this context, the Putin administration will bring to the negotiating table
on arms control a suspicious cast of mind, especially if future adminis-

trations desire the overthrow of deterrence based on offensive retaliation. On the other hand, Russia is and will remain open to reductions in the size and diversity of its strategic nuclear arsenal so long as its second-strike capability is felt to be secure and its modernization remains affordable.

FORCE STRUCTURES

The United States agreed with Russia that Russia should accept the strategic arms control obligations of the former Soviet government, undertaken in the START I and II agreements signed in 1991 and 1993, respectively. The second agreement called for the two sides to reduce their holdings of strategic nuclear weapons to ceilings in the range of 3,000 to 3,500 warheads, with additional limitations on launchers, especially MIRVed ICBMs (land-based missiles with multiple, independently targeted warheads). The United States and Russia concluded several agreements in 1997 with the objective of firming up START II and increasing the probability of its successful ratification in Russia, which finally happened in 2000. First, Washington and Moscow agreed to delay final implementation of the treaty-required reductions until December 31, 2007, instead of January 1, 2003. Related to this step, they also committed themselves to prompt negotiations on a follow-up START III agreement that would reduce each side's strategic nuclear warheads to 2,000–2,500 by 2007.[8] Both houses of the Russian parliament finally ratified START II on April 19, 2000.

Russia's ratification of START II was conditional, however. The government of President Vladimir Putin, supported by a favorable balance of power in the Russian parliament, insisted on U.S. adherence to the ABM Treaty of 1972 in its original interpretation.[9] This original interpretation precluded either side from deploying missile defense systems capable of defending its entire state or national territory from nuclear missile attack. However, President Clinton, under pressure from a Republican dominated U.S. Congress, had set a deadline of June 2000 (later postponed) for a decision whether to deploy a limited NMD system designed to defeat light attacks from "rogue" states such as Iran or North Korea. The United States hoped Russia would be willing to negotiate amendments to the ABM Treaty permissive of a limited missile defense system. In return the United States might accept Russia's preference for lower ceilings on START III offensive weapons, perhaps as few as 1,500 strategic nuclear warheads for each side. In November 2001, Presidents Bush and Putin announced their intentions to implement major reductions in strategic nuclear warheads, well below previously discussed levels. In December 2001, President Bush announced that the United States would withdraw from the ABM Treaty.

Russia's plans for modernization of its strategic nuclear forces can be estimated in general. But many specifics are undetermined as of this writing. In general terms, Russia intends, in accord with planning guidance laid down in 1998, to modernize all three legs of its strategic nuclear forces (see below for details) in order to support a strategy of second-strike, assured retaliation.[10] This implies that weapons should be survivable, emphasizing mobility and reducing the numbers of warheads per launch vehicle to the minimum. In addition, increasing the ability of retaliatory warheads to penetrate their targets will be emphasized as a possible offset to U.S. deployment of any national missile defense (NMD) system.[11] Of course, an American missile defense system might arrest the entire START process and thereby permit Russia to retain a number of its currently deployed MIRVed ICBMs, scheduled for elimination under START II guidelines.

Russian intercontinental ballistic missiles (ICBMs) remain as the backbone of its strategic retaliatory forces. The major ICBM modernization program in 1999 was the Topol-M (SS-27) single-warhead missile.[12] At the end of 1998, 19 ICBM bases held 756 missiles of five types: SS-18s, SS-19s, SS-24s and SS-27s in underground silos; rail-mobile SS-24s; and road-mobile SS-25s. START II entry into force would eliminate all SS-18s and SS-24s and all except 105 SS-19s; remaining SS-19s would be downloaded to a single warhead. Some ICBM silos may be converted to accept the SS-27 Topol-M.[13] General Vladimir Yakovlev, CINC of the Strategic Rocket Forces, has called in 1999 for a production schedule of 20 to 30 Topol-M (SS-27) becoming operational for each of the next three years, and for 30 to 40 per year for the following three years.

With regard to ballistic missile submarines, Russia's START exchange data of 1998 included 42 submarines of six classes, but the actual number of submarines available and fully operational is fewer than that. The Russian navy considers only 25 SSBNs as operational, 16 in the Northern Fleet and nine in the Pacific Fleet.[14] Operational tempos of the Russian SSBN fleet have been drastically reduced since the end of the Cold War, and Russia might have as few as 10 to 15 operational SSBNs by the end of 2003 (consisting of Delta IVs, newer Delta IIIs and Typhoons). Although the keel for the first Borey-class (Iurii Dolgoruki) SSBN was laid in November 1996, construction was suspended in 1998 at least temporarily amid official statements that the ship was being redesigned to accommodate a new type of submarine-launched ballistic missile (SLBM).[15] Russia in the autumn of 1998 was already below the START II established ceiling for warheads carried on SLBMs (1750).

The modernization plans for the Russian strategic bomber force are as vague as those for the navy. Russia claimed some 70 strategic bombers at the end of 1998, but fewer were actually operational due to lack of funds. The current generation of air-launched cruise missiles (ALCMs) is approaching the end of their service lives, adding an additional modernization requirement for airborne resources already stretched. The commander-in-chief of the Russian Air Force has announced plans to replace the Tu-95MS Bear H with a new aircraft after 2010, a rather distant date. Only two of the six Tu-160 Blackjack bombers listed as operational at the end of 1998 were actually able to take off, and plans to purchase additional Blackjacks from Ukraine fell through in 1997. The number of operational strategic bombers deployed in the next decade will surely fall below current deployments, and the possibility of Russia's going out of the bomber business entirely cannot be discounted as impossible.[16]

Compared to Russia, the United States has to undergo fewer exertions to realign its strategic nuclear forces for compliance with START II. The United States needed only to eliminate 50 Peacekeeper (MX) ICBMs, 4 Ohio-class ballistic missile submarines (SSBNs) and 28 long-range bombers with air-launched cruise missiles (ALCMs) from its START I compliant force. U.S. plans assume the downloading of Minuteman III ICBMs and Trident II SLBMs (submarine-launched ballistic missiles) and conversion of B-1B bombers to conventional missions. Because the United States can meet its START II force structure requirements by downloading or mission changes, whereas Russia must build new systems and destroy many existing ones, some Russians complain that the United States has a comparative free ride. In addition, the removed U.S. warheads could be "uploaded" fairly quickly in the event that political relations between the two states deteriorated and arms reductions came to a halt. Table 5.1 summarizes U.S. and former Soviet Union strategic nuclear forces at the beginning of 1999.

Given its limited financial resources, Russia will be unable to match unconstrained U.S. modernization of strategic nuclear forces. It may also be unable to reach the ceilings for warhead deployments permitted under START II or even START III guidelines. One expert estimated that Russia might only be able to deploy 1,300 START-compatible warheads by 2008, on 300 Topol-M ICBMs, 7 Delta IV ballistic missile submarines, and about 80 bombers. On the other hand, if Russia decides not to ratify START II, it has the option to retain its multiple warhead ICBMs. Some SS-18 and SS-19 MIRVed ICBMs could last until 2010 before expiration of their service lives.[17]

MAINTAINING PARITY AND STABILITY

Both U.S. and Russian negotiators are rightly concerned about the stability of the strategic nuclear balance at greatly reduced levels expected under START II, START III or even lower if it comes to that. Stability is a tricky concept. Comparisons of force structures do not reveal some of the properties of force *operations* that may matter for crisis management

Table 5.1
Former Soviet Union (FSU) and U.S. Strategic Nuclear Forces (as of January 1, 1999)

Delivery System	Launchers	Warheads/ Launcher	Total Warheads
		Russia and Other FSU	
ICBMs			
SS-18	180	10	1,800
SS-19	160	6	960
SS-24	90	10	900
SS-25	370	1	370
Total ICBMs	**800**		**4,030**
SLBMs			
SS-N-8	152	1	152
SS-N-18	208	3	624
SS-N-20	120	10	1,200
SS-N-23	112	4	448
Total SLBMs	**592**		**2,424**
Bombers			
Blackjack/ALCM	24	8	192
Bear/ALCM	89	8	712
Bear	4	1	4
Total Bombers	**117**		**908**
Grand Total	**1,509**		**7,362**
		United States	
ICBMs			
Minuteman II	1	1	1
Minuteman III	650	3	1,950
MX	50	10	500
Total ICBMs	**701**		**2,451**
SLBMs			
Poseidon	32	10	320
Trident I	192	8	1,536
Trident II	240	8	1,920
Total SLBMs	**464**		**3,776**
Bombers			
B-1B	91	1	91
B-2	20	1	20
B-52	48	1	48
B-52 ALCM	156*	10	1,572
Total Bombers	**315**		**1,731**
Grand Total	**1,480**		**7,958**

*Six are counted with 12 warheads each per START I accounting rules.

Source: Adapted from David B. Thomson, A Guide to the Nuclear Arms Control Treaties (Los Alamos, N.M.: Los Alamos National Laboratory, LA-UR-99–31–73, July 1999), pp. 316–317.

or deterrence. For example, the United States relies more heavily on sea-based ballistic missiles (SLBMs) and bombers as parts of its retaliatory force than does Russia, which has favored land-based missiles (ICBMs). The operational diversity of land, sea and air forces complicates the plans of attackers. Land-based missiles are fast to react but for that reason also pose a destabilizing threat of preemption. Sea-based missiles are the most survivable among launch platforms but require a degree of operational autonomy that unsettled commissars during the Cold War. The U.S. Air Force influence in defense planning ensures a prominent role for strategic bombers, which have been augmented by air-launched cruise missiles; Russia deploys comparatively fewer and less modern air forces.

Survivable Forces

Stability can be measured in various ways. We will first compare the numbers of "post–first-strike" surviving warheads delivered by U.S. and Soviet or Russian forces under the following conditions: (1) holding constant the numbers of Russian survivors and varying the number of U.S. survivors, depending upon the U.S. force structure and (2) holding constant the numbers of U.S. survivors and varying the number of Russian survivors, depending upon Russian force structure. These comparative numbers of surviving warheads and equivalent megatonnage (EMT) provide a rough estimate of the *first-strike stability* of the two states' forces. First-strike stability is a measure of the extent to which any one-sided advantage in the expected number of surviving warheads or EMT might create a hypothetical (albeit marginal) incentive for a first strike. First-strike stability is a less complicated notion than *crisis stability*. Crisis stability goes beyond force attributes and exchange calculations. It considers behavioral expectations of the two states' political leaders and military force operators. Our measures cannot hope to approximate the complexity of crisis stability, but we will measure one aspect of it.

We now compare four alternate, hypothetical U.S. and Russian START III forces in terms of their possible outcomes. Two force sizes are included in the comparison: an upper limit of 2,500 deployed strategic warheads, or a lower ceiling for each side of 1,500 warheads. The higher figure has been mentioned as the logical starting point for U.S. and Russian discussions about a baseline for any START III agreement. This lower limit is selected because Russia will probably opt for as low a force size as it can afford and still maintain parity. The alternate forces for the United States in each case are:

• A balanced triad including ICBMs, SLBMs and bombers;
• A dyad with no ICBMs;

Table 5.2
Russian Surviving and Deliverable Warheads in START III Forces

	2,500 Warheads	1,500 Warheads
Balanced Triad	675	539
No Bombers	860	609
ICBM-Heavy	803	555*
SLBM-Heavy	748	555*

*Outcomes for the 1500-warhead ICBM-heavy and SLBM-heavy forces are slightly different, but appear here as identical due to rounding. Force structures are listed in Appendix 5.1.

Source: Author, based on Steve's Nuclear Assessment Matrix (SNAM), a statistical model for calculating the results of nuclear exchanges originally developed by Dr. James J. Tritten. He is not responsible for its application here.

• A triad with no B-52 bombers;
• A force composed of SLBMs only.

The force options for Russia are:

• A balanced triad;
• A dyad without bombers;
• An ICBM-heavy triad;
• An SLBM-heavy triad.

We will use our data base to interrogate each of these forces for the numbers of survivable and deliverable warheads provided by that force, compared to a notional balanced triad on the other side. These results, for each of the eight Russian and U.S. START III forces, are summarized in Tables 5.2 and 5.3.

These results are of interest for several reasons. First, in all postures both sides can deliver enough survivable warheads and megatonnage (not shown here) to inflict socially unacceptable, and historically unprecedented, damage. This finding remains true even when defenses of modest competency are added into the START III estimates (see below). Second, there is not a great deal of variation in the outcomes across force postures, either for the Americans or for the Russians. The United States numbers of surviving and deliverable warheads are highest for a force made up entirely of submarines, but this is hypothetical since no actual force would be. The finding does suggest that the United States might shift further away from land-based forces and bombers and increase the

Table 5.3
U.S. Surviving and Deliverable Warheads in START III Forces

	2,500 Warheads	1,500 Warheads
Balanced Triad	805	497
No ICBMs	927	598
No B-52s	862	495
SLBMs Only	1,106	677

Source: Author.

proportion of SLBMs among its future retaliatory forces, other things being equal.

But other things are rarely so. The summary figures in Tables 5.2 and 5.3 measure only the gross number of warheads retaliating against any opposed target set and without specifying whether those warheads arrive promptly or are launched after riding out an attack. These considerations, timing and targeting of response, are of course important from the perspective of war planners. And it appears that there may well be an *inconsistency* between the objectives *of arms control* in reducing the numbers of deployed warheads to a minimum on both sides, on one hand, and the requirements for executing *war plans*, should deterrence fail. In the U.S. case, for example, American target planners have apparently opted (as of June 2000) to maintain an estimated 2,200 strategic warheads on alert in order to be certain of achieving the required damage expectancies against Russian and other target sets.[18] Following presidential guidance laid down in 1997, the designers of U.S. nuclear war plans assume that a force size of 2,500 deployed strategic warheads is the necessary minimum for accomplishing the military missions inferred from that guidance. Unless political directives change, it will be difficult for either the United States or Russia to get below that number of deployed nuclear weapons under a START III regime.

The issue of avoiding accidental or inadvertent war remains a live one. The U.S. government has also offered to help Russia complete an unfinished radar site in Siberia and to share additional radar warning data with Russia. The U.S. interests in making these offers are twofold: to reduce the risk of misunderstanding that might lead to accidental/inadvertent war and to help assuage Russia's frustration at the U.S. decision to abrogate the ABM Treaty of 1972 to permit limited national missile defenses against rogue state attacks.[19] The United States urged the Russians in the fall of 1999 to consider their common interest in the possibility of rogue-state ballistic missile launches against either America

or Russia from North Korea, Iran or other states with unpredictable regimes and growing ballistic missile capabilities. Russians of various political persuasions remained cool to linking nuclear transparency
measures, of which most approved, to revision of the ABM Treaty, which
many Russians regard as a cornerstone of U.S.-Russian arms control and
as a support for future strategic stability. The implications of any U.S.
missile defense deployment receive more specific consideration in the
next section.

MISSILE DEFENSE

Observers of U.S. and Russian politics might have been forgiven in
January 2000 for a sense of déjà vu. Once again, the United States and
Russia, as the nuclear arms control successor to the former Soviet Union,
were arguing about ballistic missile defenses. And, as in the latter 1960s
and early 1970s, the arguments were not only about technology, but
about principles of strategy. At issue was the question of whether strategic stability based on offensive weapons alone could suffice for deterrence. The U.S. entered the new century worried about the threat posed
by "rogue" state attacks, especially by Iran and North Korea, as well as
by China's growing nuclear power. Even if a state would not actually
launch strikes into U.S. territory, it might threaten to do so in order to
deter U.S. military intervention in regional crises. (For a chronology of
U.S. missile defense events in the 1990s and projected future milestones,
see Appendix 5.2 at the end of this chapter.)

U.S. Secretary of Defense William Cohen announced in January 1999
that the United States would commit $6.6 billion to a "three plus five"
program that would make possible a limited National Missile Defense
(NMD) system ready for deployment by the year 2005.[20] A final decision
on deployment of any U.S. NMD system was scheduled for the year
2000, permitting additional technology development and testing of proposed system components. As envisioned by DOD and BMDO (Ballistic
Missile Defense Organization) these components would be space-based
detectors for missile launch, long-range radars to track missile flight
paths, other radars for intercept tracking and non-nuclear kill interceptors.[21] (See Table 5.4 later in this chapter.)

In July 1999 President Clinton signed the National Missile Defense Act
passed by Congress and called for a U.S. NMD deployment when feasible. Clinton stated that his signature did not amount to final approval
for deployment. A final decision would be based on four criteria: technological readiness, the nature of rogue state ballistic missile threats, cost
factors, and arms control considerations.[22] On September 1, 2000, Clinton
announced that he would not make a deployment decision in 2000 but
would leave that choice to his successor. The president said the Depart-

ment of Defense would continue a vigorous program of NMD research and development. He indicated that a national missile defense system "if it worked properly" could provide extra insurance against proliferation of nuclear and other weapons of mass destruction. But Clinton also cautioned that, although the technology for NMD was promising, the "system as a whole is not yet proven."[23]

In the years immediately following the collapse of the Soviet Union, the Russian leadership gave some preliminary indications of viewing favorably missile defense deployments if they were jointly agreed by the U.S. and Russian governments. Addressing the UN Security Council in January 1992, Russian President Boris Yeltsin, after noting that the ABM Treaty was a cornerstone of stability, added that "Russia is ready to develop, then create and jointly operate a global defense system, instead of the SDI system."[24] Presidents Clinton and Yeltsin signed a statement on the need to develop a Global Protection System with the expectation of future "cooperation in developing ballistic missile defense capabilities."[25] The statement on global protection systems was also included in the preamble to the START II Treaty.

Yeltsin's second term was marked by more suspicion of American and allied NATO objectives in foreign and security policy, including nuclear arms control. The year 1999 was especially troublesome for U.S.-Russian political relations. NATO enlargement, NATO's bombing of Yugoslavia, and Russia's war in Chechnya moved the military more prominently into the security policy driver's seat. Anti-American themes were commonly articulated in the Russian Duma, and ratification of START II was temporarily held hostage to NATO's air campaign against Serbia. Boris Yeltsin's sudden resignation on December 31, 1999, opened the door to his eventual succession by Acting President Vladimir Putin in the elections scheduled for March 2000. The effect of Putin's presidency on U.S.-Russian relations and on arms control was an open book with the text to be written after Putin had the March elections safely behind him.[26] He did, at least, prod the Russian Duma to ratify START II in April 2000, opening the door to the further reductions envisioned in START III.

Russia's military leadership and defense intellectuals remain warily skeptical that any U.S. missile defense deployment could be consistent with stable deterrence. The commander-in-chief of the Russian Strategic Missile Forces (RVSN), Colonel General Vladimir Yakovlev, called in January 1999 for a global "strategic stability treaty" that would include, in addition to the United States and Russia, Britain, France and China.[27] According to Yakovlev, such an agreement would include reductions in U.S and Soviet strategic nuclear warheads even to START III levels and agreement between the two states on "the inviolability of space."[28] He specified, in regard to space arms control, the need for a pledge not to create space vehicles capable of attacking warning systems to detect missile attacks. Additional Russian skepticism about a U.S. limited national defense system was voiced by Ministry of Defense official Colonel-General Igor Valynkin, who contended in early February 1999 that a U.S. revision of the ABM Treaty to permit missile defenses would upset stability and that Russia would "undoubtedly respond."[29] Russia's military and political opposition to U.S. withdrawal from the ABM Treaty and to American NMD deployments did not deter President Bush from either move in December 2001.

The Clinton administration hoped to persuade Russian President Putin during Clinton's visit to Moscow in June 2000 to agree to amend the ABM Treaty to permit a limited U.S. national missile defense. The presumption was that the United States would offer Russia additional economic aid or other incentives to do so. One obstacle to such an agreement was the Republican Congress, including members who were determined to deploy missile defenses regardless of Russia's reaction. Congressional Republicans also felt that a "lame duck" president like Clinton should not negotiate any new arms deals, leaving that to his successor. Of course, Republicans hoped that would be George W. Bush. Russia, notwithstanding all this U.S. hoopla over as yet unproved missile defense technology, could hold out for a bargain that either (1) permitted amending the ABM Treaty but with serious constraints on the numbers and capabilities of U.S. interceptors, sensors and kill vehicles deployed or (2) allowed the Treaty to phase out in stages, during which time the United States and Russia would share missile defense and warning technology in order to provide for Russia the option of a parallel defense deployment.[30]

The George W. Bush administration committed itself to deploying missile defenses and indicated its intent to accelerate research and development toward that end. Secretary of Defense Donald Rumsfeld's research and development program investigated technologies potentially viable for boost phase, midcourse and terminal intercept of attacking warheads and/or missiles. Candidate technologies included earth- and space-based components. From the perspective of the Bush Pentagon, missile defenses are but one piece of a broader strategy for defense transformation based on advanced technology in C4I (command, control, communications, computers and intelligence), precision strike, stealth and ISR (intelligence, surveillance and reconnaissance). The Bush program also assumed that deterrence based on offensive retaliation only was no longer reliable, given the agendas of rogue states of concern to U.S. policy makers, such as Iran, Iraq or North Korea.

Defense, even granted the assumption of technologies better than Cold War defenses, is still difficult to do with high assurance of effectiveness. Space-based defense interceptors are prohibited by the ABM Treaty that remains in force; the same agreement also limits the numbers of sites and the numbers of interceptors deployed. The military tasking of defenses under any revised U.S.-Russian arms control regime will thus be restricted to accidental launches or limited attacks from rogue states armed with ballistic missiles. Even against attacks of modest sizes by Cold War standards, defenses that are very good (i.e., allow very little "leakage" of attacking warheads through the system) will not preclude historically unprecedented levels of societal damage.

The kinds of friction (after Clausewitz) that might characterize missile defense operations, even against light attacks, are summarized in Chapter 3. This is not a brief against missile defenses, but it does remind us of two things: (1) the Cold War gave offensive technology a great head start, and defenses must now play catch up and (2) the United States will have fewer obstacles, either political or military, in deploying national missile defenses against limited strikes if it does so cooperatively with Russia instead of against her wishes.

Russia has opposed U.S. national missile defenses because Russia fears that those defenses, supposedly against rogue attacks or accidental launches, could grow into credible defenses against Russia's second (retaliatory) strike. This, at least, has been the concern expressed by those who emphasize the arms control perspective in the U.S. debate on deploying defenses, and by various Russians.[31] On the other hand, proponents of American defenses contend that Russia need not fear a first-generation defense that is not intended for Russia. Pro-defense activists also note Russia's surprisingly passive reaction to U.S. withdrawal from the ABM Treaty. Critics of defenses argue that U.S. NMD will set off another round of strategic nuclear modernization in Moscow and in Washington. Proponents of defenses say that the point of NMD in the next century, as opposed to its status during the Cold War, is not deterrence but defense: rogue states may be beyond deterrence. The U.S. Ballistic Missile Defense Organization (now the Missile Defense Agency) in March 1999 envisioned a phased development of NMD systems as depicted in Table 5.4.

Force Exchanges with Defenses

How much difference would the deployment of national missile defenses by the United States to Russia, or by both make in terms of the numbers of surviving and retaliating warheads available under a START III ceiling of 2,500 warheads? We interrogated our model to answer this question, assigning a notional "leakage" rate of 20 percent to the hypothetical defenses of both sides. A leakage rate of 20 percent means that, on the average, 80 percent of the retaliating warheads will be successfully

Table 5.4
U.S. National Missile Defense Architectures

	C-1 Configuration[1]	C-2 Configuration[2]	C-3 Configuration[3]
Number of Interceptors Deployed in Alaska	20–100	100	125
Number of Interceptors Deployed in North Dakota	0	0	125
Upgraded Early-Warning Radars	Beale, CA Clear, AK Cape Cod, MA Fylingdales, UK Thule, Greenland	Beale Clear Cape Code Fylingdales Thule	Beale Clear Cape Cod Fylingdales Thule South Korea (possible new radar)
X-band Radars	Shemya, AK (Aleutians)	Shemya Clear Fylingdales Thule	Shemya Beale Clear Cape Cod Fylingdales Thule South Korea Grand Forks, ND Hawaii
Space-Based Infrared Systems-Low	No	Yes	Yes

[1] C-1 (capability 1) system is a defense against a "few, simple" warheads, where "few" refers to five or fewer warheads.

[2] C-2 (capability 2) system is a defense against a "few, complex" warheads.

[3] C-3 (capability 3) system is a defense against "many, complex" warheads. Complex warheads are those including some countermeasures against defenses.

Source: U.S. Ballistic Missile Defense Organization, from Lisbeth Gronlund and George Lewis, "How a Limited National Missile Defense Would Impact the ABM Treaty," *Arms Control Today*, November 1999, 100.

intercepted; it does not tell us the probability of successfully intercepting any individual reentry vehicle. Cell entries in Table 5.5 show the numbers of retaliating warheads that each state can place on target after absorbing a first strike and despite the other's defenses (from each of four

Table 5.5
U.S. and Russian Surviving and Retaliating Warheads with Defenses, START III, 2,500 Warhead Limit

Forces	United States	Russia
1	161	135
2	185	172
3	172	160
4	221	149

Source: Author.

force postures, as listed immediately prior to Tables 5.2 and 5.3). If the two sides' START III forces are reduced to 1,500 warheads, Table 5.6 summarizes the resulting distribution of outcomes for each side with defenses and by force posture.

These hypothetical nuclear wars fought with equally hypothetical defenses of unknown capability do not "prove" anything scientific about the relationship between nuclear offenses and anti-nuclear defenses in the twenty-first century. But they do suggest that the burden of proof remains on the proponents of defenses to show that they can compete cost-effectively with offenses, let alone threaten to overturn deterrence based on offensive retaliatory power. In the preceding tables, even a defense that is 80 percent effective (no mean feat for ground-based, non-nuclear interceptors based on kinetic kill) leaves at least 100 warheads soaking through the defender's umbrella to strike at various military, command and civilian targets.

The likely performance of defenses under fire is one issue. Perhaps new technology will eventually make defenses more cost effective than offenses, although "eventually" is unspecific. Regardless of the competency of defense technology compared to offensive, the other problematical aspect of defenses is the political one. U.S. deployment of national missile defenses may reopen a new arms race unless Russia acquiesces to American NMD deployments in favor of security cooperation on other matters. The U.S. "carrot" in this case might be to agree to reductions in force size below that preferred by the Pentagon but more affordable for Russia. However, lowering the START III ceilings to 1,500 warheads requires rethinking of U.S. nuclear war plans and may introduce some imbalance into the historically sacrosanct U.S. strategic triad of land-based, sea-based and air-delivered weapons. Third, even if Russia and the Pentagon can be finessed by defenses combined with force reductions acceptable to Russia, China's reaction to American NMD represents a

Table 5.6
U.S. and Russian Surviving and Retaliating Warheads with Defenses,
START III, 1,500 Warhead Limit

Forces	United States	Russia
1	100	107
2	119	121
3	99	111*
4	135	111*

*Rounded.

Source: Author.

third complication. China's leadership, including President Zemin in the summer of 2000, has stated emphatically its objection to U.S. NMD and to American theater missile defenses if the latter were to extend defense coverage to Taiwan. A unilateral U.S. decision to deploy NMD could cause China to back away from its prior commitments to nonproliferation and to increase its own pace of nuclear force building. Even U.S. allies in NATO have expressed reservations about possible NMD deployments that might defend North America but omit Europe.

CONCLUSION

The United States and Russia can now proceed toward the completion of planning already in progress for a START III agreement or even lower expectations. START III, once implemented, would reduce the allowable ceilings for each side's strategic nuclear warheads to 2,500. Russia would, by all indications, prefer to go lower, and the United States would prefer to get Russia to acquiesce to amendment of the ABM Treaty to permit national missile defenses. The Putin administration has taken a hard position against NMD to this writing, but some experts think that more flexibility will appear in Russian negotiating positions as Putin consolidates his domestic power base.

Russia can maintain essential strategic nuclear parity with the United States at or below START II levels, now officially agreed to. Russia for the next decade will struggle to maintain three viable legs of its nuclear strategic triad, and it may have to give up one of them for reasons of economics. Russian perceptions of START II and START III are obviously tied to future U.S. decisions about deploying national missile defenses. A worst case outcome would be U.S. defenses that were not really very effective against light attacks they are designed to prevent, but politically explosive in the Russian parliament and Putin administration. In addition to concerns about parity in offensive forces and possible U.S. defenses, Russia must also pay some attention to its nuclear command and control systems. Deterrence stability, even with equivalent U.S. and Russian strategic nuclear forces, could be undermined by fault-intolerant command systems bedeviled by synergistic error.

APPENDIX 5.1: ALTERNATE RUSSIAN AND U.S. START III FORCES

Russian Forces (2,500 Warheads)

Balanced Triad

	Launchers	Warheads per Launcher	Total Warheads
Russian Forces			
SS-11/3	0	1	0
SS-13/2	0	1	0
SS-17/3	0	4	0
SS-18/4/5	0	10	0
SS-19/3	105	1	105
SS-24 (fixed)	0	10	0
subtotal fixed land	105		105
SS-24 (rail)	0	10	0
SS-25/SS-27 (road)	490	1	490
subtotal mobile land	490		490
subtotal land-based	595		595
SS-N-6/3	0	1	0
SS-N-8/2	0	1	0
SS-N-18/2	0	1	0
SS-N-20	120	5	600
SS-N-23	112	4	448
subtotal sea-based	232		1,048
Tu-95 H6/ALCM	10	6	60
Tu-95 H16	27	16	432
Tu-160 Blackjack	4	8	32
subtotal air-breathing	41		524
Total Russian forces	**868**		**2,167**

No Bombers

	Launchers	Warheads per Launcher	Total Warheads
Russian Forces			
SS-11/3	0	1	0
SS-13/2	0	1	0

APPENDIX 5.1 (continued)

No Bombers

	Launchers	Warheads per Launcher	Total Warheads
SS-17/3	0	4	0
SS-18/4/5	0	10	0
SS-19/3	105	1	105
SS-24 (fixed)	0	10	0
subtotal fixed land	105		105
SS-24 (rail)	0	10	0
SS-25/SS-27 (road)	550	1	550
subtotal mobile land	550		550
subtotal land-based	655		655
SS-N-6/3	0	1	0
SS-N-8/2	0	1	0
SS-N-18/2	0	1	0
SS-N-20	120	8	960
SS-N-23	112	6	672
subtotal sea-based	232		1,632
Tu-95 H6/ALCM	0	6	0
Tu-95 H16	0	16	0
Tu-160 Blackjack	0	8	0
subtotal air-breathing	0		0
Total Russian forces	**887**		**2,287**

ICBM-Heavy

	Launchers	Warheads per Launcher	Total Warheads
Russian Forces			
SS-11/3	0	1	0
SS-13/2	0	1	0
SS-17/3	0	4	0
SS-18/4/5	0	10	0
SS-19/3	105	1	105
SS-24 (fixed)	0	10	0
subtotal fixed land	105		105
SS-24 (rail)	100	1	100
SS-25/SS-27 (road)	600	1	600
subtotal mobile land	700		700
subtotal land-based	805		805

APPENDIX 5.1 (continued)

ICBM-Heavy

	Launchers	Warheads per Launcher	Total Warheads
SS-N-6/3	0	1	0
SS-N-8/2	0	1	0
SS-N-18/2	0	1	0
SS-N-20	120	5	600
SS-N-23	112	4	448
subtotal sea-based	232		1,048
Tu-95 H6/ALCM	10	6	60
Tu-95 H16	27	16	432
Tu-160 Blackjack	4	8	32
subtotal air-breathing	41		524
Total Russian forces	**1,078**		**2,377**

SLBM-Heavy

	Launchers	Warheads per Launcher	Total Warheads
Russian Forces			
SS-11/3	0	1	0
SS-13/2	0	1	0
SS-17/3	0	4	0
SS-18/4/5	0	10	0
SS-19/3	105	1	105
SS-24 (fixed)	0	10	0
subtotal fixed land	105		105
SS-24 (rail)	0	10	0
SS-25/SS-27 (road)	490	1	490
subtotal mobile land	490		490
subtotal land-based	595		595
SS-N-6/3	0	1	0
SS-N-8/2	0	1	0
SS-N-18/2	0	1	0
SS-N-20	120	6	720
SS-N-23	112	5	560
subtotal sea-based	232		1,280
Tu-95 H6/ALCM	10	6	60
Tu-95 H16	27	16	432
Tu-160 Blackjack	4	8	32
subtotal air-breathing	41		524
Total Russian forces	**868**		**2,399**

APPENDIX 5.1 (continued)

U.S. Forces (2,500)

Balanced Triad

	Launchers	Warheads per Launcher	Total Warheads
U.S. Forces			
Minuteman II	0	1	0
Minuteman III	0	1	0
Minuteman IIIA	300	1	300
Peacekeeper MX	0	10	0
subtotal land-based	300		300
Trident C-4	0	4	0
Trident D-5/W-76	0	4	0
Trident D-5/W-88	336	4	1,344
subtotal sea-based	336		1,344
B-52G gravity	0	0	0
B-52G gravity/ALCM	0	0	0
B-52H gravity/ALCM	40	12	480
B-2	21	12	252
subtotal air-breathing	61		732
Total U.S. forces	**697**		**2,376**

No ICBMs

	Launchers	Warheads per Launcher	Total Warheads
U.S. Forces			
Minuteman II	0	1	0
Minuteman III	0	1	0
Minuteman IIIA	0	1	0
Peacekeeper MX	0	10	0
subtotal land-based	0		0
Trident C-4	0	4	0
Trident D-5/W-76	0	4	0
Trident D-5/W-88	336	5	1,680
subtotal sea-based	336		1,680
B-52G gravity	0	0	0
B-52G gravity/ALCM	0	0	0
B-52H gravity/ALCM	40	12	480
B-2	21	12	252
subtotal air-breathing	61		732
Total U.S. forces	**397**		**2,412**

APPENDIX 5.1 (continued)

No B-52s

	Launchers	Warheads per Launcher	Total Warheads
U.S. Forces			
Minuteman II	0	1	0
Minuteman III	0	1	0
Minuteman IIIA	300	1	300
Peacekeeper MX	0	10	0
subtotal land-based	300		300
Trident C-4	0	4	0
Trident D-5/W-76	0	4	0
Trident D-5/W-88	336	5	1,680
subtotal sea-based	336		1,680
B-52G gravity/ALCM	0	0	0
B-52H gravity/ALCM	0	12	0
B-2/ALCM	21	16	336
subtotal air-breathing	21		336
Total U.S. forces	**657**		**2,316**

SLBMs Only

	Launchers	Warheads per Launcher	Total Warheads
U.S. Forces			
Minuteman II	0	1	0
Minuteman III	0	1	0
Minuteman IIIA	0	1	0
Peacekeeper MX	0	10	0
subtotal land-based	0		0
Trident C-4	0	4	0
Trident D-5/W-76	0	4	0
Trident D-5/W-88	336	7	2,352
subtotal sea-based	336		2,352
B-52G gravity/ALCM	0	0	0
B-52H gravity/ALCM	0	12	0
B-2	0	12	0
subtotal air-breathing	0		0
Total U.S. forces	**336**		**2,352**

APPENDIX 5.1 (continued)

Russian Forces (1,500 Warheads)

Balanced Triad

Russian Forces	Launchers	Warheads per Launcher	Total Warheads
SS-11/3	0	1	0
SS-13/2	0	1	0
SS-17/3	0	4	0
SS-18/4/5	0	10	0
SS-19/3	0	1	0
SS-24 (fixed)	0	10	0
subtotal fixed land	0		0
SS-24 (rail)	0	10	0
SS-25/SS-27 (road)	490	1	490
subtotal mobile land	490		490
subtotal land-based	490		490
SS-N-6/3	0	1	0
SS-N-8/2	0	1	0
SS-N-18/2	0	1	0
SS-N-20	120	3	360
SS-N-23	112	3	336
subtotal sea-based	232		696
Tu-95 H6/ALCM	5	6	30
Tu-95 H16	16	16	256
Tu-160 Blackjack	3	8	24
subtotal air-breathing	24		310
Total Russian forces	**746**		**1,496**

No Bombers

Russian Forces	Launchers	Warheads per Launcher	Total Warheads
SS-11/3	0	1	0
SS-13/2	0	1	0
SS-17/3	0	4	0
SS-18/4/5	0	10	0
SS-19/3	0	1	0
SS-24 (fixed)	0	10	0
subtotal fixed land	0		0

APPENDIX 5.1 (continued)

No Bombers

	Launchers	Warheads per Launcher	Total Warheads
SS-24 (rail)	0	10	0
SS-25/SS-27 (road)	520	1	520
subtotal mobile land	520		520
subtotal land-based	520		520
SS-N-6/3	0	1	0
SS-N-8/2	0	1	0
SS-N-18/2	0	1	0
SS-N-20	120	4	480
SS-N-23	112	4	448
subtotal sea-based	232		928
Tu-95 H6/ALCM	0	6	0
Tu-95 H16	0	16	0
Tu-160 Blackjack	0	8	0
subtotal air-breathing	0		0
Total Russian forces	**752**		**1,448**

ICBM-Heavy

	Launchers	Warheads per Launcher	Total Warheads
Russian Forces			
SS-11/3	0	1	0
SS-13/2	0	1	0
SS-17/3	0	4	0
SS-18/4/5	0	10	0
SS-19/3	0	1	0
SS-24 (fixed)	0	10	0
subtotal fixed land	0		0
SS-24 (rail)	0	10	0
SS-25/SS-27 (road)	550	1	550
subtotal mobile land	550		550
subtotal land-based	550		550
SS-N-6/3	0	1	0
SS-N-8/2	0	1	0
SS-N-18/2	0	1	0
SS-N-20	100	3	300
SS-N-23	112	3	336
subtotal sea-based	212		636

APPENDIX 5.1 (continued)

ICBM-Heavy

	Launchers	Warheads per Launcher	Total Warheads
Tu-95 H6/ALCM	4	6	24
Tu-95 H16	16	16	256
Tu-160 Blackjack	2	8	16
subtotal air-breathing	22		296
Total Russian forces	**784**		**1,482**

SLBM-Heavy

	Launchers	Warheads per Launcher	Total Warheads
Russian Forces			
SS-11/3	0	1	0
SS-13/2	0	1	0
SS-17/3	0	4	0
SS-18/4/5	0	10	0
SS-19/3	0	1	0
SS-24 (fixed)	0	10	0
subtotal fixed land	0		0
SS-24 (rail)	0	10	0
SS-25/SS-27 (road)	450	1	450
subtotal mobile land	450		450
subtotal land-based	450		450
SS-N-6/3	0	1	0
SS-N-8/2	0	1	0
SS-N-18/2	0	1	0
SS-N-20	100	4	400
SS-N-23	112	4	448
subtotal sea-based	212		848
Tu-95 H6/ALCM	3	6	18
Tu-95 H16	10	16	160
Tu-160 Blackjack	3	8	24
subtotal air-breathing	16		202
Total Russian forces	**678**		**1,500**

APPENDIX 5.1 (continued)

U.S. Forces (1,500 Warheads)

Balanced Triad

	Launchers	Warheads per Launcher	Total Warheads
U.S. Forces			
Minuteman II	0	1	0
Minuteman III	0	1	0
Minuteman IIIA	300	1	300
Peacekeeper MX	0	10	0
subtotal land-based	300		300
Trident C-4	0	4	0
Trident D-5/W-76	0	4	0
Trident D-5/W-88	288	3	864
subtotal sea-based	288		864
B-52G gravity/ALCM	0	0	0
B-52H gravity/ALCM	9	12	108
B-2	19	12	228
subtotal air-breathing	28		336
Total U.S. forces	**616**		**1,500**

No ICBMs

	Launchers	Warheads per Launcher	Total Warheads
U.S. Forces			
Minuteman II	0	1	0
Minuteman III	0	1	0
Minuteman IIIA	0	1	0
Peacekeeper MX	0	10	0
subtotal land-based	0		0
Trident C-4	0	4	0
Trident D-5/W-76	0	4	0
Trident D-5/W-88	288	4	1,152
subtotal sea-based	288		1,152
B-52G gravity/ALCM	0	0	0
B-52H gravity/ALCM	9	12	108
B-2	20	12	240
subtotal air-breathing	29		348
Total U.S. forces	**317**		**1,500**

APPENDIX 5.1 (continued)

No B-52s

	Launchers	Warheads per Launcher	Total Warheads
U.S. Forces			
Minuteman II	0	1	0
Minuteman III	0	1	0
Minuteman IIIA	300	1	300
Peacekeeper MX	0	10	0
subtotal land-based	300		300
Trident C-4	0	4	0
Trident D-5/W-76	0	4	0
Trident D-5/W-88	300	3	900
subtotal sea-based	300		900
B-52G gravity/ALCM	0	0	0
B-52H gravity/ALCM	0	12	0
B-2	21	12	252
subtotal air-breathing	21		252
Total U.S. forces	**621**		**1,452**

SLBMs Only

	Launchers	Warheads per Launcher	Total Warheads
U.S. Forces			
Minuteman II	0	1	0
Minuteman III	0	1	0
Minuteman IIIA	0	1	0
Peacekeeper MX	0	10	0
subtotal land-based	0		0
Trident C-4	0	4	0
Trident D-5/W-88	120	4	480
Trident D-5/W-88	192	5	960
subtotal sea-based	312		1,440
B-52G gravity/ALCM	0	0	0
B-52H gravity/ALCM	0	12	0
B-2	0	12	0
subtotal air-breathing	0		0
Total U.S. forces	**312**		**1,440**

APPENDIX 5.2: U.S. BALLISTIC MISSILE DEFENSE EVENTS AND MILESTONES, 1990s AND FUTURE

The 1990s

- March 15, 1990: An independent review of SDI (Strategic Defense Initiative) endorses Brilliant Pebbles. The review also details what becomes the Global Protection Against Limited Strikes (GPALS) concept.

- January 29, 1991: President Bush announces the reorientation of SDI to GPALS—"protection from limited ballistic missile strikes, whatever their source." He anticipates GPALS would afford protection against as many as 200 long-range missiles.

- April 28–May 6, 1991: The Discovery space shuttle provides SDIO (Strategic Defense Initiative Organization) officials 17 "engine firings" against different backgrounds (earth, black space) which aid the development of sensors to detect missile launches.

- December 5, 1991: President Bush signs the Missile Defense Act of 1991 (part of H.R. 2100) which mandates DoD (Department of Defense) "develop for deployment by the earliest date allowed by the availability of appropriate technology or by Fiscal Year 1996 a cost effective, operationally effective, and Anti-Ballistic Missile (ABM) Treaty–compliant anti-ballistic missile system . . . designed to protect the United States against limited ballistic missile threats, including accidental or unauthorized launches or Third World attacks." The Act directs that Brilliant Pebbles space-based interceptors not be part of any initial deployment.

- May 1992: House Armed Services Committee Chairman Les Aspin raises the specter that "in this new [post–Cold War] world" the United States cannot assume that nuclear equipped adversaries will "always be rational or at least operate with the same logic as we do."

- July 2, 1992: Secretary of Defense Dick Cheney sends Congress a report that details the deployment strategy for an operational evaluation system capable of providing limited protection by 1997.

- July 1992: The Department of Energy cancels the last test of the six-year-old proposed X-Ray laser weapon system, effectively ending the program which had been suffering from technical problems, funding shortfalls, and competition from other non-nuclear-based technologies.

- May 1993: Secretary of Defense Les Aspin renames SDIO (Strategic Defense Initiative Organization) the Ballistic Missile Defense Organization (BMDO) and reorients its priorities to developing theater missile defenses.

- February 15, 1995: The House narrowly defeats the portion of the Republican "Contract with America" that would require deploying a nationwide missile defense "as soon as practical."

- November 1995: A National Intelligence Estimate (NIE 95–19) judges that "No country, other than the major declared nuclear powers, will develop or otherwise acquire a ballistic missile in the next 15 years that could threaten the contiguous 48 states or Canada."

- March 1996: The "Defend America Act," which declares as U.S. policy that the nation will deploy a limited missile defense by 2003, is introduced in both houses of Congress, but it does not come to a vote because of the estimated cost of deployment.
- April 1996: The Clinton Administration's "3 + 3" national missile defense plan (NMD)—three years for development and, if warranted, three more years to deploy a system—is established. The Pentagon changes the purpose of NMD from a "technology" readiness program to a "deployment" readiness program.
- April 9, 1996: BMDO (Ballistic Missile Defense Organization) is directed to establish a Joint Program Office to manage the deployment readiness program for national missile defense.
- December 1996: A congressionally chartered panel headed by former CIA Director Robert Gates concurs with the time lines estimated in the 1995 NIE (National Intelligence Estimate).
- January 21, 1997: A new version of the "Defend America Act" is introduced in the Senate, but it does not come to a vote.
- April 1, 1997: BMDO (Ballistic Missile Defense Organization) establishes the Joint Program Office (JPO) for the NMD (National Missile Defense) program. The JPO is responsible for "the design, development and demonstration of an NMD system to defend the U.S. from ballistic missile attack by 2003."
- June 24, 1997: IFT 1A flight test of "a candidate infrared sensor" is conducted using the Boeing/TRW exoatmospheric kill vehicle (EKV).
- August 6, 1997: Members of a congressionally chartered panel chaired by former Secretary of Defense Donald Rumsfeld are named to "examine the current and potential missile threat to all 50 States and to assess the capability of the U.S. intelligence community to warn policymakers of changes in this threat."
- August 11, 1997: BMDO's NMD acquisition strategy is approved, and a request for proposals for the next phase of the Lead System Integrator contract is released.
- August 21, 1997: The U.S.-Russian Standing Consultative Commission's 55th session ends with agreement on TMD-NMD demarcation and on the matter of succession to the ABM Treaty.
- September 25, 1997: The Pentagon-created "Task Force on Reducing Risk in Ballistic Missile Defense Flight Test Programs" (the Welch panel) meets for the first time.
- September 26, 1997: The United States, Russia, Belarus, Kazakhstan, and Ukraine sign the August 21 agreements in New York.
- January 15, 1998: IFT 2 (Integrated Flight Test) is conducted using the Raytheon (Hughes) EKV (Exoatmospheric Kill Vehicle).
- February 1998: In the first of what will be annual reviews, the Welch DOD advisory panel criticizes shortcomings and overambitious timelines that amount to a "rush to failure" in various missile defense programs.

- March 19, 1998: Senator Thad Cochran (R-MS) introduces the American Missile Protection Act which says it will be "U.S. policy to deploy, as soon as technologically possible, a National Missile Defense system."
- April 1998 : Integrated Ground Test 1A. Primary objectives are testing system discrimination and ability to handle unsophisticated Capability 1 threats.
- April 30, 1998: In a contract worth $1.6 billion (but potentially as much as $6 billion), the Pentagon names Boeing the lead systems integrator for NMD.
- May 13, 1998: The attempt to debate the "American Missile Protection Act" is defeated by a single vote in the Senate.
- July 15, 1998: The Rumsfeld Commission states that the ballistic missile threat to the United States could emerge with little warning and likely will appear sooner than U.S. intelligence agencies have estimated. Some panel members dissent.
- July 27, 1998: The Pentagon announces the selection of the booster for the NMD Ground-based Interceptor (GBI).
- August 31, 1998: North Korea launches a Taepo Dong 1 three-stage missile over Japan, but the third stage malfunctions and fails to put the satellite payload in orbit.
- September 9, 1998: In the aftermath of the North Korean launch, Senate Republicans again try to begin debate on the "American Missile Protection Act" but again fail by one vote.
- January 20, 1999: The Pentagon requests more money for NMD programs, delays the target date for achieving initial operating capability from 2003 to a "more realistic" 2005 and sets a June 2000 date for a deployment decision by the Administration.
- February 5, 1999: The Air Force cancels its contracts with TRW and Boeing to design and develop the prototype satellites for SBIRS-Low.
- February 10, 1999: BMDO conducts Risk Reduction Flight 5, which is designed to reduce the technical risks inherent in NMD.
- March 16, 1999: "The National Missile Defense Act of 1999," which declares as U.S. policy that America will "deploy as soon as technologically possible an effective National Missile Defense system," passes the Senate.
- March 17, 1999: The House of Representatives approves a measure committing the United States to deploy national missile defenses.
- May 20, 1999: The House approves legislation stating that it is the policy of the United States to field limited national missile defenses as soon as technically feasible.
- July–August 1999: Integrated Ground Test 4
- July 23, 1999: In signing "The National Missile Defense Act of 1999," President Clinton states the four criteria he will consider in making his decision to deploy: the threat, the cost, the technological status of NMD and adherence to a renegotiated ABM Treaty.
- August 17, 1999: The United States and Russia resume strategic arms talks that include a modification of the ABM Treaty to allow the United States to deploy a limited national missile defense system.

- September 1999: The Welch panel's second look at the reconfigured timelines for NMD again concludes that the program is "high-risk" and recommends that the president's June 2000 decision be considered a "feasibility" rather than a "readiness to deploy" judgment. A new NIE (National Intelligence Estimate), "Foreign Missile Developments and the Ballistic Missile Threat to the United States Through 2015," judges that "during the next 15 years the United States most likely will face ICBM threats from Russia, China, and North Korea, probably from Iran, and possibly from Iraq."
- October 1999: Integrated Ground Test 5.
- October 2, 1999: The first Integrated Flight Test (IFT 3) that attempts to bring down a target missile employing elements of the proposed NMD system is hailed by the Pentagon as an unqualified success. Later it is revealed that the kill vehicle initially homed in on the single decoy released by the target.

The 2000s

- January 18, 2000: The second attempted Integrated Flight intercept (IFT 4) fails when the infrared sensor on the kill vehicle malfunctions. The Pentagon nevertheless declares the test a success because it "learns" so much even from a failure.
- February 14, 2000: Philip Coyle, Director of the Pentagon's Office of Operational Test and Evaluation, tells Congress that "undue pressure has been placed on the [NMD] program" by the requirement to meet the artificial deployment deadline of 2005.
- June 13, 2000: The third Welch panel report states that the "technological capability to develop and field" a limited NMD system to handle "the defined threat" is available, but that meeting the 2005 target date for Initial Operational Capability (IOC) "remains high risk." The panel also points out that flight tests encompass only "a limited part of the required operating envelope."
- June 2000: Administration lawyers conclude that initial work connected with constructing the X-band tracking and discrimination radar on Shemya Island in the Aleutians will not violate the ABM Treaty.
- July 7, 2000: The third Integrated Flight intercept (IFT 5), delayed twice from the original April test date, fails. The EKV (exoatmospheric kill vehicle) does not separate from the surrogate booster and therefore does not activate its sensors. Additionally, the Mylar decoy on the target rocket fails to inflate.
- August 2000: A new NIE (National Intelligence Estimate) on the emerging ICBM threat to the United States is completed and sent to the president. Mr. Clinton will consider its findings as part of his decision on whether to proceed with preparations for the X-band radar site on Shemya Island.
- September 1, 2000: Citing the status of technology, the refusal by Russia to agree to modify the ABM to permit deployment of an NMD system, and the reluctance of our closest allies to endorse NMD unless strategic stability can be assured through a modified ABM Treaty, President Clinton decides not to authorize work to begin on deploying NMD.

- September 27, 2000: Risk Reduction Flights 9 and 10 were declared successes by the Pentagon. RRF 9 tested the discrimination capabilities of the Ground Based Radar prototype against 20 objects while RRF-10 "exercised" all NMD system target, tracking, and communications elements except those of the GBI (Ground-based Interceptor).

- January 2001: With IFT 5 a failure, the Pentagon projects it may not be able to conduct another test until the beginning of 2001.

- February 2001: Integrated Ground Test 6.

- Summer 2001: The Defense Acquisition Board (DAB) will consider a decision to purchase elements of the system to be deployed.

- 2003: The DAB will evaluate whether to build and deploy interceptors. This milestone rests on successful testing of a production interceptor mated with the kill vehicle against a target.

- 2005: Target date for deploying the Capability 1 system with 20 interceptors. In his September 1, 2000 announcement, President Clinton spoke of a deployment in "2006 or 2007."

- 2007: Target date for deploying the Expanded Capability 1 (C-1) system with 100 interceptors. The addition of an expanded Ballistic Missile Command, Control and Communication package, together with the 100 ground-based interceptors to be deployed by this year, would "convert" the Expanded C-1 system to the Capability 2 system.

- 2011: Target date for deploying the Capability 3 system with 125 interceptors at each of 2 sites (in Alaska and North Dakota), 3 command centers, 5 communications relay stations, 15 radars (6 early warning and 9 high-resolution UHF or X-band), and 29 satellites (Space-Based Infrared High and Low).

Source: Colonel Daniel Smith, USA (Ret.), Center for Defense Information, December 1, 2000. Reprinted by permission.

NOTES

1. Economic problems may also affect the safety and security of Russia's nuclear arsenal. See Deborah Yarsike Ball, "How Safe Is Russia's Nuclear Arsenal?" *Jane's Intelligence Review*, No. 12 (December 1999): 10–11.

2. *RFE/RL Newsline*, Vol. 3, No. 197, Part I, October 8, 1999, newsline @list.rferl.org.

3. Martin Nesirsky, "Short of Conventional Weapons, Russia Reassesses Security Strategy," *Reuters*, October 8, 1999, via *Russia Today*, http://www.russia today.com, October 10, 1999.

4. *Reuters*, Moscow, October 12, 1999, via *Russia Today*, http://www.russia today.com, October 12, 1999.

5. On Russia's draft October 1999 and April 2000 military doctrine, see S.J. Main, *Russia's Military Doctrine* (Camberley: Conflict Studies Research Centre, Royal Military Academy Sandhurst, April 2000); Celeste A. Wallander, *Russian National Security Policy in 2000*, PONARS Policy Memo Series No. 102 (Cam-

bridge, Mass.: Program on New Approaches to Russian Security, Davis Center for Russian Studies, January 2000), esp. p. 3; Mark Kramer, *What Is Driving Russia's New Strategic Concept?*, PONARS Policy Memo No. 103 (Cambridge, Mass.: Program on New Approaches to Russian Security, Davis Center for Russian Studies, January 2000).

6. Stephen J. Blank, *Threats to Russian Security: The View from Moscow* (Carlisle Barracks, Pa.: Strategic Studies Institute, U.S. Army War College, July 2000), p. 3.

7. Putin, *Moscow Vek*, in Russian, November 26, 1999, FBIS-SOV, November 29, 1999, cited in Blank, *Threats to Russian Security*, p. 21.

8. Jack Mendelsohn, "The U.S.-Russian Strategic Arms Control Agenda," *Arms Control Today* (November/December 1997): 12.

9. Michael R. Gordon, "In a New Era, U.S. and Russia Bicker over an Old Issue," *New York Times*, April 25, 2000, pp. A1, A6.

10. Nikolai Sokov, *Russian Strategic Modernization: The Past and Future* (Lanham, Md.: Rowman and Littlefield, 2000), pp. 157–172.

11. Ibid., pp. 166–167.

12. Pavel Podvig, "Russian Nuclear Forces in Ten Years with and without START II," Program on New Approaches to Russian Security, Harvard University, Policy Memo No. 92, downloaded from web site, www.armscontrol.ru, March 15, 2000.

13. *NRDC Nuclear Notebook*, Vol. 55, No. 2 (March/April 1999), pagination uncertain due to electronic transmission.

14. Ibid.

15. Podvig, "Russian Nuclear Forces in Ten Years with and without START II," p. 1.

16. *NRDC Nuclear Notebook*, Vol. 55, No. 2 (March/April 1999) pagination uncertain due to electronic transmission.

17. Podvig, "Russian Nuclear Forces in Ten Years with and without START II," p. 2.

18. Bruce Blair, "Going Backwards: Number of U.S. Nuclear Targets Has Grown Since 1993," *Manchester Guardian*, June 16, 2000, http://www.cdi.org/issues/proliferation/goingbckbb.html.

19. Steven Mufson and Bradlay Graham, "U.S. Offers to Help Russia Complete Radar Site," *Philadelphia Inquirer* from *Washington Post News Service*, October 17, 1999, p. A7.

20. Douglas J. Gillert, "Cohen Announces National Missile Defense Plan," *Armed Forces Press Service*, January 21, 1999, DEFENSE-PRESS-SERVICE-L@DTIC.MIL.

21. Ibid.

22. *Arms Control Today*, July/August 1999, p. 22.

23. Gerry J. Gilmore, "President Defers Missile Defense System," American Forces Press Service, Washington, D.C., September 1, 2000, afisnews_sender @DTIC.MIL.

24. Paul Podvig, *A History of the ABM Treaty in Russia* (Cambridge, Mass.: Davis Center for Russian Studies, Harvard University, Program on New Approaches to Russian Security, February 2000), p. 2.

25. Ibid., 3.

26. Alexander Pikayev, *The Prospects for ABM Treaty Modification* (Cambridge,

Mass.: Davis Center for Russian Studies, Harvard University, Program on New Approaches to Russian Security, February 2000), pp. 3–4.

27. *Interfax*, Moscow, January 26, 1999, via medusa.x-stream.co.uk, February 2, 1999.

28. Ibid.

29. Medusa.x-stream.co.uk, February 4, 1999.

30. For additional perspective on this, see Celeste A. Wallander, *Russian Policy and the Potential for Agreement on Revising the ABM Treaty* (Cambridge, Mass.: Harvard University, PONARS Policy Memo No. 134, May 2000).

31. J. Peter Scoblic with Jennifer Gauck, "Russian Officials Continue to Oppose Changes to ABM Treaty," *Arms Control Today* (November 1999): 21, 26.

Chapter 6

Russian Nuclear Command and Control: Policy and Strategy Perspectives

INTRODUCTION

The Russian nuclear command and control system was one of the most dependable dinosaurs of the Cold War. Redundant in its extensive network of sensors, communications and political checks and balances against accidental or unauthorized use of nuclear weapons, it was nevertheless politically accountable to a Communist Party and state leadership, of which the military high command was an integral part.[1] The end of the Cold War and the breakup of the Soviet Union subdivided the dinosaur's tail, limbs and brain into widely scattered and underfunded components. Expert analysts and some Russian officials have expressed concerns about the crisis stability and political reliability of the Russian nuclear C3 (command, control and communications) system during the 1990s and beyond.[2] The transition from the Yeltsin to the Putin administration and the more assertive Russian military doctrine and national security concepts of 1999 also raise the significance of Russian nuclear command and control issues for Western observers.

In this chapter, we first review the generalized functions that any nuclear command and control system must perform, with special reference to the U.S. and Russian cases. Under this heading we discuss the problems of delegation of nuclear command authority and of devolution of nuclear control. Second, we interrogate the "so what" issue with regard to the possible political or military outcomes affected by deficiencies in nuclear command and control. In this section we consider the possibility of Russian hyper-dependency on prompt retaliatory launch, and we also note that the deployment of missile defenses by the U.S., by Russia or by both in the next decade or two has certain implications for crisis command and control stability.

MISSIONS OF STRATEGIC NUCLEAR COMMAND AND CONTROL

Positive and Negative Control

The first requirement for a strategic nuclear C3 system is the ability to balance the requirements for positive and negative control. This can be discussed as two separate requirements, although they are intimately related. Negative control is the prevention of any nuclear release or launch except by duly authorized command. Positive control means that forces are promptly and reliably responsive to authorized commands. In some discussions this is characterized as the "always–never" problem: always ensuring that forces are responsive when required, but never permitting actions that are unintended by political and/or military leaders.[3] Confusion can be introduced into the discussion by the term "positive control launch" which is actually a form of negative control, as described here. Positive control launch, as in SAC Cold War "fail safe" procedures, restrains an attack from taking place unless a specific coded message authorizes the attack, even after bomber aircraft have been loaded with weapons and routed to preliminary airborne destinations.

There is inherent tension between the requirements for negative and positive control at the margin, especially during the alerting of military forces.[4] Nuclear weapons make this tension acute. Steps taken to make forces ready for prompt retaliation after enemy attack can remove some of the controls against accidental or unauthorized use. More significant than changes in hardware are changes in the expectations of the people who operate forces and their associated command and control systems. As a confrontation between two states looms, military operators will shift their expectations from latent to manifest awareness of the worst possible performance of the system for which they are responsible. Forces will be exercised to guard against worst-case possibilities. However, too much alerting can wear out forces and reduce their actual readiness for war. Forces and command systems can only be maintained at high alert levels for a very short time before performance degradation sets in.

If alerts are extended beyond the "knee of the curve" for ready forces, then deteriorated performance, including performance capable of causing accidents, is a possible outcome. People get tired, machinery wears, and nerves are frayed. Stress levels rise. Interpretations of events are influenced by the strained condition of physical and human systems. Introduce the additional complexity of an attack by one side on the information bytes of the other, exacerbating stress and tension. One possible result of stress compounded by misinformation is the tendency to rationalize or falsely explain whatever action was recently taken. Another possible result is cognitive or motivational bias in assessments of the status of forces and command/control systems, including information networks.[5] A cognitive bias is a bias in the logical explanation for an event or forecast of a future event. Motivational bias is based on emotional needs of the observer that distort his or her perception of what is being observed.

First-strike fears compounded by information malaise and motivational or cognitive bias can also contribute to an outbreak of accidental/ inadvertent war. If leaders believe that the opponent will attack at their weakest moment of preparedness, and if they are further persuaded that their command system is becoming a sewer pipe of enemy disinformation, they may shut down channels or networks that maintain negative control under stressful conditions. Consider, for example, the problem of crisis-time communication with ballistic missile submarines. The possible disruption of these communications in time of war, and the equally strong possibility of prompt enemy attacks against the other side's SSBN (fleet ballistic missile submarine) force, led Cold War U.S. policy makers to enable submarines to launch their weapons under approved "fail deadly" procedures. This meant that, faced with disrupted communications and under presumed attack from enemy attack submarines, U.S. ballistic missile submarines (under certain restrictive guidelines) might fire at predesignated targets. PALs (permissive action links, essentially electronic locks that could only be bypassed by encoded messages from the U.S. National Command Authority) were not installed on U.S. SSBNs during the Cold War, although they were in place on land-based and air-delivered weapons.[6]

The U.S. Navy argued that the environment in which maritime operations were carried out precluded PALs or other devices that depended upon the fidelity of shore-to-ship communications in wartime. In addition, the Navy contended that procedural safeguards against accidental/ inadvertent war were more important than mechanical or electronic locks. Navy training and tradition were the guarantors against nuclear usurpation.[7] This argument was not entirely self-serving. In the largest sense, the entire U.S. government depends upon the training and tradition of its military as the fundamental guarantees of civil supremacy in times of peace or war. The modern military has always had the physical power or capability to overthrow the government (or, at least, to overthrow the civilian leadership in Washington, D.C., temporarily) but never the inclination since the end of the Civil War.

The problem of accidental/inadvertent escalation of a crisis into war, or of a mistaken decision for nuclear preemption, is more complicated than simple military overthrow of civil power. Slippage of negative control in the direction of accidental or inadvertent war or escalation can occur in stages and without any lapse of military loyalty to civil authority. Disjunction between the intent of political leaders and military operators can take place when commanders are carrying out logical procedures under unusual, but possible, conditions.[8] Consider the management of U.S. naval forces during the Cuban missile crisis. Standard operating procedure called for the U.S. Navy to force any Soviet submarines within the quarantine line to the surface. Commanders proceeded quite logically from this standpoint to do exactly that. It was not fully appreciated by policy makers or by navy commanders that this could lead to inadvertent escalation and war.[9] Soviet submarines signaled by depth charges might respond not by surfacing as required but by attacking U.S. vessels. At one point in the crisis this was perceived by President Kennedy, who reportedly exclaimed "almost anything but that" when the possibility of military clashes between U.S. forces and Soviet submarines was mentioned.[10]

Warning and Attack Assessment

A second requirement for the avoidance of accidental/inadvertent nuclear war or mistaken nuclear preemption is the validity of warning and attack assessment. Leaders must have confidence that they can distinguish between false and true warning of attack. They must also expect, once they have received valid warning of attack, that they will have time to respond appropriately. U.S. nuclear warning and attack assessment evolved during the Cold War into a tightly coupled system of warning sensors, analysis and fusion centers, communications links, commanders and command posts. The nerve center of U.S. Cold War warning and assessment was NORAD, located in an underground and hardened shelter complex at Cheyenne Mountain, Colorado. NORAD even after the Cold War is the chef d'oeuvre of the elaborate U.S. warning system for surprise attack.

The problem of warning is related to the timing and character of response. Although warning and response can be separated for purposes of analysis, operational warning and response are closely related. The development of long-range, nuclear-tipped missiles required rethinking of many of the basic premises of warning and response on the part of U.S. officials. The time between launch of Soviet ICBMs and their detonations on North American soil would be 20 minutes or less; submarine-launched missiles might arrive even sooner, depending upon their assigned targets and launch positions. Warning had therefore to be automated to some extent, but the "person in the loop" could not be extracted without control passing to a machine. In addition, with such short timelines for warning and response, the initial warning decision and the responsive forces should be assigned to different commands. Thus, for example, the United States assigned to NORAD the strategic warning function, and to SAC and the Navy the responsive forces and weapons. The function of NORAD was to establish the plausibility of warning within certain parameters and to initiate a series of conferences among political and military leaders.

The problem of mistaken warning and retaliation based on that mistake was taken very seriously by U.S., and presumably by Soviet, Cold War military and political leaders. The compensatory approach to possibly mistaken warning chosen by the United States was phenomenal redundancy, or "dual phenomenology." This locution meant that indicators of a possible attack would have to be confirmed from more than a single source of input data. For example, U.S. early warning (DSP) satellites would first detect the exhaust plume of land or sea-based missiles rising from their Soviet points of origin. Minutes later, ballistic missile early warning radars (BMEWS) at Fylingdales Moor, England; Thule, Greenland; and Clear, Alaska would confirm the initial observations by satellite and provide additional details about the size and character of the attack. The United States also deployed specialized radars for the detection of submarine-launched ballistic missiles, presumably off the Atlantic and Pacific coasts of the continental United States. The presumption of phenomenal redundancy was that even if a single part of the system gave wrong indications or were out of operation at a particular time, the remainder of the system could effectively confirm, or disconfirm, that an attack was under way.

Warning having been confirmed by more than one source, the problem of assessment remained. What kind of attack was in progress: was it a massive surprise strike against a comprehensive target set, or was it a "limited" strike intended for coercive purposes with follow-up attacks held in reserve? U.S. and Soviet leaders in the Cold War also would have been concerned about two possible kinds of errors in attack assessment. A Type I error results in delayed or flawed launch in response to actual attack. A Type II error results in premature or mistaken launch although no actual attack is in progress.[11] The significant thing about Type I and Type II error probabilities is that they are relational. Steps taken to minimize the likelihood of one kind of error often increase the probability of the other type of mistaken decision. For example, building in more elaborate and redundant checks against false warning of attack (Type I) may slow down the decision-making process, thereby increasing the chance of a reaction too late for retaliatory forces to carry out their assigned missions.

The problem of valid warning and appropriate response is complicated by the tight coupling of sensors, assessment centers and response system. Certain high-technology organizations are especially prone, according to sociologist Charles Perrow, to "normal accidents."[12] So-called normal accidents occur in these kinds of organizations when individual component failures cause other components also to fail, but in unexpected ways. The result is a systemic dysfunction not anticipated by the designers of the system. Accident-prone high-technology organizations, according to Perrow, share two attributes: interactive complexity and tight coupling. Interactive complexity of these organizations increases the frequency of unexpected or seemingly anomalous interactions among the parts, including the human parts. Tight coupling implies (1) parts of the system interact quickly, (2) sequences of activity are invariant—there is only one right way to do things, (3) little organizational "slack" is available to compensate for error, and (4) safety devices, including redundant checks and balances against failure, are limited to those planned for, and designed into, the system.[13] The Three Mile Island nuclear power disaster, airline crashes, space shuttle malfunctions, electric power grid brownouts, and other "normal accidents" may be inevitable in organizations dependent upon advanced technology and highly interactive parts. The Cold War U.S. nuclear warning, assessment and response systems are also examples of high-risk, high-technology systems prone to normal accidents. Yet, despite this documented failure propensity for these kinds of organizations, normal accidents in the U.S. nuclear command and control system were apparently rare, and obviously none were catastrophic.[14]

Three possible explanations exist for the avoidance of catastrophic failure in nuclear warning and attack assessment during the Cold War. First, the situation was overdetermined. Even the most dullard national political leadership would search for any way out before authorizing a nuclear attack, or a retaliation based on warning of attack. Second, redundancy built into the system ensured against any retaliation based on mistaken warning. Indeed, numerous false warnings became routine business during the Cold War for both U.S. and Soviet organizations charged with warning. Some might argue that the two sides became so habituated to false warning and the low likelihood of actual attack that they dropped their guards. This charge was laid by Gorbachev against the Soviet military after an intrepid West German pilot flew his Cessna aircraft into Red Square, through and under Soviet radar nets and interceptor squadrons. U.S. military leaders were not lulled into complacency about the possibility of accidental nuclear war. But evidence suggests that their confidence in the ability of the decision-making process to compensate for errors in warning and attack assessment, possibly contributory to accidental nuclear war, was excessive.[15]

A third possible explanation is that the United States and the Soviets got lucky. No lethal combination of mistaken warning *and* a nuclear crisis occurred simultaneously. The interactive complexity of both sides' warning systems was never fully road-tested under Gran Prix conditions. Paul Bracken makes a related and significant point with regard to the judgment here. The interaction between the U.S. warning and assessment system *and* its Soviet counterpart became a separate and dangerous part of the Cold War nuclear complex. That is, the cat watched the rat, and the rat watched the cat. All of this took place in very quick time. The potential for the two sides' interactively complex systems to set one another off, like new wave smoke detectors that reacted not only to smoke but also to the alarm of another detector, was considerable.

Delegation of Authority

Thus far we have established two requirements for the avoidance of accidental or inadvertent nuclear war or mistaken preemption, managing the trade-off between positive and negative control, and coping with the complexity of nuclear warning and attack assessment. A third requirement for strategic nuclear command and control systems is correct management of the problem of delegation of authority and, related to that, the issue of devolution of command.

The president, as head of the executive branch of the U.S. government, may delegate any of his or her responsibilities almost without limit. The U.S. Constitution and the Presidential Succession Act of 1947 have established a constitutional order of succession in case of presidential death, disability or removal from office. The vice president stands at the head of this order of succession, followed by the speaker of the House of Representatives and the president pro tempore of the Senate. After that, the heads of cabinet departments are enumerated from the oldest department to the youngest: State, Treasury, Defense (War originally), and so forth. The president is the only lawful person who can authorize nuclear release to force commanders and retaliatory attacks using nuclear weapons. However, the president is not a singular actor in this regard; he or she requires the cooperation of various other levels of command and responsibility. This need for more than a singular center of competency for nuclear decision, in case of presidential death or disability, overlaps the military chain of *command* with the civilian chain of *succession* in nuclear matters.

The death of a president or even the entire civilian political leadership in a surprise strike on Washington, D.C. cannot be permitted to paralyze U.S. retaliation, for the obvious reason that such vulnerability might invite attack. Therefore, predelegated or devolved command arrangements for nuclear *authorization* (or authentication) and *enablement* must be possible from other sources in extremis. Authorization means that the person or office conveying a command to a subordinate unit is lawfully entitled to do so. Enablement provides the necessary release mechanisms

that allow operators to circumvent mechanical or electronic locks assigned to weapons in peacetime to prevent accidental or unauthorized
use.[16] For example, an authorization code from the "football" or suitcase
carried by a presidential aide tells the receiver that the president has,
indeed, sent the indicated command. Enabling commands include the
"unlock" codes to bypass electronic locks such as Permissive Action
Links (PALs) or other use-control devices.

Devolution is a complicated matter because, at least in the U.S. Cold
War case, authorization and enablement codes were usually not held by
the same persons or at the same levels of command. The president and
the secretary of defense, for example, can authorize nuclear release, but
they have neither physical possession nor effective custody of nuclear
weapons. Possession is related to custody, but not necessarily identical
to it. Custody implies control over the weapon, whether in one's possession or not. For example, tactical nuclear weapons may be deployed
in storage sites guarded by personnel other than those who would actually use those weapons once authorized and enabled to do so. In theory, authorization and enablement commands would be unambiguous
and those lower on the chain of command should automatically carry
out orders from higher echelons. The matter is not so simple in practice:
human operators, not automatons, are in the chain of command. And
actual custody or physical possession of the weapons is the responsibility
of lower echelons who are, in any military situation, capable of resistance
of various kinds in response to orders. Even nuclear age Willie and Joe
have some discretion and may decide, mutatis mutandis, to think for
themselves, once nuclear charges begin to move from storage sites to
launch platforms.[17]

As orders cascade downward and outward through bureaucratic organizations, honest misconstructions and organizational self-interest are
inevitable concomitants of crisis-time mobilization. Organizations will do
what they have been prepared to do: this normative model dictates that
nuclear force commanders will follow orders to retaliate once given without even thinking about what they are doing. This model works for a
situation of unambiguous clarity: warheads have begun detonating on
U.S. soil, the president has identified the transgressor and authorized
retaliation, and public support for nuclear response can be assumed.
Prior to the actual arrival of nuclear destruction on American targets,
the expectations become more confused, within and among bureaucratic
compartments. One can imagine some elements taking the "wait and
see" position given the Cold War history of false alarms. Other elements
might delay response and demand additional authentication for so significant an order. Psychological paralysis on the part of some persons in
the face of orders to unleash nuclear death and destruction, knowing
that their own kith and kin were at risk from enemy strikes of a similar

kind, would be almost predictable, and entirely human. Table 6.1 depicts various loci in the Russian and U.S. nuclear command and control systems by function and tabulates their respective kinds of influence.

The U.S. nuclear command system works, according to one expert analyst, like a revolver. The function of the presidential center is "not to act as *a trigger to launch nuclear weapons*, but as a *safety catch preventing other triggers from firing*."[18] In times of peace and relaxed tension, the trigger safety is "on" so that the weapon cannot be fired; negative control reigns supreme. As a crisis develops the controls are progressively relaxed to permit faster reaction to emergency: positive control becomes more important. This process becomes apparent in the U.S. Defense Condition gradations for management of alerts: from level five (lowest, peacetime conditions) to level one (highest, ready for imminent war). As policy makers authorize the military to proceed from lower to higher levels of alert, restraints on force movement and preparedness are "unwrapped" and the criterion of readiness for combat takes precedence relative to peacetime safety and security. Alert management is a tricky business, and the United States, with as much experience as anybody, had its own share of snafus despite high levels of military personnel reliability and numerous checks and balances in the system.

The former Soviet nuclear C3 system had a number of built-in checks and balances against any accidental nuclear release or, for obvious reasons, against political usurpation of authority. There were also protections against impetuous behavior from one or more levels of command. For a decision to launch nuclear weapons to be taken and followed through to conclusion, senior military and political leaders representing different departments or arms of service would have had to assent. In addition, the command and control system divided responsibility for the technical maintenance of the nuclear forces from the responsibility for combat command of those forces. The General Staff was normally responsible for the former, and the nuclear CINCs for the latter.[19] One reason why the abortive coup of 1991 was not even more terrifying was that, in the Soviet Union at that time, the power to authorize a nuclear attack was not tantamount to the degree of control necessary to cause implementation of that order. Thus, the nuclear CINCs of the Strategic Rocket Forces and other nuclear-capable arms of service essentially did a sit-down strike with regard to any launch commands from the "Extraordinary Committee" of coup plotters.

On the other hand, the Soviet nuclear command and control system was also not paralyzed during the coup. If necessary, even under attack the system could have provided for prompt retaliation:

In the event of enemy nuclear attack the CGS and CINC SRF (Chief of the General Staff and Commander-in-Chief of the Strategic Rocket Forces) still had the

Table 6.1
U.S. and Russian Nuclear C3 (Command, Control and Communication) Command Functions and Capabilities

	AUTHORITY (lawful source of command for nuclear release)	VETO (effective ability to nullify orders from authorities)	PHYSICAL CAPABILITY (effective ability to use weapons and/or launch vehicles)
Constitutional authorities/U.S. president and secretary of defense/Russian Federation president and defense minister	yes	no	no
Enabling code holders[1]/U.S. and Russian nuclear commanders-in-chief	no, unless authority is predelegated	yes	no
Authorizing code holders[2]/U.S. Joint Chiefs of Staff/Russian General Staff	no, unless authority is predelegated	no	possible, if they also hold enabling codes and can transmit an apparently authentic order down the chain of command
Weapon holders/U.S. and Russian air and missile forces, plus custodial units in charge of weapons storage in peacetime	no, unless authority is predelegated	yes	possible, if weapons lack use-control devices or if codes have already been given out

[1] Some levels of command may hold authorization codes as well, for example, commanders in chief of unified and specified commands in the U.S., or the General Staff and nuclear CINCs in Russia.

[2] Some levels of command may hold enablement codes as well, for example, commanders in chief of unified and specified commands or the General Staff and nuclear CINCs in Russia.

Sources: Peter Douglas Feaver, *Guarding the Guardians: Civilian Control of Nuclear Weapons in the United States* (Ithaca, N.Y.: Cornell University Press, 1992); Bruce G. Blair, *The Logic of Accidental Nuclear War* (Washington, D.C.: Brookings Institution, 1993), pp. 82–86 and 95–96; and Peter Vincent Pry, *War Scare: Russia and America on the Nuclear Brink* (Westport, Conn.: Praeger Publishers, 1999). For checks and balances in the former Soviet nuclear C3 system, see Ibid, p. 82 and passim.

capability to generate the requisite preliminary and direct codes. Together they could have disseminated the launch authorization and unlock codes. Alternatively, the command system might have switched over to the automatic mode of operation in the event of an enemy attack that had inflicted severe damage to the chain of command.[20]

The extent to which the present-day Russian nuclear C3 system has the same complex interdependence of checks and balances as the former Soviet one is speculative. It cannot be reassuring for Russian commanders that their nuclear retaliatory forces are much less capable than their former Soviet counterparts, nor that they are backed up by less comprehensive radar and satellite early warning systems against nuclear attack.

Former Russian Minister of Defense Igor Sergeev proposed in 1998 a new command structure for strategic nuclear forces. His proposal would have created a Joint Strategic Command (JSC) Strategic Deterrent Force (SDF), possibly outside of the General Staff and reporting directly to the president of the Russian Federation. Sergeev's plan was preceded by measures taken in 1997 to unite Space Troops and Ballistic Missile Defense (BMD) Troops with the Strategic Rocket Forces (SRF). The 1997 unification and Sergeev's 1998 plan were both motivated, at least in part, by a perceived need to improve and streamline strategic C3 and to increase the flexibility of all of Russia's strategic deterrent forces as an instrument of the political and military leadership.[21] Sergeev's plan for a joint command for SDF was temporarily approved by then President Yeltsin in 1998 but has been since shelved. It has drawn opposition from sources among the military leadership and from certain political circles.

Sergeev's 1998 plan for a new joint command for SDF may emerge from bureaucratic battles as a partial victory for reformers. One of the controversial aspects of the plan was to make the proposed commander in chief, SDF, independent of the General Staff chain of command. This created a dilemma for modernizing nuclear C3. Under present auspices, the General Staff's C3 system is shared by fleet ballistic missile submarines, strategic aviation and conventional forces. The Strategic Rocket Forces' C3 system is apparently separate from the General Staff system and based on different technology.[22] In addition to these technical problems, an independent "CINC" (commander in chief) for all strategic deterrent forces would create a newly empowered political actor to challenge the chief of the General Staff and the defense minister. Other complications might arise from the unique operational environments or command arrangements of the Navy and Air Force. SSBNs (ballistic missile submarines) not under the operational control of the Navy might be more vulnerable to enemy anti-submarine warfare (ASW) because those ships are highly dependent upon conventional naval forces for their protection against ASW. In the Air Force case, a unified SDF command raises the possibility of a divided reporting chain for dual-capable conventional and nuclear strategic bombers: one to SDF, and one to the commander in chief of the Air Force.[23]

The Fog of Assessment

Each of the requirements for the effective performance of any strategic nuclear command and control system (balancing positive and negative control, making an action upon valid warning and attack assessment, and maintaining authoritative and responsive delegation of authority and/or devolution of command) is potentially at risk in the fog of information that marks crisis communications between states and within states, among those authorized to participate in the relevant decisions about nuclear warning and response.

First, the balance between positive and negative control becomes a more complicated juggling act as alert levels are raised. Some components of the force, say ICBMs, are permanently at high levels of readiness for prompt launch. Others, such as the bomber force, require a great deal of care and feeding under stressful conditions before they are launch ready. Nuclear armed sea-based cruise and ballistic missiles can be readied to fire in a short time provided that the submarine is on station, but some submarines may need to proceed from port to station and others may be moved in connection with targeting requirements or possible threats to their survivability. Elements of the command system also require synchronized movement across disparate services and civilian departments. If NATO alerts are involved in addition to U.S. forces, as they would have been during any Cold War confrontation with the Soviets, the management of alert phasing and timing becomes even more complicated.

Ambiguous information introduced into this alerting process has the potential to disestablish the desirable balance between positive and negative control as forces are gradually empowered to go to war. From an enemy perspective, this might be considered a good thing: confuse the American alerting process and make the wartime command system only partly ready for battle by means of "information warfare." That is conventional, not nuclear, logic.

In a nuclear crisis, the two sides have a *shared interest in avoiding nuclear war* as well as a competitive desire to prevent one another's gains. Accordingly, each will want the other to maintain assured control over the balance between unlocking the cocked pistol for retaliation and preserving control over the military movements and actions that might trigger inadvertent war. And those military movements and actions are dangerous precisely because their inherent danger might not be so obvious. As Thomas Schelling has noted, war can begin not as a deliberate decision by policy makers, but as the result of a process over which neither side has full control. The possible loss of control to be feared here is not military usurpation of civil authority or military disregard of authorized commands. Instead, it is a lack of correct foresight that results in a sequence of events foreseen by neither side, creating a new and more adverse climate of expectations about future behavior.[24]

If the two sides in a nuclear crisis get into a sequence of events not correctly foreseen by either and seek to interpret those events correctly, information warfare will be harmful, not helpful, to correct interpretation. An example is perceptions management by one side designed to suggest to the media, public and legislature of the other side that the first side's intentions are only honorable.[25] The second side, according to this carefully orchestrated set of perceptions fed from one side to another, is really the "aggressor" or the "uncooperative" partner. And the media and political elites of the second side might believe the image created by enemy perceptions management, calling upon leaders to stand down forces and accept the demands of the opponent. Or, leaders of the second side might be outraged at the cyber-propaganda of the first side, escalate their demands, and become more intransigent. As Robert Jervis has noted:

A state tends to see the behavior of others as more planned, coordinated, and centralized than it is. Actions that are accidental or the product of different parts of the bureaucracy following their own policies are likely to be perceived as part of a coherent, and often devious, plan. In a nuclear crisis, the propensity to see all of the other side's behavior as part of a plan would be especially likely to yield incorrect and dangerous conclusions.[26]

Messages may be received as intended, but their political effect is not necessarily predictable. Hitler's propaganda efforts to dissuade British and French military reactions to his occupation of Czechoslovakia worked as intended in the short run, but established in the Nazi dictator's mind misleading impressions of the two states' weakness in resisting any further tearing up of the map of Europe. Boomeranged perceptions management appeared in Soviet Cold War forgeries of diplomatic and military communications between the United States and its allies. Most of these were transparent, and once found out, gave additional evidence of Soviet diplomatic perfidy to hawkish U.S. politicians and commentators.

Forces poised for immediate retaliation to possible surprise attack also interact with warning systems looking outward for indications of such an attack. False indicators planted by the other side's infowarriors to bring down air defense systems and missile attack warning radars, are harbingers of disaster once forces and command systems have been tweaked to war expectant levels. Under those conditions, the vanishing of information from radar screens or fusion centers could be assumed as the first info-wave of a nuclear attack, calling forth a preemptive response. Blank screens and obstructed communications leaving personnel in the dark for orders helped the United States in Desert Storm to clear the way for its air strikes against targets in Baghdad and at other locations within Iraqi state territory. The same phenomena might create unacceptable panic if the stakes were vulnerability to nuclear instead of conventional attack. Terrible pressures would rise from lower to higher command levels to "use them or lose them" before communications between and among NCA (National Command Authority), CINCs and geographically dispersed force commanders were completely severed. The U.S. president might be loath to order into effect any retaliation under these or similar circumstances, but this legal consolation might not make much practical difference.

In theory, no president would authorize the firing of nuclear forces on the basis of ambiguous warning information. But in the exigent circumstances, while clarification of the status of schizoid information systems was sought, force commanders would not be idle. At DefCon 3 or higher they would be taking appropriate measures to protect their divisions, fleets and air wings from enemy surprise. These moves would almost certainly be noticed by the other side's intelligence and warning, *even if* no U.S. or allied nuclear weapons were released, moved or loaded.

Few if any military experts ever thought that a war would begin with a nuclear "bolt from the blue," not preceded by a period of high political tension and based on a cold, calculated decision to strike at a favorable moment. Any accidental/inadvertent nuclear war in the years between 1946 and 1990 would have almost certainly begun at the level of foot patrols wandering off the map into restricted areas, maritime collisions on the heels of U.S.-Soviet "dodge-em" games at sea, or inadvertent strays by one side into restricted air space of the other.[27] Confrontations at the tip of the lance have an entirely different meaning higher up the chain of command if links in the chain have been deliberately confused, or their inter-link communications distorted, by cyber-pathological strikes. As Bruce G. Blair has noted:

Central authorities cannot reasonably expect military organizations simply to carry out orders, however rational the orders may be. Organizations are not that pliant. Any attempt to assert positive or negative control in a way that requires major abrupt changes in operating procedures, a situation more likely to occur if operating routines escape attention in peacetime, would invite confusion and disorder.[28]

Consider, for example, the impression created by Presidents Clinton and Yeltsin, pursuant to their agreement of 1994, that U.S. and Russian strategic nuclear missiles are no longer aimed at targets on one another's state territory. The agreement may have symbolic value, but it did little to change essential procedures for missile targeting.[29] Although Russian missiles are supposedly set on "zero flight plan," the missiles' memory banks still store wartime targets. The Russian General Staff can, from command posts in Moscow and elsewhere, override the de-targeting by means of a Signal-A computer network, re-aiming silo-based missiles at U.S. targets within 10 seconds.[30] U.S. missiles can be retargeted against Russia just as rapidly.

In addition, Russian operational practice permits its command system about three or four minutes for detection of an attack, and another three or four minutes for high-level decision making. Russia's command system and early warning network have obviously deteriorated since the end of the Cold War, along with the rest of Russia's military, raising the potential for accidents or inadvertence. For example, in January 1995, the firing of a Norwegian scientific rocket triggered the first-ever Russian strategic alert of their prompt-launch forces, an emergency conference including the Russian president and other principal leaders, and activation of the Russian equivalent to the U.S. nuclear "football" or suitcases assigned to national command authorities.[31] According to U.S. press reports in April 1997, Russia's present-day nuclear command and control system was in danger of breaking down. A retired Strategic Rocket Forces officer charged that at least one recent system malfunction caused parts of the nuclear arsenal to go spontaneously into "combat mode."[32]

Finally, the problem of delegation of authority or devolution of command is exacerbated by information distortion, either purposeful or unintentional, in the command system of either side. In the case of the U.S. nuclear command system, for example, the "cocked pistol" analogy implies that the pistol will fire back at the highest levels of alert unless authorized commands hold back retaliation.[33] An enemy seeking to paralyze U.S. retaliation by confusing the information networks for nuclear command would, instead, have an equal chance of cutting the command and control system into pieces. Each piece and the forces with which it could connect would then be a sovereign, post-attack entity, firing back with whatever resources remained to it at targets of opportunity. Commanders unable to communicate with one another might assume that their counterparts were already dead or hopelessly cut off from proper orders. A dumb, blinded and disaggregated nuclear response system would then take over from what had been a singular chain of nuclear command and control.

Less was known during the Cold War about the Soviet nuclear command and control system, compared to the American system. This relative ignorance applied both to the technical aspects of the Soviet system as well as to its operational ethos. Since the end of the Soviet Union and the development of a distinctly Russian military, some additional information has surfaced about how the Soviet and Russian systems might have operated in the past, and about how the Russian system might perform in the future. Broadly speaking, the contemporary Russian nuclear command and control system was thought by some experts, both American and Russian, to be oriented in its ethos and procedures more in the direction of positive control than toward negative control. That is, the emphasis in the Russian post–Cold War system was thought to be on guaranteeing retaliation under any circumstances of surprise attack, as opposed to preventing accidental or inadvertent nuclear escalation or war.[34] By itself this finding might not cause many exertions in Whitehall or in Washington. But, in addition, the Russian command and control system may place in the hands of the General Staff the capability, although not the legal authority, to initiate nuclear release or to launch nuclear strikes even if the president of Russia were not involved.[35]

Stylized descriptions of nuclear warfare in the Cold War literature followed predictable scripts. One side's first strike subtracted weapons from the second side's inventory; the second strike fired back with its survivors; the first side struck again with its remaining forces, and so forth. These stylistic descriptions of force exchanges (including my own) sometimes overlooked the differences among peacetime, crisis and wartime assessments. Assessment is a qualitative process, dependent upon accurate and timely flow of information. It demands both central coordination, so that all arms of the military machine are operating according to a shared concept of alertness or battle, and decentralized operation or execution of orders. The loss of information necessary for crisis or wartime assessment may not take place in discrete and measurable stages, but in weird nonlinear ways. Accordingly, leaders in a crisis or early wartime situation literally *may not know what it is that they do not know.*[36]

An important aspect of the difference between conventional and nuclear deterrence is that the strategic problematique is so much more linear in the conventional case. The object of the military in a conventional war is to obtain dominant battlespace awareness and to deny the opponent the opportunity to use cyberspace effectively.[37] On the other hand, the problem of avoiding accidental/inadvertent nuclear war is more nonlinear, perhaps even chaotic, with regard to the information spectrum.[38] Exploitation of information, including electronic, is both a cooperative and a competitive activity when the avoidance of nuclear war is equally as significant as the accomplishment of one's military object, should war occur. One side does not necessarily want to drive the other side's information regime off the field, or to corrupt it into a Mad Hatter's Tea Party of misinformation. Further, the distinction between "offensive" and "defensive" infowar may be more muddled in the case of nuclear deterrence and the avoidance of accidental war or escalation compared to the more straightforward task of prevailing in war, should it occur.

CONSEQUENCES OF FAILED C3 SYSTEMS

Information Environments and Command/Control Failures

What difference might it make, at the margin, if U.S. or Russian nuclear command and control systems failed to function properly? There are several kinds of effects in which leaders and military planners might be interested. First, command and control system failures might lead to inappropriately taken decisions for alerting or firing forces. Second, malfunctioning command and control might adversely affect a state's ability to respond to attack in a timely and effective manner, consistent with its war plans. If a state feared loss of its command and control early in a crisis, it might be more prone to interpret unintended or unsanctioned behavior on the other side as deliberate and malicious.

A preliminary model was used to estimate the effects of C3 system failure for the United States and for Russia under different assumptions about the kinds of forces the two states might field, consistent with the requirements of START I (existing protocol until the Russian Duma finally ratified START II in the spring of 2000), START II and START III at two levels: 2,500 and 1,500 warhead ceilings. Each force was statistically interrogated for its survivability after a first strike following a period of political crisis. We then subjected each surviving "normal" force, thus far unaffected by the distortion of partial command/control failure, to three kinds of C3 "hits," each degrading one attribute of post-strike force performance: (1) reduced alert levels, (2) fewer first-strike survivors, and (3) fewer working launchers and/or warheads. We made realistic but arbitrary assumptions about the statistical "penalty" that each side might pay, given what is known about their force operations, as a result of each C3 failure mode. The results are summarized for the various force structures and kinds of C3 errors in Table 6.2. Cell entries are the numbers of surviving and retaliating warheads in each case.

For the case of the Russian strategic nuclear command and control system, the problem of nuclear command system deficiency and its relationship to possible catastrophe is important because Russian military planners and political leaders already feel acutely threatened. The post–Cold War economic aftershock has punched holes in their early warning radar network. Reportedly Russia has no satellite coverage of the oceans and must depend on land-based early warning radars for warning of any U.S. submarine-launched ballistic missile (SLBM) attack on Russian territory. Funds have been lacking to modernize obsolete communica-

Table 6.2
Surviving Warheads after C3 System Failures

	Reduced Alert Levels	Fewer First-Strike Survivors	Fewer Work (Reliability)
START I			
Both affected	798/681	878/973	1,007/942
Russia affected	798/1,938	878/1,938	1,007/1,938
U.S. affected	1,639/681	1,639/973	1,639/942
START II			
Both affected	495/394	580/532	652/523
Russia affected	495/1,063	580/1,063	652/1,063
U.S. affected	1,069/394	1,141/532	1,069/523
START III (2,500)			
Both affected	404/390	422/466	477/477
Russia affected	404/930	422/930	477/930
U.S. affected	779/390	779/466	779/477
START III (1,500)			
Both affected	276/203	289/249	336/254
Russia affected	276/497	289/497	336/497
U.S. affected	539/203	539/249	539/254

The calculations are done with a force exchange model but the model does not drive itself. The investigator must enter qualitative assumptions about system performance by converting them into quantitative judgments suitable for analysis. Thirty-six different model variations result, summarized in Table 6.2 in the interest of parsimony.

Source: Author.

tions and computer equipment required for the control of nuclear forces; one result may have been an increase in the number of false signals transmitted by the system during the last few years. In addition, pay in arrears and horrible living conditions for service personnel in the Russian armed forces have reduced morale and have led, in at least one case, to a walkout by the staff of the Institute that had designed the nuclear control and communications for the former Soviet and now Russian strategic nuclear forces. According to Bruce G. Blair, a U.S. expert on the subject of nuclear command and control who is familiar with the problems of Soviet and Russian nuclear C3:

How close has Russia slipped to the edge of a failure, a serious catastrophic failure of command and control? It's really not possible to calculate, but we know the trends are adverse. And we know, I believe, that it's only reasonable that the command system cannot endure this stress indefinitely.[39]

In addition to these factors tending to raise the random probability of Russian error synergy in a nuclear crisis, there is the tendency in Russian (and former Soviet) military planning guidance and doctrine toward reliance upon prompt launch (launch on warning) in case of presumed nuclear attack on Russia. Launch on warning means that Russian retaliatory forces would be launched in response to reliable detection of any missile attack but before the attacking missiles and their reentry vehicles had reached their intended targets in Russia. Launch on warning is a more time-urgent choice for political and military leaders compared to launch after riding out a first strike, which allows leaders more time to validate and authenticate the attack. Launch on warning increases the likelihood of a mistaken decision for retaliation based on false warning or of a mischaracterized attack resulting in a choice among retaliatory options that is not optimized for the exigent circumstances.

Possible Russian reliance on launch on warning is particularly troublesome now, when their early warning and attack assessment systems are in such rickety condition. It is also especially important because the United States and Russia have both ratified START II, increasing the likelihood of further reductions to 2,000–2,500 warheads each or even fewer under an agreed START III regime. The only important obstacle remaining in the way of fully implementing START II and moving on to START III is disagreement over the U.S. request to amend the ABM Treaty of 1972 to permit deployment of a limited national missile defense system.

Missile Defenses and Command/Control

The George W. Bush defense strategy calls for a broad military transformation based on advanced technology in sensors, weapons, computers and other systems that support military operations and deterrence. National missile defenses based on a variety of physical principles are one component of this transformative military strategy. The Bush strategy intends to proceed with prompt deployment of current or near term missile defense technologies while several possible "leapfrog" technologies for next generation defenses are studied and evaluated.

Even prior to a leap forward into the next generation of technology, how much difference might hit-to-kill exoatmospheric defenses of the kind proposed by Clinton and George W. Bush, but expanded in numbers, make? Let us consider a hypothetical situation. Suppose that a U.S. or Russian defense system could operate with an average leakage rate of 20 percent: 80 percent of attacking or retaliating warheads would be

Table 6.3
Defense Leakage vs. U.S. and Russian Surviving Warheads

	Russian Warheads Surviving and Penetrating U.S. Defenses	U.S. Warheads Surviving and Penetrating Russian Defenses
START I	327	387
START II	228	212
START III (2,500)	155	186
START III (1,500)	107	99

Pertinent force structures are listed in Appendix 6.1.

Source: Author.

destroyed by the BMD/NMD system. In terms of crisis or arms race stability, U.S. and Russian leaders would be most concerned about the potential of the defense to nullify their second (retaliatory) strike. A defense good enough to nullify the other state's retaliation, even if the defense is inadequate to defeat the other side's first strike, poses acute problems for Russian or American planners. One incentive created by a counter–second-strike defense is that, if only deployed by one side, the other side is tempted to attack the defense *first* in order to preserve its own retaliatory deterrent. This temptation reduces crisis stability. And with regard to arms-race stability, there is no technology plateau on which the United States or Russia can stand with its version of a deployed NMD technology that does not invite competitors to do one or more of the following: (1) introduce countermeasures specifically tailored to defeat the defense, (2) steal the technology after the United States has completed the hard work of research and development, or (3) design and deploy a defense technology of its own.

How much of an impact would our hypothetical counter–second-strike defenses have on U.S. or Russian deterrence stability. One way to ask that question is to tabulate how many U.S. or Russian warheads would get through a defense with an overall leakage rate of 20 percent, after either state has absorbed a first strike and retaliated? The results from our model of this process are summarized in Table 6.3.

These findings point to the following conclusions with regard to stability and defenses. First, neither the United States nor Russia has to fear the loss of its second-strike capability at START III levels. Second, U.S. and Russian START III forces cannot be negated by the kind of limited nationwide BMD system proposed by the Clinton administration. But Russia's fears about expansion beyond that system are legitimate and need to be taken into account. Therefore, and third, the United States and Russia should pursue serious discussions about the implications of offense–defense mix for future nuclear arms control. It is possible that the Putin government will moderate its opposition to U.S. missile defenses in return for U.S.-Russian security cooperation on anti-terrorism and for a new NATO-Russia consultative forum.

Fourth, it deserves further emphasis beyond this chapter that the introduction of strategic defenses into the equation of nuclear-strategic deterrence adds another layer of complexity into the command and control problem. This additional complexity may result from the first strike vulnerability of the defenses themselves, from uncertainty about their actual performances under the stress of crisis or war, or from the inherent complexity of defensive C3 technology given the high demands for performance and the small fault tolerance that policy makers and commanders would almost certainly insist on.

CONCLUSIONS

What are the implications of these findings for nuclear command and control? The attainment of reduced START III levels of strategic retaliatory forces becomes a foreseeable accomplishment in the next decade. Even at reduced (1,500 warheads) START III levels as illustrated here, Russian forces will remain more ICBM-heavy and therefore more dependent on prompt launch than their U.S. counterparts. This is not necessarily destabilizing so long as those modernized ICBMs are single warhead missiles and many are mobile (thus more survivable than silo-based ICBMs).

However, Russia's first-strike fears may have more to do with political encirclement than they do with the technical character of Russia's forces or C3 systems. Care must be taken in future decisions about the enlargement of NATO and/or in avoiding the appearance of demonstrative support for hostile states or non-state actors within, or near, Russia's borders. Russia's security perceptions include threats from within and without its borders, and these perceptions are based on some realistic recognition of Russia's military weaknesses.

What can the United States do with regard to command stability in Russia? Options for the United States are limited, but worth undertaking. First, technical assistance is needed to help ensure that C3 equipment, including cyber-equipment, is modernized and capable of carrying the load. Second, shared early warning information is vital so that the imaginations of crisis-time commanders do not take the place of hard data providing reassurance that no real attack is in progress. Third, further reductions in nuclear weapons inventories and implementation of the Comprehensive Test Ban (CTB) agreement would contribute to the shared interest of Russia and the United States in nuclear nonproliferation. Nonproliferation has many benefits, one of which is the reassurance to the United States and to Russia that they can remain first among equals among nuclear armed states without re-igniting the arms race.

APPENDIX 6.1: U.S. AND RUSSIAN STRATEGIC NUCLEAR FORCES*

		START I Forces	
	Launchers	Warheads per Launcher	Total Warheads
Russian Forces			
SS-11/3	0	1	0
SS-13/2	0	1	0
SS-17/3	0	4	0
SS-18/4/5	154	10	1,540
SS-19/3	0	6	0
SS-24 (fixed)	60	10	600
subtotal fixed land	214		2,140
SS-24 (rail)	36	10	360
SS-25 (road)	715	1	715
subtotal mobile land	751		1,075
subtotal land-based	965		3,215
SS-N-6/3	0	1	0
SS-N-8/2	0	1	0
SS-N-18/2	96	7	672
SS-N-20	120	6	720
SS-N-23	160	4	640
subtotal sea-based	376		2,032
Tu-160 Blackjack bomb	70	8	560
Bear-H6 ALCM	130	8	1,040
Tu-160 Blackjack ALCM	70	16	1,120
subtotal air-breathing	270		2,720
Total Russian forces	**1,611**		**7,967**
U.S. Forces			
Minuteman II	0	1	0
Minuteman III	0	1	0
Minuteman IIIA	500	3	1,500
Peacekeeper MX	0	10	0
subtotal land-based	500		1,500
Trident C-4	192	8	1,536
Trident D-5/W-76	0	8	0

*Forces in this appendix are generally similar to those summarized in Appendix 3.1, with some modifictions specific to the research objectives of this chapter.

APPENDIX 6.1 (continued)

START I Forces

	Launchers	Warheads per Launcher	Total Warheads
Trident D-5/W-88	144	8	1,152
subtotal sea-based	336		2,688
B-2	10	16	160
B-52G gravity/ALCM	0	0	0
B-52H gravity/ALCM	95	20	1,900
B-1	97	24	2,328
subtotal air-breathing	202		4,388
Total U.S. forces	**1,038**		**8,576**

START II Forces

	Launchers	Warheads per Launcher	Total Warheads
Russian Forces			
SS-11/3	0	1	0
SS-13/2	0	1	0
SS-17/3	0	4	0
SS-25 silo	90	1	90
SS-19/3	105	1	105
SS-25 silo	0	1	0
subtotal fixed land	195		195
SS-24 (rail)	0	10	0
SS-25/SS-27 (road)	605	1	605
subtotal mobile land	605		605
subtotal land-based	800		800
SS-N-6/3	0	1	0
SS-N-8/2	0	1	0
SS-N-18/2	176	3	528
SS-N-20	120	6	720
SS-N-23	112	4	448
subtotal sea-based	408		1,696
Tu-95 H6	20	6	120
Tu-95 H16	35	16	560
Blackjack	6	12	72
subtotal air-breathing	61		752
Total Russian forces	**1,269**		**3,248**

APPENDIX 6.1 (continued)

START II Forces

	Launchers	Warheads per Launcher	Total Warheads
U.S. Forces			
Minuteman II	0	1	0
Minuteman III	0	1	0
Minuteman IIIA	500	1	500
Peacekeeper MX	0	10	0
subtotal land-based	500		500
Trident C-4	0	4	0
Trident D-5/W-76	0	4	0
Trident D-5/W-88	336	5	1,680
subtotal sea-based	336		1,680
B-52G gravity	0	0	0
B-52H/ALCM	32	20	640
B-52H/ALCM	30	12	360
B-2	21	12	252
subtotal air-breathing	83		1,252
Total U.S. forces	**919**		**3,432**

START III Forces (2,500 Warhead Limit)

	Launchers	Warheads per Launcher	Total Warheads
Russian Forces			
SS-11/3	0	1	0
SS-13/2	0	1	0
SS-17/3	0	4	0
SS-18/4/5	0	10	0
SS-19/3	105	1	105
SS-24 (fixed)	0	10	0
subtotal fixed land	105		105
SS-24 (rail)	0	10	0
SS-25/SS-27 (road)	490	1	490
subtotal mobile land	490		490
subtotal land-based	595		595
SS-N-6/3	0	1	0
SS-N-8/2	0	1	0
SS-N-18/2	0	1	0
SS-N-20	120	8	960
SS-N-23	112	4	448
subtotal sea-based	232		1,408

APPENDIX 6.1 (continued)

START III Forces (2,500 Warhead Limit)

	Launchers	Warheads per Launcher	Total Warheads
Tu-95 B/G gravity	0	2	0
Tu-95 H16	31	16	496
Tu-160 Blackjack	0	8	0
subtotal air-breathing	31		496
Total Russian forces	**858**		**2,499**
U.S. Forces			
Minuteman II	0	1	0
Minuteman III	0	1	0
Minuteman IIIA	300	1	300
Peacekeeper MX	0	10	0
subtotal land-based	300		300
Trident C-4	150	4	600
Trident D-5/W-76	150	4	600
Trident D-5/W-88	132	4	528
subtotal sea-based	432		1,728
B-52G gravity/ALCM	0	0	0
B-52H gravity/ALCM	40	8	320
B-2	15	12	180
subtotal air-breathing	55		500
Total U.S. forces	**787**		**2,528**

START III Forces (1,500 Warhead Limit)

	Launchers	Warheads per Launcher	Total Warheads
Russian Forces			
SS-11/3	0	1	0
SS-13/2	0	1	0
SS-17/3	0	4	0
SS-18/4/5	0	10	0
SS-19/3	0	1	0
SS-24 (fixed)	0	10	0
subtotal fixed land	0		0
SS-24 (rail)	0	10	0
SS-25/SS-27 (road)	490	1	490
subtotal mobile land	490		490
subtotal land-based	490		490

APPENDIX 6.1 (continued)

START III Forces (1,500 Warhead Limit)

	Launchers	Warheads per Launcher	Total Warheads
SS-N-6/3	0	1	0
SS-N-8/2	0	1	0
SS-N-18/2	0	1	0
SS-N-20	120	3	360
SS-N-23	112	3	336
subtotal sea-based	232		696
Tu-95 H6/ALCM	5	6	30
Tu-95 H16	16	16	256
Tu-160 Blackjack	3	8	24
subtotal air-breathing	24		310
Total Russian forces	**746**		**1,496**
U.S. Forces			
Minuteman II	0	1	0
Minuteman III	0	1	0
Minuteman IIIA	300	1	300
Peacekeeper MX	0	10	0
subtotal land-based	300		300
Trident C-4	0	4	0
Trident D-5/W-76	0	4	0
Trident D-5/W-88	288	3	864
subtotal sea-based	288		864
B-52G gravity/ALCM	0	0	0
B-52H gravity/ALCM	9	12	108
B-2	19	12	228
subtotal air-breathing	28		336
Total U.S. forces	**616**		**1,500**

NOTES

1. For a variety of sources on this topic in addition to those cited below see Stephen J. Cimbala, ed., *Soviet C3* (Washington, D.C.: AFCEA International Press, 1987).

2. See, for example, Peter Vincent Pry, *War Scare: Russia and America on the Nuclear Brink* (Westport, Conn.: Praeger Publishers, 1999). For purposes of this discussion and in the interest of brevity, we use the term C3 system to include

C3I systems (command, control, communications and intelligence) or C4I systems (command, control, communications, computers and intelligence).

3. Peter Douglas Feaver, *Guarding the Guardians: Civilian Control of Nuclear Weapons in the United States* (Ithaca, N.Y.: Cornell University Press, 1992), p. 12.

4. John D. Steinbruner, "Choices and Trade-Offs," in Ashton B. Carter, John D. Steinbruner and Charles A. Zraket, eds., *Managing Nuclear Operations* (Washington, D.C.: Brookings Institution, 1987), pp. 535–554, esp. pp. 539–541.

5. On the relationship between deterrence and stress see Richard Ned Lebow and Janice Gross Stein, *We All Lost the Cold War* (Princeton, N.J.: Princeton University Press, 1994), pp. 331–338.

6. Scott D. Sagan, *Moving Targets: Nuclear Strategy and National Security* (Princeton, N.J.: Princeton University Press, 1989), pp. 164–165.

7. Ibid.

8. Bruce G. Blair, *The Logic of Accidental Nuclear War* (Washington, D.C.: Brookings Institution, 1993), passim; Blair, *Strategic Command and Control: Redefining the Nuclear Threat* (Washington, D.C.: Brookings Institution, 1985), pp. 65–78. Blair's 1993 book is the most detailed on operations of the Soviet and now Russian nuclear C3 systems.

9. Steinbruner, "Choices and Trade-Offs," in Carter, Steinbruner and Zraket, eds., *Managing Nuclear Operations*, pp. 542–543.

10. Graham T. Allison, *Essence of Decision* (Boston: Little, Brown, 1971), p. 137.

11. Ashton B. Carter, "Sources of Error and Uncertainty," in Carter, Steinbruner and Zraket, eds., *Managing Nuclear Operations*, p. 628.

12. Charles Perrow, *Normal Accidents: Living with High-Risk Technologies* (New York: Basic Books, 1984). Perrow's concept is further developed and applied to nuclear accident theory in Scott D. Sagan, *The Limits of Safety: Organizations, Accidents and Nuclear Weapons* (Princeton, N.J.: Princeton University Press, 1993), pp. 31–36.

13. Sagan, *The Limits of Safety*, p. 34; Perrow, *Normal Accidents*, pp. 93–96.

14. But see Sagan, *The Limits of Safety*, pp. 228–246.

15. Ibid., p. 248.

16. Feaver, *Guarding the Guardians*, p. 38.

17. I suspect that Russian nuclear force commanders are worried about Ivan and Boris in this regard; if not, they ought to be, given the current morale of the Russian military. Russian Defense Minister Igor Rodionov declared in January 1997 that the possibility of a breakdown in the nuclear command and control system was very real.

18. Paul Bracken, *The Command and Control of Nuclear Forces* (New Haven, Conn.: Yale University Press, 1983), p. 196.

19. Blair, *The Logic of Accidental Nuclear War*, p. 91.

20. Ibid., p. 85.

21. Mikhail Tspkin, "Military Reform and Strategic Nuclear Forces of the Russian Federation," *European Security*, No. 1 (Spring 2000): 22–40, esp. pp. 26–27.

22. Ibid., p. 28.

23. Ibid., p. 29.

24. The most original thinking about this problem has been contributed by

Thomas C. Schelling. See Schelling, *Arms and Influence* (New Haven, Conn.: Yale University Press, 1966), esp. pp. 99–111.

25. See Brian D. Dailey, "Deception, Perceptions Management, and Self-Deception in Arms Control: An Examination of the ABM Treaty," in Brian D. Dailey and Patrick J. Parker, eds., *Soviet Strategic Deception* (Lexington, Mass.: D.C. Heath, 1987), pp. 225–260, esp. pp. 230–231. The author overstates the degree of Soviet deception involved in their approach to ABM Treaty negotiation, but the discussion of the concept of perceptions management remains useful.

26. Robert Jervis, *The Meaning of the Nuclear Revolution* (Ithaca, N.Y.: Cornell University Press, 1989), p. 155.

27. None of these illustrations is hypothetical. The first happened to U.S. forces in East Germany acting as authorized military observers; the second, to U.S. and Soviet naval forces in Cold War encounters too numerous to mention; the third, to KAL 007 in 1983, suspected by the Soviets (so they claimed) of espionage for the Korean CIA and for the United States.

28. Blair, *Strategic Command and Control*, p. 69.

29. According to Blair, the 1994 de-targeting agreement "was entirely cosmetic and symbolic and had absolutely no effect on the combat readiness of U.S. and Russian nuclear forces, or on the danger or risk of unauthorized or accidental or inadvertent use of those weapons." Blair, transcript of interview, *Frontline*, "Russian Roulette," February 23, 1999, 6, http://www.pbs.org/wgbh/pages/frontline/shows/russia/etc/script.html.

30. Testimony of Bruce G. Blair, Senior Fellow in Foreign Policy Studies, Brookings Institution, before House National Security Committee, March 13, 1997, from Committee on Nuclear Policy, Policy Brief, Vol. 1, No. 3:1.

31. Ibid., pp. 1–2.

32. James T. Hackett in *Wall Street Journal*, March 28, 1997, cited in *Russian Reform Monitor*, No. 251 (Washington, D.C.: American Foreign Policy Council, April 4, 1997). The term "combat mode" does not necessarily reveal very much about the actual operational status of Russian forces. Soviet forces of the Cold War years used the term combat readiness (*boevaya gotovnost'*) to include at least three different levels of preparedness for troops: routine, increased, and full combat readiness.

33. Bracken, *The Command and Control of Nuclear Forces*, pp. 196–197.

34. Extensive documentation for this appears in Pry, *War Scare*, esp. pp. 150–157.

35. Ibid., p. 152.

36. Ibid., esp. pp. 114–116, is especially good on this point.

37. Jeffrey Cooper, "Dominant Battlespace Awareness and Future Warfare," in Stuart E. Johnson and Martin C. Libicki, eds., *Dominant Battlespace Knowledge: The Winning Edge* (Washington, D.C.: National Defense University Press, 1995), pp. 103–119, esp. pp. 115–116. See also John Arquilla and David Ronfeldt, eds., *In Athena's Camp: Preparing for Conflict in the Information Age* (Santa Monica, Calif.: RAND, 1997); Alvin Toffler and Heidi Toffler, *War and Anti-War: Making Sense of Today's Global Chaos* (New York: Warner Books, 1993), esp. p. 166; and Arquilla and Ronfeldt, *Cyberwar Is Coming!* (Santa Monica, Calif.: RAND, 1992), p. 6.

38. On the issue of nonlinear relationships and their potential relationship to

deterrence, see Robert Jervis, "Systems and Interaction Effects," in Jack Snyder and Robert Jervis, eds., *Coping with Complexity in the International System* (Boulder, Colo.: Westview Press, 1993), pp. 25–46, esp. pp. 32–33.

39. Blair, interview, *Frontline*, "Russian Roulette," pp. 8–9.

Chapter 7

Cyberwar and Nuclear Deterrence

The twentieth century was the century of total war, and one result was the "perfection" of mass destruction in the form of nuclear weapons. It soon became clear to policy makers and to their military advisors, as explained in earlier chapters, that nuclear weapons were the basis for military stalemate instead of victory. Victory as defined in the age of pre-nuclear combat was not attainable at an acceptable cost. The Gulf war of 1991 and U.S. victory over Iraq suggested to some the arrival of a post-nuclear age, in which clueless weapons of mass destruction would be superseded by smart weapons of precision aim and limited collateral damage. A "system of systems" or infosphere would interconnect the various parts of the American war machine with such fidelity, while blinding and deafening the war-making capabilities of opponents, that U.S. enemies might be defeated in virtual reality before, or instead of, suffering the indignity of actual bombing.

This chapter considers another possible outcome, one far more pessimistic with regard to international peace and security. The other possible outcome is coexistence and, to a certain extent, co-determination of information warfare and nuclear deterrence. New state actors and others may acquire nuclear weapons in order to equalize the advantage of high-technology conventional warfare now held by the United States (Chapter 8 considers this issue in more detail as it relates to proliferation). But in addition to the risks inherent in more nuclear armed states, another product of the coexistence of nuclear deterrence with information warfare may be co-determination of crisis instability. Cyberwar combined with weapons of mass destruction could be the equivalent of an automated nuclear dinosaur.

INFORMATION WARFARE AND NUCLEAR DETERRENCE

Will the information revolution make nuclear weapons obsolete? Military analysts and academic experts in security studies have described a post–Cold War world dominated by a "Revolution in Military Affairs" based on high technology, conventional weapons and nearly complete knowledge of the wartime environment.[1] Other experts have suggested that nuclear and other weapons of mass destruction are the past tense of military art: information based non-nuclear weapons, in this vision, are the future of war.[2] The assumption of entirely separate paths for nuclear weapons and for information warfare may be correct in general, but incorrect for some kinds of situations, including crises between nuclear armed states. In nuclear crises or arms races, nuclear power and information strategies may come together to create a new, and potentially terrifying, synthesis.

For present purposes, information warfare can be defined as activities by a state or non-state actor to exploit the content or processing of information to its advantage in time of peace, crisis and war, and to deny potential or actual foes the ability to exploit the same means against itself.[3] This is intended as an expansive and permissive definition, although it has an inescapable bias toward military and security-related issues. Information warfare can include both *cyberwar* and *netwar*. Cyberwar, according to John Arquilla and David Ronfeldt, is a comprehensive, information-based approach to battle, normally discussed in terms of high intensity or mid-intensity conflicts.[4] Netwar is defined by the same authors as a comprehensive, information-based approach to societal conflict.[5] Cyberwar is more the province of states and conventional wars, netwar, more characteristic of non-state actors and unconventional wars.[6]

There are at least three reasons why the issues of information warfare and its potential impact upon nuclear deterrence are important. First, there is the growing significance of information warfare as a speculative construct for military-strategic thinking, especially in countries with high-technology militaries. Along with this trend is the emergence of technologies which have made policy makers and planners more sensitive to the significance of communications, computers and networks of information in time of peace, crisis and war.

Second, there is some appreciation on the part of the U.S. defense community, at least, that infowar may have *strategic* potential. This means that infowar could, by itself, bring about fundamental or decisive changes in the peacetime balance of power, or in friendly or enemy *perceptions* of the balance. In addition, in time of war, infowar could be a major, if not decisive, factor in determining the outcome of a military conflict. The Gulf war of 1991 has been called, not without reason, the first information war.[7] However, compared to what is conceivable or potentially available for future infowarriors, Desert Storm was an early-generation dress rehearsal.[8] The United States and its allies must assume that other states will be able to acquire and to use infowar technologies: leadership in present day infowar is no assurance of future preeminence. This warning against infowar complacency is especially timely now, when direct military challenges to U.S. security are seemingly nonexistent. Military-strategic surprise is, by definition, almost never anticipated by the victim.[9]

The assertion that information warfare is an issue of potentially strategic significance for U.S. planners and policy makers is not an endorsement of the idea that the United States is vulnerable to an imminent info-driven Pearl Harbor. The U.S. national information infrastructure (NII) "has yet to suffer a major attack or anything close to it despite numerous smaller attacks."[10] Although some military functions are vulnerable to attacks against part of the NII, a "strategic" disruption of the entire U.S. computer and communications system by hackers would require fictional capabilities not yet available. The more realistic aspect is that partial attacks could distort policy makers' and commanders' perceptual universes or information flows in crises or wartime situations, leading to faulty decision.[11] Even the carrying out of successful attacks is not easy. As Martin C. Libicki has noted:

Can communications be sufficiently disrupted to retard or confound the nation's ability to respond to a crisis overseas? An enemy with precise and accurate knowledge of how decisions are made and how information is passed within the U.S. military might get inside the cycle and do real damage—but the enemy must understand the cycle very well. Even insiders can rarely count on knowing how information is routed into a decision; in an age in which hierarchical information flow is giving way to networked information flow the importance of any one predesignated route is doubtful.[12]

A third reason for the significance of the infowar/deterrence relationship is the continuing reality of nuclear deterrence in the world after the Cold War. Contrary to some expectations, nuclear weapons and arms control issues have not vanished over the horizon in a post–Desert Storm euphoria. There are a number of reasons for this continuing relevancy of nuclear weapons and deterrence for American policy makers and military planners. First, Russia still has many thousands of nuclear weapons, including those of intercontinental range. Second, other acknowledged nuclear powers, in addition to the United States and Russia, show no inclination to abandon nuclear weapons as ultimate deterrents. A third reason for the continued importance of nuclear deterrence is the spread of nuclear weapons among "opaque" proliferators and the potential for additional non-nuclear states to acquire these and other weapons of mass destruction. India and Pakistan have now joined the club of declared nuclear states: Iran, North Korea, Iraq and others are judged to be nuclear aspiring. Israel is widely acknowledged as an unacknowledged member of the nuclear club.

Fourth, nuclear deterrence remains important because non-state actors, including terrorists, interstate criminal organizations (ICOs), and revolutionary actors of various sorts may acquire nuclear or other weapons of mass destruction.

The general parameters of the problem have been established. The sections that follow offer three more specific perspectives on the relationship between information warfare and nuclear deterrence: (1) crisis management, (2) preemption, and (3) conflict termination. These are not mutually exclusive categories, and some illustrative material could be just as easily provided under one heading as under another. Since no nuclear weapons have been fired in anger since Nagasaki, placement of illustrations or cases is more like a moving finger of historical analogy than a scientific experiment. For example, it is quite reasonable that the same incident could illustrate pertinent points about crisis management or the risk of preemption, or of both.

INFORMATION WARFARE AND CRISIS MANAGEMENT

Crisis management, including nuclear crisis management, is both a competitive and cooperative endeavour between military adversaries. A crisis is, by definition, a time of great tension and uncertainty.[13] Threats are in the air and time pressure on policy makers seems intense. Each side has objectives that it wants to attain and values that it deems important to protect. During crisis, state behaviors are especially interactive and interdependent with those of another state. It would not be too far-fetched to refer to this interdependent stream of interstate crisis behaviors as a system, provided the term "system" is not reified out of proportion. The system aspect implies reciprocal causation of the crisis time behaviors of "A" by "B," and vice versa.

One aspect of crisis management is the deceptively simple question: what defines a crisis as such? When does the latent capacity of the international order for violence or hostile threat assessment cross over into the terrain of actual crisis behavior? It may be useful to separate traffic jams from head-on collisions. A traffic jam creates the potential for collisions but leaves individual drivers with some steering capacity for the avoidance of damage to their particular vehicles. A breakdown of general deterrence in the system raises generalized threat perceptions among salient actors, but it does not guarantee that any particular state-to-state relationship will deteriorate into specific deterrent or compellent threats.

Therefore Patrick Morgan's concept of "immediate" deterrence failure is useful in defining the onset of a crisis: specific sources of hostile intent have been identified by one state with reference to another, threats have been exchanged, and responses must now be decided upon.[14] The passage into a crisis is equivalent to the shift from Hobbes' world of omnipresent potential for violence to the actual movement of troops and exchanges of diplomatic demarches.

The first requisite of successful crisis management is clear signaling. Each side must send its estimate of the situation to the other in a way that the other correctly interprets. It is not necessary for the two sides to have identical or even initially complementary interests. But a sufficient number of correctly sent and received signals are prerequisite to effective transfer of enemy goals and objectives from one side to the other. If signals are poorly sent or misunderstood, steps taken by the sender or receiver may lead to unintended consequences, including miscalculated escalation.

The first requirement for effective crisis management includes high-fidelity communication between adversaries, and within the respective decision-making structures of each side. High-fidelity communication in a crisis can be distorted by everything that might interfere physically, mechanically or behaviorally with accurate transmission. Electromagnetic pulses that disrupt communication circuitry or physical destruction of communication networks are obvious examples of impediments to high-fidelity communication. Cultural differences that prevent accurate understanding of shared meanings between states can confound deterrence as practiced according to one side's theory. As Keith B. Payne notes, with regard to the potential for deterrence failure in the post-Cold War period:

Unfortunately, our expectations of opponents' behavior frequently are unmet, not because our opponents necessarily are irrational but because we do not understand them—their individual values, goals, determination and commitments—in the context of the engagement, and therefore we are surprised when their "unreasonable" behavior differs from our expectations.[15]

A second requirement of successful crisis management is the reduction of time pressure on policy makers and commanders so that no untoward steps are taken toward escalation mainly or solely as a result of a misperception that "time is up." Policy makers and military planners are capable of inventing fictive worlds of perception and evaluation in which "h hour" becomes more than a useful benchmark for decision closure. In decision pathologies possible under crisis conditions, deadlines may be confused with policy objectives themselves: ends become means, and means, ends. For example, the war plans of the great powers in July 1914 contributed to a shared self-fulfilling prophecy among leaders in Berlin, St. Petersburg, and Vienna that only by prompt mobilization and attack could decisive losses be avoided in war. Plans so predicated on the inflexibility of mobilization timetables proved insufficiently flexible for policy makers who wanted to slow down the momentum of late July/early August toward conciliation and away from irrevocable decision in favor of war.

A third attribute of successful crisis management is that each side should be able to offer the other a safety valve or a "face-saving" exit from a predicament that has escalated beyond its original expectations. The search for options should back neither crisis participant into a corner from which there is no graceful retreat. For example, President John F. Kennedy was able, during the Cuban missile crisis of 1962, to offer Soviet Premier Khrushchev a face-saving exit from his overextended missile deployments. Kennedy publicly committed the United States to refrain from future military aggression against Cuba and privately agreed to remove and dismantle Jupiter medium-range ballistic missiles previously deployed among U.S. NATO allies.[16] Kennedy and his ExComm advisors recognized, after some days of deliberation and clearer focus on the Soviet view of events, that the United States would lose, not gain, by public humiliation of Khrushchev that might, in turn, diminish Khrushchev's interest in any mutually agreed solution to the crisis.

A fourth attribute of successful crisis management is that each side maintains an accurate perception of the other side's intentions and military capabilities. This becomes difficult during a crisis because, in the heat of a partly competitive relationship and a threat-intensive environment, intentions and capabilities can change. As Robert Jervis has explained, the process by which beliefs that war was inevitable might have created a self-fulfilling Cold War prophecy:

The superpowers' beliefs about whether or not war between them is inevitable create reality as much as they reflect it. Because preemption could be the only rational reason to launch an all-out war, beliefs about what the other side is about to do are of major importance and depend in large part on an estimate of the other's beliefs about what the first side will do.[17]

Intentions can change during a crisis if policy makers become more optimistic about gains or more pessimistic about potential losses during the crisis. Capabilities can change due to the management of military alerts and the deployment or other movement of military forces. Heightened states of military readiness on each side are intended to send a two-sided signal: of readiness for the worst if the other side attacks, and of a nonthreatening steadiness of purpose in the face of enemy passivity. This mixed message is hard to send under the best of crisis management conditions, since each state's behaviors and communications, as observed by its opponent, may not seem consistent. Under the stress of time pressure and of military threat, different parts of complex security organizations may be taking decisions from the perspective of their narrowly defined, bureaucratic interests. These bureaucratically chosen decisions and actions may not coincide with policy makers' intent, nor with the decisions and actions of other parts of the government.

If the foregoing is accepted as a summary of some of the attributes of successful crisis management, information warfare has the potential to attack or to disrupt crisis management on each of the preceding attributes.

First, information warfare can muddy the signals being sent from one side to the other in a crisis. It can do this deliberately or inadvertently. Suppose one side plants a virus or worm in the other's communications networks.[18] The virus or worm becomes activated during the crisis and destroys or alters information. The missing or altered information may make it more difficult for the cyber-victim to arrange a military attack. But destroyed or altered information may mislead either side into thinking that its signal has been correctly interpreted, when it has not. Thus, side A may be intending to signal "resolve" instead of "yield" to its opponent on a particular issue. Side B, misperceiving a "yield" message, decides to continue its aggression, meeting unexpected resistance and causing a much more dangerous situation to develop.

Infowar can also destroy or disrupt communication channels that impede successful crisis management. One way infowar can do this is to disrupt communication links between policy makers and force commanders during a period of high threat and severe time pressure. Two kinds of unanticipated problems, from the standpoint of civil-military relations, are possible under these conditions. First, political leaders may have predelegated limited authority for nuclear release or launch under restrictive conditions: only when these few conditions obtain, according to the protocols of predelegation, would force commanders be authorized to employ nuclear weapons distributed within their command. (See the discussion of conflict termination, below, for related points about predelegation.) Clogged, destroyed or disrupted communications could prevent top leaders from knowing that force commanders perceived a situation to be far more desperate, and thus permissive of nuclear initiative, than it really was. For example, during the Cold War, disrupted communications between U.S. National Command Authority and ballistic missile submarines, once the latter came under attack, could have resulted in a joint decision by submarine officers and crew to launch in the absence of contrary instructions.

Second, information warfare during a crisis will almost certainly increase time pressure under which political leaders operate. It may do this actually, or it may affect the perceived time lines within which the policy-making process can take its decisions. Once either side sees parts of its command, control and communications (C3I) system being subverted by phony information or extraneous cyber-noise, its sense of panic at the possible loss of military options will be enormous. In the case of U.S. Cold War nuclear war plans, for example, disruption of even portions of the strategic command, control and communications system could have prevented competent execution of parts of the SIOP (the strategic nuclear war plan). The Single Integrated Operational Plan (SIOP) depended upon finely orchestrated time on target estimates and precise damage expectancies against various classes of targets. Partially misinformed or disinformed networks and communications centers would have led to redundant attacks against the same target sets and, quite possibly, unplanned attacks on friendly military or civil ground zeros.

A third potentially disruptive impact of infowar on nuclear crisis management is that infowar may reduce the search for available alternatives to the few and desperate. Policy makers searching for escapes from crisis denouements need flexible options and creative problem solving. Victims of information warfare may have diminished ability to solve problems routinely, let alone creatively, once information networks are filled with flotsam and jetsam. Questions to operators will be poorly posed, and responses will (if available at all) be driven toward the least common denominator of previously programmed standard operating procedures.

The propensity to search for the first available alternative that meets minimum satisfactory conditions of goal attainment ("satisficing") is strong enough under normal conditions in nonmilitary bureaucratic organizations.[19] In civil-military command and control systems under the stress of nuclear crisis decision making, the first available alternative may quite literally be the last. Or, so policy makers and their military advisors may persuade themselves. Accordingly, the bias toward prompt and adequate solutions is strong. During the Cuban missile crisis, for example, a number of members of the ExComm presidential advisory group favored an air strike and invasion of Cuba during the entire thirteen days of crisis deliberation. Had less time been available for debate and had President Kennedy not deliberately structured the discussion in a way that forced alternatives to the surface, the air strike and invasion might well have been the chosen alternative.[20]

Fourth, and finally on the issue of crisis management, infowar can cause flawed images of each side's intentions and capabilities to be conveyed to the other, with potentially disastrous results. This problem is not limited to crisis management, as we shall see. A good example of the possible side effects of simple misunderstanding and noncommunication on U.S. crisis management will suffice for now. At the most tense period of the Cuban missile crisis, a U-2 reconnaissance aircraft got off course and strayed into Soviet airspace. U.S. and Soviet fighters scrambled and a possible Arctic confrontation of air forces loomed. Khrushchev later told Kennedy that Soviet air defenses might have interpreted the U-2 flight as a prestrike reconnaissance mission or bomber, calling for a compensatory response by Moscow.[21] Fortunately Moscow chose to give the United States the benefit of the doubt in this instance and to permit U.S. fighters to escort the wayward U-2 back to Alaska. The question of why this scheduled U-2 mission had not been scrubbed once the crisis began has never been fully answered; the answer may be as simple as bureaucratic inertia compounded by noncommunication down the chain of command by policy makers who failed to appreciate the risk of "normal" reconnaissance under these extraordinary conditions.

All crises are characterized to some extent by a high degree of threat, short time for decision and a "fog of crisis" reminiscent of Clausewitz's "fog of war" that confuses crisis participants about what is happening. Before the discipline of "crisis management" was ever invented by modern scholarship, historians had captured the rush-to-judgment character of much crisis-time decision making among great powers.[22] The influence of nuclear weapons on crisis decision making is therefore not so dramatic as has been sometimes supposed. The presence of nuclear forces obviously influences the degree of destruction that can be done, should crisis management fail. Short of that catastrophe, the greater interest of scholars is in how the presence of nuclear weapons might affect the decision-making process in a crisis. The problem is conceptually overdetermined: there are so many potentially important causal factors relevant to a decision with regard to war or peace.

Despite the risk of explanatory overkill for successful cases of crisis management, including nuclear ones, the firebreak between crises under the shadow of potential nuclear destruction, and those not so overshadowed, remains important. Infowar can be unleashed like a pit bull against the command, control, communications, computers, intelligence, surveillance and reconnaissance (C4ISR) of a potential opponent in conventional conflicts with fewer risks compared to the case of a nuclear armed foe. The objective of infowar in conventional warfare is to deny enemy forces battlespace awareness and to obtain dominant awareness for oneself, as the United States largely was able to do in the Gulf war of 1991.[23] In a crisis with nuclear weapons available to the side against which infowar is used, crippling the intelligence and command and control systems of the potential foe is at best a necessary, and certainly far from a sufficient, condition for successful crisis management or deterrence. And under some conditions of nuclear crisis management, crippling the C4ISR of the foe may be simply unwise. What do we think the Russians will do when their bunkers go bonkers? The answer lies only partly in hardware: the mind-sets of people, their training and their military-strategic culture must also be factored in.[24]

With or without nuclear weapons, it bears repeating that states are not simply seeking to avoid war once they have entered into a crisis; they are trying to accomplish their objectives without war, if possible, or to position themselves during the crisis so that if war occurs they will be favorably disposed to fight it. These two objectives are in tension at the margin. Nuclear weapons and the complexity of modern command and control systems make this tension more acute. Other aspects of these systems are noted below, but especially pertinent to crisis management are several attributes of nuclear weapons and delivery systems in addition to their high lethality. First, once launched they cannot be recalled. Second, no defenses against large nuclear attacks are presently feasible. Third, governments and their command/control apparatuses are more fragile than forces. Governments and military commanders steering through a nuclear crisis are aware as never before that they are plausible specific and prompt targets of enemy war plans and that these attacks, once launched, cannot be blunted. This concentrates the mind wonderfully, but how effectively?[25]

How should we operationalize or measure the possible effects of information warfare on nuclear crisis management? One possible approach is to ask how information warfare related to crisis management might impact upon expected war outcomes, should deterrence fail. An example of information warfare related to crisis management would be infowar that affected the quality of one or both sides' warning and alertness. To simulate and model this process, we developed U.S. and Russian START I, START II and START III compatible strategic nuclear forces—two versions of START III, with ceilings of 2,500 warheads and 1,500 warheads respectively. We interrogated each of these forces with a model that compared the postattack surviving warheads for the United States and Russia. We then introduced a surrogate variable for infowar that affected either the Russian level of alertness, the U.S. level, or both. The results of this analysis are summarized in Table 7.1.

INFORMATION WARFARE AND PREEMPTION

Preemption is the taking of a decision for nuclear first strike in the expectation that the opponent has already ordered its forces into attack. Preemption thus differs from preventive, or premeditated, war to forestall a possible attack at a future time.[26] Although preventive war was occasionally advocated by high U.S. officials during the Cold War, no American president ever approved a war plan based on that assumption. Preemption was, for the United States and for the Soviet Union, a more serious and continuing concern.[27]

Table 7.1

Effects of Information Warfare on Alertness (cell entries are Russian/U.S. first-strike surviving warheads)

	Both Affected	Russia Affected	United States Affected
START I	798/681	798/1,938	1,639/681
START II	495/394	495/1,063	1,069/394
START III (2,500)	404/390	404/925	779/390
START III (1,500)	252/232	252/497	539/232

Force structures are provided in Appendix 7.1. The model permits focussed comparison of the poststrike surviving warheads and equivalent megatonnage (EMT) for the United States and Russia and calculates other indicators of interest to the investigator. It was originally developed by Dr. James J. Tritten and has been modified by the author; Dr. Tritten bears no responsibility for its use here.

Source: Author, using Steve's Nuclear Assessment Matrix (SNAM).

The first requirement for the avoidance of nuclear preemption is that neither side conclude that war is "inevitable" or that the opponent has already begun it. The "war is inevitable" conclusion and the decision that the opponent has already begun a war are related, but not necessarily the same. Leaders with a fatalistic bent might conclude that war was inevitable well before actual troop movements or shooting started. Something of this sort seems to have gripped the Austro-Hungarians and the Germans in the weeks immediately preceding the outbreak of World War I. The judgment that one's possible adversaries have already begun to fight, correct or not, can also lead to a decision for war. In late July 1914, Germany judged Russian mobilization on the basis of Germany's own mobilization planning: mobilization for Germany was tantamount to war.[28] Russia's mobilization envisioned a concentration of forces near the frontiers in order to hold a defensive position, but not necessarily a decision to attack into enemy territory. Understanding Russia's mobilization through its own conceptual lenses, the Kaiser and his advisors judged that war had, in fact, begun, although Russia's Tsar was still vacillating.[29]

A second requirement for the avoidance of nuclear preemption is that each side's forces and strategic command, control and communications (C3) be survivable against any conceivable surprise attack. This is a tall order, and only the U.S. and Soviet systems in the Cold War years could aspire to meet the requirement against a large and diverse arsenal. The second part of the requirement, survivable command and control systems, is much harder to attain. Much depends upon the standard of

Table 7.2
U.S. Cold War Views of Nuclear Deterrence

	Image of Soviets	Weapons/C3 Requirements	Character of U.S.-Soviet Deterrence
Assured destruction	aggressive but cautious	destroy USSR as a modern society	basically strong, but shaky at the margin
War fighting	bold, potentially undeterrable	match or exceed Soviet counterforce capabilities across conflict spectrum	precarious, at risk from Soviet counterforce advantage
Finite deterrence	fearful of nuclear war	several hundred warheads on Soviet cities	overdetermined by excessive numbers of U.S. and Soviet weapons

Source: Based on and adapted from Richard Ned Lebow and Janice Gross Stein, *We All Lost the Cold War* (Princeton, N.J.: Princeton University Press, 1994), pp. 348–368. See also David W. Tarr, *Nuclear Deterrence and International Security* (London: Longman, 1991), chs. 5–7.

survivability expected of the components of any command and control system: physical infrastructure (bunkers, computers, landlines); organizational hierarchy (chain of command); communications networks (vertical and horizontal or lateral); and, not least, people (personal reliability, professional ethos).[30] One of these components could fail while others performed up to the expected standard, whatever that was. For example, the destruction of physical infrastructure would not necessarily disrupt the entire chain of command nor change the personal reliability of individuals.

The standard of survivability for forces and command systems can be set high or low. At one extreme, the simple requirement to strike back with a minimum retaliatory force against the cities of the opponent might satisfy the requirements of policy makers. At another extreme, policy makers might demand nuclear forces and command systems sufficient to fight an extended nuclear war through many stages. Richard Ned Lebow and Janice Gross Stein, among others, classify U.S. schools of thought about the military requirements of nuclear deterrence into three groups: (1) mutual assured destruction, (2) nuclear war fighting, and (3) finite deterrence.[31] Table 7.2 summarizes the tenets of the various schools of thought in terms of each school's (1) images of Soviet foreign and security policy objectives, (2) weapons and C3 requirements, and (3) presumed character of U.S.-Soviet nuclear deterrence.

The model of minimum deterrence never appealed to U.S. presidents once nuclear weapons and delivery systems became plentiful in number; they wanted options in addition to several hundred retaliatory strikes against cities.[32] On the other hand, despite considerable hubris in declaratory policy, no U.S. forces and command systems ever met the standard of being able to conduct an "extended" large-scale nuclear war.[33] For the most part, strategists and government officials judged that this was neither necessary nor advisable for deterrence. Most U.S. strategists and policy makers agreed, notwithstanding other differences of opinion, that forces and command systems had to be survivable enough to guarantee "unacceptable" retaliation against a variety of enemy target sets. Arguments about degrees of damage that would meet the standard of "unacceptable" continued throughout the Cold War.[34]

A third requirement for the avoidance of preemption is that the management of nuclear alerts must be competent. This means that the alerting process itself must allow for gradations of military activity, and that such activities must take place according to the guidance previously established by political leaders for the operation of nuclear forces.[35] Alerts also send to the other side, intentionally or not, signals about intent: is the alert of side A a precautionary measure on account of its fears of side B, or is it an ominous sign that side A is preparing to attack? Alerts are open to ambiguous interpretation. For example, as German forces massed on the western borders of the Soviet Union in the spring of 1941, Soviet and foreign intelligence sources warned the Kremlin of Hitler's plans to attack. Stalin chose to ignore those warnings, and the launch of Operation Barbarossa on June 22, 1941, caught Soviet border forces premobilized and unprepared.[36] On account of security, nuclear alerts may be more opaque than prenuclear ones, with equal possibilities of ambiguity in intelligence assessment of their significance.

A fourth requirement for the avoidance of preemption is the timely and accurate communication of the activities and status of military forces at the sharp end of the spear to higher political and military authorities. Political leaders are, on the evidence, often ignorant of the operational details and standard operating procedures by which their own militaries alert, move, feed, transport and hide.[37] Two problems here are breadth versus narrowness of vision, and time lines. At the strategic level of command, one is concerned with the "big picture" of fleets, armies and air wings moving in combined arms formations. At the tactical level, things are more immediately dangerous and personal. The term "GI" may have survived as slang because it expressed succinctly the world view of the grunt. Differences in time horizon also matter in ascertaining the status of one's own forces during times of peace, crisis or war. The time lines of the high command are extended; those of tactical commanders, dominated by the imminent likelihood of being under fire.

The operation of U.S. maritime forces during the Cuban missile crisis offers one illustration of this difference in time and perspective between center and periphery. President Kennedy and his advisors were concerned to avoid, if possible, a direct confrontation at sea between Soviet and American forces. To that end, they exercised a degree of close supervision over U.S. navy forces in the theater of operations that some in the navy chain of command, including the chief of naval operations, found objectionable. From the perspective of Admiral Anderson and some of his tactical commanders, operating a blockade was a dangerous exercise that had to be left to military experts if it was to be carried out successfully. The standpoint of Kennedy and McNamara was that this was no ordinary tactical operation; shooting between Soviet and American naval forces in the Caribbean could have strategic consequences.[38]

A fifth requirement for the avoidance of nuclear preemption is that flexible options be available to policy makers and to force commanders. This requirement has two parts. First, policy makers and their military advisors must be aware of flexible options and believe that they can be carried out under the exigent conditions. Second, those actually holding custody of nuclear weapons or operating nuclear forces must understand the options and be prepared actually to carry them out once told to do so. Each of these requirements is not necessarily easy to meet. Policy makers may not know the availability of options or may be reluctant to order the military into unpreferred choices under duress. For example, Kaiser Wilhelm II, in the late stage of the crisis preceding the outbreak of World War I, ordered his Chief of the General Staff, General Helmuth von Moltke, to reverse the direction of the main German mobilization, from west to east (against Russia, instead of France). The astonished von Moltke responded that "it cannot be done." Moltke meant that it could not be done without disrupting the intricate railway timetables for moving forces and supplies that had been painfully worked out according to the prewar Schlieffen Plan, based on an assumed prompt offensive westward against France through Belgium.

A second aspect of this requirement is that those holding custody of nuclear weapons, including nuclear force commanders once weapons have been released to them, understand those flexible options of interest to policy makers and are prepared to implement them. Policy makers have sometimes engaged in wishful thinking about available military options: because flexibility is deemed necessary, it is therefore assumed to be possible. An example of misbegotten assumptions of this sort is provided by the behavior of Russia's high command in the last week of the July 1914 crisis. Foreign Minister Sergei Sazonov sought a partial mobilization including only Russia's western military districts, directed against Austria-Hungary but not against Germany. The intent was to send a message to Austria of Russia's determination not to permit further Austrian aggression against Serbia. Sazonov was unaware that the Russian General Staff had in fact done no serious planning for a partial mobilization under these or similar circumstances of possible multi-front war against Germany and Austria. Neither Russia's war minister nor the chief of the General Staff warned Sazonov to this effect. When the tsar at Sazonov's urging ordered into effect a partial mobilization, the General Staff and the rest of the military chain of command sat on their hands, hoping it would be superseded by an order for general mobilization that they were prepared to implement.[39]

Nuclear war plans of the Cold War were equally elaborate as the Schlieffen Plan, and policy makers' lack of familiarity with them is well documented. Few presidents received more than a once-and-done briefing on the SIOP.[40] Faced with a serious nuclear crisis or actual war, presidents would have been presented with a short menu of options and advised that other options could not be improvised on the spot. U.S. presidents and Soviet premiers of the Cold War years thus had political control only over the actual decision to start a nuclear war, but little effective control over the military execution of that command once given.

Information warfare might contribute to a failure on the part of policy makers or the command system to meet each of these requirements for the avoidance of preemption.

First, infowar might raise first-strike fears based on the mistaken assumption by one side that the other had concluded that "war is inevitable." It might do this in one of two ways. First, deliberate attack on the information systems of the other side in a crisis might lead the victim to conclude mistakenly that war had already begun. The United States has had some experience with infowar against itself of this sort. In 1979 and in 1980, misplayed tapes or failed computer chips resulted in false warnings of attack at the North American Aerospace Defense Command (NORAD). In the June 3, 1980, incident, indicators of attack from Soviet land- and sea-based missiles spread from NORAD to other key nuclear command posts. U.S. military commands prepared for retaliation in case of valid attack warning. Minuteman launch control officers were alerted to be ready for possible launch orders, and bomber crews on bases throughout the United States ran to alert aircraft and started their engines.[41] Fortunately no crisis was in progress at the time, and operators were quickly able to calm fears throughout the nuclear chain of command.

A second way in which infowar might raise first-strike fears is by confusion of the enemy's intelligence and warning (see also, below, for the discussion of this factor in relation to accidental/inadvertent war), but in unexpected ways. If warning systems and the fusion/analysis centers to which they are connected overreact to confusion in their shared information nets, interpreters might conclude that the other side has already launched a first strike or an "infoattack" preparatory to preemptive attack. And this logic might not, in the abstract, be totally flawed. From the perspective of traditional military strategy, it makes sense to attack the enemy's command and control system, including warning systems, in the early stages of a war. A blinded and misinformed opponent can be defeated in battle faster and at lower cost, as U.S. air strikes in the Gulf war of 1991 demonstrated.

Weaknesses in the contemporary Russian warning and information systems for nuclear conflict suggest that the danger of feared attacks against Russia's command and control system is not hypothetical. Russia's military leadership has acknowledged slippage in the reliability of personnel in the Strategic Nuclear Forces, including the Strategic Rocket Forces responsible for land-based, long-range missiles. Inadequate pay and poverty living conditions for the troops are compounded by insufficient funding for replacements and upgrades to computers and electronics that tie together warning systems, communications and commanders. Cleavage of Ukraine and the Baltics from Russia's western perimeter cost Moscow important warning radar sites, and key satellite tracking stations formerly under Moscow's control now reside in the newly independent states of Georgia, Kazakhstan and Ukraine. These technical and personnel problems in Russia's warning and response system are compounded by Russia's proclivities in military strategy related to nuclear weapons. Russia's approved military doctrine expressly permits nuclear first use under some conditions, and Russia's Strategic Rocket Forces remain on a hair trigger, launch on warning posture capable of nuclear preemption.[42]

Third, infowar might contribute to preemption by complicating the management of alerting operations. Even the alerting of conventional forces on the part of major powers requires many complex interactions among force components. Nuclear forces must be alerted under separate protocols that ensure safety and security of those weapons and that alerted nuclear forces do not invite attack on themselves. Ground-launched and most air-delivered weapons must be moved from storage sites and mated with launch vehicles. Submarines will be surged from port enroute to their holding stations or probable launch positions. As one side's forces and command systems surge to higher levels of activity, the other side's intelligence sensors will be taking in more and more raw information. With strategic nuclear forces and command systems as complicated as those of the Cold War Americans and Soviets, the potential for mischievous misconstruction of alerting operations existed even without present and foreseeable potential for infowar.

What, for example, were the Soviets to make of the massive U.S. military alert of U.S. conventional air, ground and naval forces during the Cuban missile crisis, poised for an invasion of Cuba if the president so decided? U.S. leaders at the time viewed the preparations as precautionary, should the Soviets refuse to remove the missiles and the crisis turn uglier. Soviet leaders understandably saw things differently. They concluded by October 27 that the United States was definitely preparing for an invasion of Cuba. U.S. participants in Cuban missile crisis decision making aver that there were preparations for invasion but no plan for invasion, as such, had been approved. This distinction, from the Soviet and Cuban standpoint, might have been distinction without a difference.[43]

Now imagine a rerun of this crisis with more up-to-date information warfare techniques: a "holodeck" version with the same political setting but with technology of the year 2010. In the holodeck version, U.S. planners might insert corruptions into Soviet information networks that simulated an overwhelming attack force about to strike at Cuba, when in fact such a force was far from being fully prepared. And Khrushchev, aided by manipulation of U.S. information systems, might have simulated a full-scale nuclear alert of Soviet forces in order to intimidate Washington. We know now that, if the United States had actually invaded Cuba or if the Soviets had actually gone to full nuclear alert in the Cuban missile crisis, the probability of a mutually acceptable outcome short of war would have been reduced. U.S. planners were unaware for much of the crisis period of certain tactical nuclear weapons deployed with Soviet ground forces and authorized for use in case of an American invasion of Cuba.[44] And it was helpful to the avoidance of fear of preemption that the U.S. alerting of its nuclear forces, including at least one alert broadcast en clair, was not matched by as boisterous a military statement from Moscow.[45]

Related to the third factor in avoiding preemption—careful alert management—is the fourth: timely and accurate communication of force status. Leaders must know the status of their own forces and must correctly communicate this to the adversary (unless, of course, they are deliberately attempting to conceal force status because they are actually planning to attack). For example, during the Soviet orchestrated invasion of Czechoslovakia in 1968 by forces of the Warsaw Pact, NATO was careful to avoid provocative overflights or troop movements that could be misunderstood as a responsive military intervention. A disquieting example during the Cuban missile crisis was the apparent firing of a test ICBM from Vandenberg Air Force base over the Pacific. Although this missile was not weaponized, Soviet observers could be forgiven if they had assumed otherwise in the middle of the worst crisis of the Cold War. Fortunately, Soviet air defense or other watchers never detected the launch or, if they did, chose not to make an issue of it.[46] One can, on the other hand, overdo the issue of making clear to the opponent the preparedness of one's forces. The U.S. SAC commander who broadcast alerting orders in the clear during the Cuban missile crisis, doubtless to

impress his Soviet interlocuters, was trying too hard. Such braggadocio
was unintended by his superiors and, under more trying circumstances,
could only have contributed to Soviet fears of attack (or of an out of
control U.S. commander with nuclear weapons, thus overlapping with
the problem of accidental/inadvertent war).

A fifth requirement for the avoidance of preemption, the availability
of flexible options, might also be put at risk by information warfare.
Logic bombs, worms or viruses that attack information might also deny
policy makers and high commanders of the other side an accurate reading on their own command system and forces. It was hard enough to
convince Cold War U.S. leaders, on the evidence, that they had options
other than those of massive nuclear retaliation. SIOP planners, convinced
that nuclear flexibility was the road to defeat in war by overcomplicating
the command system, had little or no interest in preparing mini–nuclear
strike packages. As a result, in an actual crisis, the president might have
wanted smaller or more selective options than actually existed on the
available menu. Former Secretary of Defense Robert McNamara recalled,
with reference to the Cuban missile crisis, that he considered the SIOP
options then available irrelevant to the crisis.[47] This is quite a statement,
considering that McNamara had just overseen a major overhaul of nuclear war plans with the very object of introducing selective nuclear options.

The issue of flexibility can be misconstrued and that is to be avoided
in this context. Flexibility is a two-edged sword. Nuclear flexibility does
not imply that any nuclear war would or could be waged at an acceptable cost. It means, to the contrary, that however terrible a smaller nuclear war would be, a larger one would be that much worse. This issue
should not sidetrack us. The present point is that an infowarrior could
"persuade" his opponent that the opponent's information system is full
of electronic junk or that his command/control system for nuclear response is about to die off. So persuaded, preemption for fear of death
could appeal to leaders even before the other side had made its own
irrevocable decision for war.

Preemption for lack of information on account of cyber-distortion, intended by the other side as intimidation, is a possible path to war in an
age of information complexity. Even the Cuban missile crisis, taking
place in an environment of comparative information simplicity, was dangerous enough in this regard. For example, U.S. leaders at one stage
wondered whether Khrushchev was still in control in Moscow.[48] Fear
existed that he had been overruled by a more hard-line faction within
the Politburo, after a relatively conciliatory message from Khrushchev
on Friday, October 26, was followed by another message from the Soviet
premier the next day, harsher in tone and more demanding in substance.
In Moscow, some Soviet leaders feared that Kennedy was a virtual pris-

Table 7.3
Effects of Information Warfare on Preemption (cell entries are Russian/U.S. first-strike surviving warheads)

	Both Affected	Russia Affected	United States Affected
START I	878/973	878/1,938	1,639/973
START II	580/532	580/1,063	1,141/532
START III (2,500)	422/463	422/925	779/463
START III (1,500)	289/249	289/497	539/249

Source: Author.

oner of hawkish forces that might overthrow his regime unless he acquiesced to an air strike or invasion of Cuba. Fortunately these mistaken images were not compounded by infowarriors using perceptions management to make them more convincing.

As with the potential impact of information warfare on crisis management, we attempted to operationalize and to measure the potential impact of information warfare on preemption. In this case, we used as a surrogate variable the calculation that each side would have to make about the probable decrease in force survivability that would result from the other side's preemptive strike prompted by infowar. The results of this analysis are summarized in Table 7.3.

INFORMATION WARFARE AND CONFLICT TERMINATION

Conflict termination as used here refers to war termination: hostilities have already begun, and a point is reached at which at least one side prefers to cease firing. Conflict or war termination is difficult enough to accomplish in a conventional war, especially one between great powers that are more or less equivalent in military capability. A nuclear war would obviously differ from a non-nuclear conflict with respect to war termination, although it is not obvious how.[49] The destruction attendant to a small number of nuclear explosions, especially against heavily populated areas, would be total or nearly so for small powers. For large countries with diverse and survivable arsenals like the Cold War Americans and Soviets, the choice of war termination might present itself after the initial salvos. Although historically unprecedented damage would have been done, much additional damage could be prevented if leaders came to their senses in time.

War termination was the Achilles heel of U.S. and arguably Soviet nuclear strategy in the Cold War, for different reasons. Much U.S. nuclear strategic planning was oriented to the worst-case possibility: a "bolt from the blue" against the military forces, war supporting industry and economic infrastructure of North America. Although planners acknowledged that other kinds of attacks were more probable, this extreme condition drove much policy, force planning and targeting.[50] Soviet planners, although not unmindful of the possibility of a massive U.S. surprise attack, did not consider that this was the main, or most probable, contingency against which they had to prepare.[51] Instead, Soviet expectations were for an outbreak of conventional war in Europe, pitting NATO against Soviet and allied Warsaw Pact forces. This war would begin conventionally but in all likelihood would escalate rather quickly to a nuclear conflict, first in the Western TVD (theater of military action) and then globally. Soviet military strategists averred that it was NATO's dependency on forward-deployed, tactical nuclear weapons that would cause prompt escalation from conventional to nuclear warfare, and not a Soviet preference for that means of fighting a theater military campaign in Europe.[52]

Thus the political backdrop for war termination was somewhat different, in terms of state policy objectives, as between the Soviet Union and the United States.[53] Notable policy differences also existed within the NATO alliance. The United States preferred a nuanced strategy of flexible nuclear response even after the firebreak between conventional and nuclear war had been crossed. Many Europeans argued that the idea of any firebreak, between large-scale conventional war on the Eurasian mainland and global war against the Soviet Union, would weaken deterrence. Many Europeans also felt unwilling or unable to pay for the improved conventional defenses that might make it possible to prolong the conventional phase of a war before the decision for nuclear first use had to be taken.[54] France departed from the NATO military command structure in 1966 and declared that the decision to use French nuclear weapons would be made independently of the alliance and only in French national interest.

Given this political background, bringing any war to a conclusion would have challenged alliance unity (in the West) and defied the suspicious mind sets that had grown up between Cold War antagonists. Notwithstanding these difficulties, let us review some of the requirements for nuclear war termination and consider how information warfare might make it more difficult to meet those requirements. These are accurate and timely communications of a willingness to cease fire, military compliance with settlement, stable command and control during war, and, fourth, verification of behavior called for in armistice. In any real situation of war termination, these processes would be commingled, and the ensuing discussion reflects the fact.

The first requirement for war termination is the accurate and timely communication of an interest in cease-fire. Unless and until most forces in any war can be made to cease fire, policy makers' desire to stop a war is more theory than reality. In a conventional war fought mostly or entirely between professional armed forces accountable to civil authorities, this should be a comparatively simple matter of communication between heads of state. Even in this case, however, there are many variables to consider. Armies may or may not be promptly responsive to directives from their superiors to stop shooting. Disengagement of forces and virtual disarmament of troops on both sides may be necessary before serious negotiations over policy issues can begin. The problem is exacerbated if, within the country of one or more combatants, there exist factions opposed to any peace settlement short of victory or death. For example, in World War II, a die-hard faction in the Imperial Japanese military leadership resisted surrender even after Hiroshima and Nagasaki. Germany's surrender in World War II was made more difficult because the "die hard" was Hitler himself, who preferred to see his country destroyed, along with his own life, rather than agree to terms.[55]

The problem of communicating an intent to cease fire and a willingness by the sides to disarm recalcitrant troops and noncompliant field commanders is exacerbated if the conflict is an unconventional one. In revolutionary or guerrilla warfare (not identical, but similar in their dissimilarity from conventional war) or in terrorism, obtaining the proper "address" to which to send communications can be difficult. Guerrilla and revolutionary leaders not infrequently have difficulty enforcing labor discipline over their forces, and for understandable reasons.[56] The essence of unconventional warfare includes reliance on intelligence and combat support from paramilitary elements that may have few, if any, of the rudiments of professional soldiering. They are civilians armed for a cause, and once the cause has taken on a momentum of its own, military discipline may not be reimposed without excessive costs. In Bosnia between 1992 and 1995 the difficulty of obtaining cease-fire and disarming regulars, partisans, ruffians and renegades finally called forth a major NATO military intervention to impose at least a temporary peace.

A nuclear conflict between major powers would have aspects of both conventional and unconventional warfare. It would in all likelihood be fought between states, with militaries supposedly under the operational control of duly constituted civil authorities. However, once a nuclear war had begun, the empowered nuclear commanders would have been converted into potential nuclear ministates. This is especially so in the case of nuclear force commanders in a state without a democratic tradition of political accountability of the armed forces. More will be said about the problem of politico-military control below, but the present point is about the ability to communicate a timely and accurate sense of one side's willingness to stop fighting. If there are plural instead of singular effective fighting forces in the field with whom to communicate, cease-fire becomes harder to obtain. Russia's frustration in attempting to negotiate a cease-fire with rebels in Chechnya, and not only in this century, makes the point.

Therefore, a second requirement for war termination is military compliance with the terms of armistice and, ultimately, the peace settlement. If disarmament and peace can be imposed upon the losers by the victors, as in World War II, then the issue of military compliance is solved by diktat. Under somewhat different conditions, the issue of military compliance may be solved for the defeated military of the loser, but may remain as a sore point among one or more military elements of the winning side. Militaries bound by an alliance agreement may find their commanders straining at the leashes in advocacy of their preferred strategies for victory as the war nears its termination and the writing of history is anticipated. In World War II, the allied armies from Normandy to the Rhine were marked by contention, caused both by personality differences and by serious differences in operational appreciations of the situation. These differences were not only apparent in the field, but in Whitehall and in Washington. Only Eisenhower's brief to deal with Churchill as something approaching a military proconsul for Europe (pro tem, and with occasional intrusive oversight) was able to resolve the differences that sparked disagreements among high-strung field commanders and among allied chiefs of service in Europe.

The U.S. and allied militaries did comply with the terms of settlement in Europe, of course, in part because everyone had had enough of fighting by this time and because the last symbol of Hitler's resistance had been crushed by the Soviets in Berlin. Also, Japan remained to be dealt with, and U.S. leaders assumed that Soviet cooperation would be needed to finish the war against Japan. Therefore issues that might have been provocative of immediate postwar disagreement, as between the Western allies and the Soviets, were papered over for later argument. However, a good historian could easily concoct a "counterfactual" scenario in which U.S. and Soviet forces fought at the Elbe instead of shaking hands across it. Where that would have led is speculative. If Field Marshal Montgomery's preference for a sudden and spectacular thrust into Germany's vital regions in late 1944 had been followed, instead of Eisenhower's preference for a slower and surer pushing of Germany's defenses across a broad front, would faster moving U.S. and British forces have threatened Stalin's plans for an East-West dividing line? And if they had, what would Stalin have done about it?

The termination of World War II in Europe did not involve military noncompliance with civil authority. The latter stages of World War I are another story. The mutinies of the French army in 1917 forced a change to a less aggressive and casualty-intensive operational art on the Western front, and a reshuffling of the French military high command.[57] The widely politicized and demoralized Russian army walked away from the field of battle, and many soldiers joined workers in Russia's cities in revolt against the provisional government. The soldiers' and workers' soviets that seized power in Petrograd in November 1917 prolonged the war by withdrawing the Soviet Union from the conflict in the spring of 1918, according to the terms of Brest-Litovsk. This defection from the entente almost dealt a mortal blow to Germany's enemies. Russia's willingness to sue for peace counted as a rationale for later British, U.S. and Japanese intervention in the Russian civil war, prolonging and exacerbating that conflict and poisoning U.S.-Soviet relations for more than a decade.[58]

An even more interesting case is the situation in Germany after the armistice. Since Germany's military had not been annihilated in the field, many Germans believed that a dishonorable peace had been agreed to by an insufficiently patriotic civil government. Germany's military leadership played this "undefeated in battle" card effectively in the period between the two world wars. The German army became a state within a state even within a supposedly liberal-democratic political order. In the 1920s the army and the social democrats proved to be the pillars on which a reconstructed state could be built: the army had respect, and the social democrats, more or less, could govern under the constraints of the Versailles peace treaty. Ironically, the military combined this institutional autonomy with ideological neutrality. They would serve any duly elected or appointed civil masters, including Hitler, but not as his political enforcers. Thus Hitler was, before and during World War II, forced to turn to paramilitaries other than the Wehrmacht for the suppression of his political enemies.

The preceding cases are not historical excursions off the map, but germane to the second requirement for nuclear, or other, war termination: military compliance. The contrast between the first and second world wars shows that, whereas a more ambitious war aim (unconditional surrender) may be harder to impose in battle, it leaves fewer ambiguities both during and after the fighting. Disarmed and dead troops and deposed cabinets can no longer resist. On the other hand, the proclamation of unconditional surrender as a wartime policy objective may cut the ground out from under peace proponents within the government or military of the other side.

In the case of a nuclear conflict between powers in possession of large arsenals and ample numbers of delivery systems, conditional surrender may be difficult, if not impossible, to arrange. Nuclear weapons not yet fired must be rounded up and returned to storage sites. Troops capable of firing those weapons will have to stand down. Commanders will have to yield their weapons and codes to some representatives of the other side or to neutral arbiters, despite less than complete knowledge of the degree of disarmament and compliance by their opposite numbers in uniform. One of the most death-defying scenarios to write is the regathering of nuclear weapons among Cold War NATO forces in Europe, after they had been given out during a crisis that led to conventional fighting but before nuclear escalation had taken place, once governments had decided to cease fire.

Related to the second requirement for war termination—military compliance with settlement—is the third: stable command and control during war. There are at least two aspects to this requirement: stability of central control, and preservation of continuing control over widely dispersed forces on the periphery of the command, control and communications links. Of course, if central control falls apart, so too will control over the peripheral actions of armed forces engaged in combat. Central control could fail due to destroyed command posts or communications, or both, among other possibilities. Peripheral control might fail if embattled commanders and troops were cut off from central authority, as is quite conceivable under many circumstances in war and has occurred more than once in military history. There is a mistaken assumption that, with the plethora of communication links that exist today, forces of great powers on one side of the globe could not be disconnected from their owners and operators on the other side. This view assumes incorrectly that only simple messages need to get through from center to periphery, and vice versa.

For central and regional commands to make intelligent decisions about fighting or about war termination, they would need to exchange with field commanders highly precise and often technical information about status of forces and other variables. In addition, it might be prudent or even necessary for these kinds of information exchanges to take place between or among opposed field commanders, and between each of them and their respective central commands. Sorting out confusion within the same chain of command is difficult enough as a war nears its presumed end. For example, the timing of the cease-fire in the Gulf War of 1991 caught the commanders of the U.S. XVIII Airborne Corps and VII Corps off balance. Deputy CENTCOM Lieutenant General Calvin Waller regarded the decision as premature on operational grounds.[59] CENTCOM General Norman Schwartzkopf, according to one account, was prepared "to subordinate the final destruction of the Republican Guard to the administration's political goals" such as avoiding images of U.S. brutality and avoiding American and Iraqi casualties.[60] Some Washington policy makers were operating under the mistaken assumption that the crack Republican Guard Iraqi armoured divisions had in essence been destroyed by the time the cease-fire took place.

Intelligence failures can contribute to wartime confusion between center and periphery in the latter stages of a war. The Battle of the Bulge beginning in December 1944 is an example. Neither field commanders nor allied command Europe anticipated that seemingly exhausted and virtually defeated German forces would attempt one final, desperate offensive that prolonged the war and shook allied confidence. Initial reports from forward units suddenly caught off guard and committed to furious fire fights were at first disbelieved or misconstrued by Army intelligence as a result of preconceptions about German capabilities, based on recent performance.[61] The assumption that Germany was down to its shoe leather was correct; what was missed was that resources remained to be called out, including previously untapped manpower both old and young, for Hitler's final throw of the dice.[62]

A fourth requirement for war termination can be deduced easily from what has been argued so far: verification of behavior in compliance with a cease-fire and subsequent peace settlement. In conventional wars this is done by exchanges of military observer personnel. Doubtless this would be difficult to accomplish in a fast-paced and highly destructive nuclear conflict. Substitutes for observers, especially in the early stages of any war termination, would have to be found. Overhead reconnaissance by satellites and aircraft, if any satellites remained functional and aircraft could count on flying safely, would provide some necessary verification of compliance with agreed cease-fire protocols. However, any reconnaissance or surveillance is highly selective. One must have a conceptual roadmap for what to look at, and in wartime this is all the more significant than in peace. Just as moving targets are harder to hit than stationary ones, so too are mobile and movable missiles and command posts harder to verify than fixed forces or sites. In addition, some platforms used for nuclear launch might not be locatable at all: the virtue of submarines in time of peace, stealthy defiance of location detection, could become an obstacle to locking down a truce or cease-fire in war.

Illustrative of the overlap between the requirements for war termination is the essential nature of reliable and uncorrupted communications links for sending a message of intent to terminate, and for monitoring compliance with termination agreements. Quite obviously, then, each side would have to be able to verify that its own communication links were operating with fidelity and fully under its own control at the endgame of negotiation as well as when negotiation feelers are first put out. Ghosts in the machine that spoofed or distorted information could slow down or bring to a halt the process of arranging a cease-fire.

Information warfare has been identified previously as a threat to successful crisis management and as a potential cause of preemption or accidental/inadvertent war. Infowar may also make war termination impossible or more difficult to attain than it would otherwise be.

First, information warfare could prevent the timely and accurate communication of any interest in a cease-fire or peace settlement. In a nuclear war between the Cold War Americans and Soviets, the targeting of command posts and command/control assets, including communications links between U.S. or Soviet NCA and retaliatory forces, was a two-sided coin. Military strategy á la Clausewitz would call for early strikes against critical command and control systems in order to paralyze as much of the enemy's nuclear stinger as possible. Strikes against command posts, communications and other aspects of C3 might be defended as "economy of force" operations providing a nullifying effect equivalent to much more costly counterforce strikes. The downside of this approach is that it might work too effectively. A knockout blow against the other side's command and control system could, as noted previously, make it more difficult for the opponent to organize a stable post-attack government with which reliable negotiations could be carried on.

Of course, this latter concern is only pertinent to a limited, as opposed to a total, nuclear war; thus the apparently greater interest on the part of U.S., as opposed to Soviet, military theorists in the entire concept of limited nuclear war. Soviet forces had the tools with which to fight a limited nuclear war, but neither Soviet military nor political leadership exhibited any serious inclination to do so. This disinterest in limited nuclear war may have reflected Marxist-Leninist precepts about wars between capitalism and socialism that the military, along with the civilians, or in some cases even more so, adopted as part of their sociopolitical worldview.[63] The comparative Soviet disinterest in limited nuclear war may also have been an example of intended "echo" effects. Publicly proclaimed skepticism about less than total war, originally intended to dissuade U.S. interest in the subject, became more persuasive to its original authors after being repeated back to them by sympathetic U.S. audiences.[64] Regardless of the assumed cause, Soviet assumptions that any war in Europe would quickly escalate into theater nuclear war, and that it would be difficult to impossible to prevent expansion of theater into strategic-intercontinental warfare, were widely shared among party, government and military elites.

The significance of the preceding point is that destruction of the wartime Soviet high command or its key military and political nodes would have made war termination more difficult. Almost certain Soviet attacks against central and regional U.S. and allied NATO command posts, communications and other C3 assets would have had a similar outcome. Direct attacks against command posts and commanders are not, strictly speaking, part of "information warfare" if that term is restricted to possible future netwars and cyberwars. One might say that attacks on command posts and commanders are an older form of information warfare; but they are important to the task of understanding how information warfare affects nuclear deterrence, and therefore, however old-fashioned, are included here. Attacks against command posts, commanders and their communications to field forces also affect other attributes of war termination, including military compliance, stable wartime command and control, and verification.

Military compliance with settlement terms could also be affected by information warfare. This might occur because the enemy had spoofed information networks by introducing false or misleading messages into them. Or, it might occur because peripheral forces reluctant to surrender held out and deliberately cut off their communications with central authorities. Nuclear force commanders being fired upon would be understandably reluctant to trust or credit messages from headquarters suggesting that firing be held back to expedite peace feelers. Enemy dissidents equally reluctant to quit fighting might help friendly "holdouts" from side A by disrupting or manipulating their communications with their own central authorities, by perceptions management of the intent of their own (side B) government (represented as more implacable than it actually is), or by creating false images in information networks of newly planned attacks by either side. Phony speeches promising war to the death could be played into information networks and passed along to forces already skeptical about cease-fires and bombing pauses.

Information warfare (Old Style) can interfere with stable wartime command and control by destroying command posts, commanders and communications. More artful and less physical means of information warfare can accomplish some of the same objectives. One might paralyze the other side's retaliatory forces by getting control of the satellite uplinks and downlinks which serve as the eyes and ears for military reconnaissance and communications. A side blinded and deafened in the preliminary stages of a nuclear war would be even more at risk than were Iraqi forces in the early hours of Desert Storm. Enemy awareness of being blinded and deafened even prior to attack might induce a more reasonable, or compliant, posture with political demands. Once war had begun, however, a blinded opponent would have difficulty, even with the best of intentions, in agreeing to terms for a cease-fire or in conducting any other negotiations.

As in the case of stable command and control, verification also would be at risk from information warfare, New Style. Neither side could trust the other's compliance by means of verification systems (photographic, electronic or cybernetic) that were suspect of being under the control of the opponent. It would make more sense to fight on in the hope of recapturing information integrity. Without verification of compliance with cease-fires, any agreed terms for cease-fire or peaceful settlement would be at the mercy of the first corrupt megabyte under enemy control. And how would either side establish, in the aftermath of even small nuclear

Table 7.4
Context for War Termination: Post-attack Forces Remaining after Second
Strikes (cell entries are Russian/U.S. second-strike surviving warheads)

	Both Affected	Russia Affected	United States Affected
START I	626/817	626/1,938	1,639/817
START II	471/441	471/1,063	1,069/441
START III (2,500)	324/418	324/930	779/418
START III (1,500)	252/232	252/497	539/232

Source: Author.

strikes and partly destroyed communications, that its remaining command and control apparatus, having survived infowar Old Style, was
still proof against infowar New Style? Experts might not be available
when and where they were needed in order to verify the integrity of
information networks and the security of information protocols. They
might, along with some policy makers and commanders, be buried in
rubble or psychologically unable to react, much less choose intelligently.

Making operational the aspect of war termination and its potential
impact on policy makers' and commanders' estimates of probable war
outcomes is not a simple matter. The process of war fighting exerts considerable influence on the decisions taken by combatants about when
and where to cease fire. The difficulties inherent in terminating any war
would be drastically compounded in a nuclear conflict. Nevertheless, for
illustrative purposes we show in Table 7.4, one possible approach. We
forced our exchange model through two cycles: a first cycle in which
each side absorbed the first strike of the other; and a second cycle, in
which we compared the surviving warheads available to each side after
a second strike. This is the probable context within which negotiations
for conflict termination would have to take place. The remaining numbers of warheads for the United States and for Russia were small in
comparison to the survivors in Tables 7.1 and 7.3 for the cases of the
impact of information warfare on alertness and survivability.

CONCLUSIONS

Military capabilities and intentions of states in conflict can come together in unexpected ways, and with unpredictable side effects. The preceding discussion has argued that the combination of information
warfare with nuclear deterrence may produce military malapropisms.
Among these possibly unexpected synergies are nuclear preemption, a

Table 7.5
Potential Problems for Nuclear Deterrence from Information Warfare (by category)

Crisis Management
- confuse signals, destroys or disrupts communications
- increase time pressure
- omit face-saving exit
- distort perceptions

Preemption
- create "war is inevitable" feeling
- raise fear of vulnerable C3, forces
- inept alert management
- inaccurate knowledge of force movement, dispositions
- inflexible perception of available options

Conflict termination
- untimely or inaccurate communication of intent to cease fire/settle on terms
- military noncompliance with settlement
- unstable command and control
- inability to verify

Source: Author.

failure of crisis management, or an increase in the difficulty of terminating a conflict between nuclear armed states that is about to go nuclear, or already has. These hypotheses and findings are summarized in Table 7.5.

The same findings are supported by the data analysis of possible impacts of information warfare on the viability of the U.S. or Russian nuclear deterrents. Even highly "successful" information attacks against the warning, command and control and response systems of either side would fall short of creating the paralysis that would preclude a devastating and unacceptable retaliation after any attack. The case of war termination does show, on the other hand, that at START III levels and after several attacks, both sides' inventories of surviving weapons run down rather quickly. If destruction of national and military information infrastructures had eliminated too many components of either side's brain and central nervous system, there might be only an unofficial ending to the war when previously empowered commanders finally ran out of weapons.

APPENDIX 7.1: FORCES IN THE ANALYSIS*

| | START I Forces | | |
	Launchers	Warheads per Launcher	Total Warheads
Russian Forces			
SS-11/3	0	1	0
SS-13/2	0	1	0
SS-17/3	0	4	0
SS-18/4/5	154	10	1,540
SS-19/3	0	6	0
SS-24 (fixed)	60	10	600
subtotal fixed land	214		2,140
SS-24 (rail)	36	10	360
SS-25 (road)	715	1	715
subtotal mobile land	751		1,075
subtotal land-based	965		3,215
SS-N-6/3	0	1	0
SS-N-8/2	0	1	0
SS-N-18/2	96	7	672
SS-N-20	120	6	720
SS-N-23	160	4	640
subtotal sea-based	376		2,032
Tu-160 Blackjack bomb	70	8	560
Bear-H6 ALCM	130	8	1,040
Tu-160 Blackjack ALCM	70	16	1,120
subtotal air-breathing	270		2,720
Total Russian forces	**1,611**		**7,967**
U.S. Forces			
Minuteman II	0	1	0
Minuteman III	0	1	0
Minuteman IIIA	500	3	1,500
Peacekeeper MX	0	10	0
subtotal land-based	500		1,500
Trident C-4	192	8	1,536
Trident D-5/W-76	0	8	0
Trident D-5/W-88	144	8	1,152
subtotal sea-based	336		2,688
B-2	10	16	160
B-52G gravity/ALCM	0	0	0
B-52H gravity/ALCM	95	20	1,900

*Forces in this appendix are generally similar to those summarized in Appendix 3.1, with some modifications specific to the research objectives of this chapter.

APPENDIX 7.1 (continued)

	START I Forces		
	Launchers	Warheads per Launcher	Total Warheads
B-1	97	24	2,328
subtotal air-breathing	202		4,388
Total U.S. forces	**1,038**		**8,576**

	START II Forces		
	Launchers	Warheads per Launcher	Total Warheads
Russian Forces			
SS-11/3	0	1	0
SS-13/2	0	1	0
SS-17/3	0	4	0
SS-25 silo	90	1	90
SS-19/3	105	1	105
SS-25 silo	0	1	0
subtotal fixed land	195		195
SS-24 (rail)	0	10	0
SS-25/SS-27 (road)	605	1	605
subtotal mobile land	605		605
subtotal land-based	800		800
SS-N-6/3	0	1	0
SS-N-8/2	0	1	0
SS-N-18/2	176	3	528
SS-N-20	120	6	720
SS-N-23	112	4	448
subtotal sea-based	408		1,696
Tu-95 H6	20	6	120
Tu-95 H16	35	16	560
Blackjack	6	12	72
subtotal air-breathing	61		752
Total Russian forces	**1,269**		**3,248**
U.S. Forces			
Minuteman II	0	1	0
Minuteman III	0	1	0
Minuteman IIIA	500	1	500
Peacekeeper MX	0	10	0
subtotal land-based	500		500

APPENDIX 7.1 (continued)

START II Forces

	Launchers	Warheads per Launcher	Total Warheads
Trident C-4	0	4	0
Trident D-5/W-76	0	4	0
Trident D-5/W-88	336	5	1,680
subtotal sea-based	336		1,680
B-52G gravity	0	0	0
B-52H/ALCM	32	20	640
B-52H/ALCM	30	12	360
B-2	21	12	252
subtotal air-breathing	83		1,252
Total U.S. forces	**919**		**3,432**

START III (2,500 Warhead Limit)

	Launchers	Warheads per Launcher	Total Warheads
Russian Forces			
SS-11/3	0	1	0
SS-13/2	0	1	0
SS-17/3	0	4	0
SS-18/4/5	0	10	0
SS-19/3	105	1	105
SS-24 (fixed)	0	10	0
subtotal fixed land	105		105
SS-24 (rail)	0	10	0
SS-25/SS-27 (road)	490	1	490
subtotal mobile land	490		490
subtotal land-based	595		595
SS-N-6/3	0	1	0
SS-N-8/2	0	1	0
SS-N-18/2	0	1	0
SS-N-20	120	8	960
SS-N-23	112	4	448
subtotal sea-based	232		1,408
Tu-95 B/G gravity	0	2	0
Tu-95 H16	31	16	496
Tu-160 Blackjack	0	8	0
subtotal air-breathing	31		496
Total Russian forces	**858**		**2,499**

APPENDIX 7.1 (continued)

START III (2,500 Warhead Limit)

	Launchers	Warheads per Launcher	Total Warheads
U.S. Forces			
Minuteman II	0	1	0
Minuteman III	0	1	0
Minuteman IIIA	300	1	300
Peacekeeper MX	0	10	0
subtotal land-based	300		300
Trident C-4	150	4	600
Trident D-5/W-76	150	4	600
Trident D-5/W-88	132	4	528
subtotal sea-based	432		1,728
B-52G gravity/ALCM	0	0	0
B-52H gravity/ALCM	36	8	288
B-2	15	12	180
subtotal air-breathing	51		468
Total U.S. forces	**783**		**2,496**

START III (1,500 Warhead Limit)

	Launchers	Warheads per Launcher	Total Warheads
Russian Forces			
SS-11/3	0	1	0
SS-13/2	0	1	0
SS-17/3	0	4	0
SS-18/4/5	0	10	0
SS-19/3	0	1	0
SS-24 (fixed)	0	10	0
subtotal fixed land	0		0
SS-24 (rail)	0	10	0
SS-25/SS-27 (road)	490	1	490
subtotal mobile land	490		490
subtotal land-based	490		490
SS-N-6/3	0	1	0
SS-N-8/2	0	1	0
SS-N-18/2	0	1	0
SS-N-20	120	3	360
SS-N-23	112	3	336
subtotal sea-based	232		696

APPENDIX 7.1 (continued)

START III (1,500 Warhead Limit)

	Launchers	Warheads per Launcher	Total Warheads
Tu-95 H6/ALCM	5	6	30
Tu-95 H16	16	16	256
Tu-160 Blackjack	3	8	24
subtotal air-breathing	24		310
Total Russian forces	**746**		**1,496**
U.S. Forces			
Minuteman II	0	1	0
Minuteman III	0	1	0
Minuteman IIIA	300	1	300
Peacekeeper MX	0	10	0
subtotal land-based	300		300
Trident C-4	0	4	0
Trident D-5/W-76	0	4	0
Trident D-5/W-88	288	3	864
subtotal sea-based	288		864
B-52G gravity/ALCM	0	0	0
B-52H gravity/ALCM	9	12	108
B-2	19	12	228
subtotal air-breathing	28		336
Total U.S. forces	**616**		**1,500**

NOTES

The author gratefully acknowledges John Arquilla, RAND, and Peter Feaver, Duke University, for helpful comments and references on earlier drafts. They bear no responsibility for arguments or errors here.

1. Dorothy E. Denning, *Information Warfare and Security* (Reading, Mass.: Addison-Wesley, 1999), pp. 21–42 explains the theory of information warfare. Information has, of course, always been an important part of war and crisis management. But, as Steven Metz and James Kievit have explained, the informational aspect of RMA may "alter the traditional relationship between operational complexity and effective control" as new means of acquiring, analyzing and distributing information allow for added complexity in military action without sacrificing control or timing. See Metz and Kievit, *Strategy and the Revolution in Military Affairs: From Theory to Policy* (Carlisle Barracks, Pa.: U.S. Army War College, June 27, 1995), p. 4 and passim.

2. Alvin Toffler and Heidi Toffler, *War and Anti-War: Making Sense of Today's Global Chaos* (New York: Warner Books, 1993), passim.

3. For an introduction to this topic, see John Arquilla and David Ronfeldt, "A New Epoch—and Spectrum—of Conflict," in Arquilla and Ronfeldt, eds., *In Athena's Camp: Preparing for Conflict in the Information Age* (Santa Monica, Calif.: RAND, 1997), pp. 1–22. See also, on definitions and concepts of information warfare, Martin Libicki, *What Is Information Warfare?* (Washington, D.C.: National Defense University, ACIS Paper 3, August 1995); Libicki, *Defending Cyberspace and Other Metaphors* (Washington, D.C.: National Defense University, Directorate of Advanced Concepts, Technologies and Information Strategies, February 1997); Toffler and Toffler, *War and Anti-War*, pp. 163–207; Arquilla and Ronfeldt, *Cyberwar Is Coming!* (Santa Monica, Calif.: RAND, 1992); and David S. Alberts, *The Unintended Consequences of Information Age Technologies: Avoiding the Pitfalls, Seizing the Initiative* (Washington, D.C.: National Defense University, Institute for National Strategic Studies, Center for Advanced Concepts and Technology, April 1996); and Gordon R. Sullivan and Anthony M. Coroalles, *Seeing the Elephant: Leading America's Army into the Twenty-First Century* (Cambridge, Mass.: Institute for Foreign Policy Analysis, 1995). A roadmap to information resources related to strategy and other military topics appears in James Kievit and Steven Metz, *The Strategist and the Web Revisited: An Updated Guide to Internet Resources* (Carlisle Barracks, Pa.: U.S. Army War College, Strategic Studies Institute, Army After Next Project, October 17, 1996).

4. Arquilla and Ronfeldt, "A New Epoch—and Spectrum—of Conflict," p. 6.

5. Arquilla and Ronfeldt, "The Advent of Netwar," in Arquilla and Ronfeldt, eds., *In Athena's Camp*, pp. 275–294.

6. Ibid., passim.

7. Thomas A. Keaney and Eliot A. Cohen, *Revolution in Warfare? Air Power in the Persian Gulf* (Annapolis, Md.: Naval Institute Press, 1995), pp. 188–212. See also Kenneth Allard, *Command, Control and the Common Defense*, rev. ed. (Washington, D.C.: National Defense University Press, 1996), pp. 273–303. For appropriate cautions, see Jeffrey Cooper, *Another View of the Revolution in Military Affairs* (Carlisle Barracks, Pa.: U.S. Army War College, Strategic Studies Institute, July 15, 1994), esp. pp. 8 and 36.

8. Martin C. Libicki, "DBK and Its Consequences," in Stuart E. Johnson and Martin C. Libicki, eds., *Dominant Battlespace Knowledge: The Winning Edge* (Washington, D.C.: National Defense University Press, 1995), pp. 27–58.

9. Richard K. Betts, *Surprise Attack: Lessons for Defense Planning* (Washington, D.C.: Brookings Institution, 1982).

10. Libicki, *Defending Cyberspace and Other Metaphors*, p. 10.

11. David S. Alberts, *Defensive Information Warfare* (Washington, D.C.: National Defense University, Directorate of Advanced Concepts, Technologies and Information Strategies, August 1996), p. 12.

12. Libicki, *Defending Cyberspace and Other Metaphors*, p. 30.

13. Alexander L. George, ed., *Avoiding War: Problems of Crisis Management* (Boulder, Colo.: Westview Press, 1991).

14. See Patrick M. Morgan, *Deterrence: A Conceptual Analysis* (Beverly Hills, Calif.: Sage Publications, 1983) and Lebow and Stein, *We All Lost the Cold War*, pp. 351–355.

15. Keith B. Payne, *Deterrence in the Second Nuclear Age* (Lexington: University Press of Kentucky, 1996), p. 57. See also Col. David Jablonsky, *Strategic Rationality*

Is Not Enough: Hitler and the Concept of Crazy States (Carlisle Barracks, Pa.: Strategic Studies Institute, U.S. Army War College, August 8, 1991), esp. pp. 5–8 and 31–37.

16. Lebow and Stein, *We All Lost the Cold War*, pp. 122–123.

17. Robert Jervis, *The Meaning of the Nuclear Revolution: Statecraft and the Prospect of Armageddon* (Ithaca, N.Y.: Cornell University Press, 1989), p. 183.

18. A virus is a self-replicating piece of software intended to destroy or alter the contents of other software stored on floppy disks or hard drives. Worms corrupt the integrity of software and information systems from the "inside out" in ways that create weaknesses exploitable by an enemy.

19. James G. March and Herbert A. Simon, *Organizations* (New York: John Wiley and Sons, 1958), pp. 140 and 146.

20. Lebow and Stein, *We All Lost the Cold War*, pp. 335–336.

21. Graham T. Allison, *Essence of Decision: Explaining the Cuban Missile Crisis* (Boston: Little, Brown, 1971), p. 141. See also Scott D. Sagan, *Moving Targets: Nuclear Strategy and National Security* (Princeton, N.J.: Princeton University Press, 1989), p. 147, and Lebow and Stein, *We All Lost the Cold War*, p. 342.

22. For example, see Richard Ned Lebow, *Between Peace and War: The Nature of International Crisis* (Baltimore, Md.: Johns Hopkins University Press, 1981); Michael Howard, *Studies in War and Peace* (New York: The Viking Press, 1971), pp. 99–109; Gerhard Ritter, *The Schlieffen Plan: Critique of a Myth* (London: Oswald Wolff, 1958); and D.C.B. Lieven, *Russia and the Origins of the First World War* (New York: St. Martin's Press, 1983).

23. As David Alberts notes, "Information dominance would be of only academic interest, if we could not turn this information dominance into battlefield dominance." See Alberts, "The Future of Command and Control with DBK," in Johnson and Libicki, *Dominant Battlespace Knowledge*, pp. 77–102, citation p. 80.

24. As Colin S. Gray, has noted, "Because deterrence flows from a relationship, it cannot reside in unilateral capabilities, behavior or intentions. Anyone who refers to *the* deterrent policy plainly does not understand the subject." Gray, *Explorations in Strategy* (Westport, Conn.: Greenwood Press, 1996), p. 33.

25. Ashton B. Carter, "Assessing Command System Vulnerability," in Carter, John D. Steinbruner and Charles A. Zraket, eds., *Managing Nuclear Operations* (Washington, D.C.: Brookings Institution, 1987), pp. 555–610.

26. Richard Ned Lebow, *Nuclear Crisis Management: A Dangerous Illusion* (Ithaca, N.Y.: Cornell University Press, 1987), p. 25.

27. Ibid., pp. 31–74. See also David Alan Rosenberg, "The Origins of Overkill: Nuclear Weapons and American Strategy, 1945–1960," *International Security*, No. 4 (Spring 1983), in Steven E. Miller, ed., *Strategy and Nuclear Deterrence* (Princeton, N.J.: Princeton University Press, 1984), pp. 113–182, esp. pp. 135 and 143–144.

28. Donald Kagan, *On the Origins of War and the Preservation of Peace* (New York: Doubleday, 1995), p. 197.

29. L.C.F. Turner, "The Significance of the Schlieffen Plan," in Paul M. Kennedy, ed., *The War Plans of the Great Powers* (London: Allen and Unwin, 1979), pp. 199–221; and Holger M. Herwig, "The Dynamics of Necessity: German Military Policy during the First World War," in Allan R. Millett and Williamson Murray, eds., *Military Effectiveness*, Vol. I (London: Unwin Hyman, 1988), pp. 80–

115. See also Kennedy's note that German planning was unique and tantamount to war in his introduction to *The War Plans of the Great Powers*, pp. 15–16.

30. See Martin Van Creveld, *Command in War* (Cambridge, Mass.: Harvard University Press, 1985), passim.

31. Lebow and Stein, *We All Lost the Cold War*, pp. 349–351.

32. Desmond Ball, "The Development of the SIOP, 1960–1983," in Ball and Jeffrey Richelson, eds., *Strategic Nuclear Targeting* (Ithaca, N.Y.: Cornell University Press, 1986), pp. 57–83.

33. Colin S. Gray, "Targeting Problems for Central War," in Ball and Richelson, eds., *Strategic Nuclear Targeting*, pp. 171–193.

34. Lawrence Freedman, *The Evolution of Nuclear Strategy* (New York: St. Martin's Press, 1981), pp. 245–256.

35. Bruce G. Blair, "Alerting in Crisis and Conventional War," in Carter, Steinbruner and Zraket, eds., *Managing Nuclear Operations*, pp. 75–120; Scott D. Sagan, *Moving Targets: Nuclear Strategy and National Security* (Princeton, N.J.: Princeton University Press, 1989), pp. 148–149.

36. Col. David M. Glantz, ed., *The Initial Period of War on the Eastern Front, 22 June–August 1941* (London: Frank Cass, 1993), esp. pp. 28–37 and 40–50.

37. Martin Van Creveld, *Technology and War: From 2000 B.C. to the Present* (New York: The Free Press, 1989), p. 247.

38. Lebow and Stein, *We All Lost the Cold War*, p. 341; Allison, *Essence of Decision*, pp. 138–139.

39. L.C.F. Turner, "The Russian Mobilization in 1914," in Kennedy, ed., *The War Plans of the Great Powers*, pp. 252–268, argues that the distinction between Russian partial and general mobilization was essentially meaningless, in terms of Germany's understanding of Russia's actions. See also Marc Trachtenberg, *History and Strategy* (Princeton, N.J.: Princeton University Press, 1991), pp. 80–87 and 94–95. Luigi Albertini refers to the plan for partial mobilization as "this bright idea of Sazonov's" and argues that the Russian General Staff had never worked up a plan for mobilization only against Austria-Hungary. See Albertini, *The Origins of the War of 1914*, Vol. 2, translated and edited by Isabella M. Massey (London: Oxford University Press, 1953), pp. 292–293.

40. Lebow, *Nuclear Crisis Management*, p. 150.

41. Sagan, *The Limits of Safety*, pp. 228–231.

42. Bruce W. Nelan, "Nuclear Disarray," *Time*, May 19, 1997, pp. 46–48.

43. Lebow and Stein, *We All Lost the Cold War*, p. 132. Raymond L. Garthoff, who participated in U.S. Cuban missile crisis decision making as a State Department official, contends that "no U.S. plan for an invasion of Cuba was under way" but acknowledges that previously laid down U.S. contingency plans for military action against Cuba were being refined, updated and rehearsed. Garthoff, *Reflections on the Cuban Missile Crisis*, rev. ed. (Washington, D.C.: Brookings Institution, 1989), pp. 50–51. See, in particular, his discussion of the memorandum from McNamara on contingencies for military action against Cuba, referred by the Joint Chiefs to CINCLANT (Commander in Chief, Atlantic).

44. General Anatoli I. Gribkov and General William Y. Smith, *Operation ANADYR: U.S. and Soviet Generals Recount the Cuban Missile Crisis* (Chicago: Edition Q Publishers, 1994), pp. 62–63, and Appendix 1, Documents 1–3. See also Mark Kramer, "Tactical Nuclear Weapons, Soviet Command Authority, and the

Cuban Missile Crisis," *Cold War International History Project Bulletin*, No. 3 (Fall 1993): 40, 42–46; and James G. Blight, Bruce J. Allyn and David A. Welch, "Kramer vs. Kramer: Or, How Can You Have Revisionism in the Absence of Orthodoxy?" *Cold War International History Project Bulletin*, No. 3 (Fall 1993): 41, 47–50. The best evidence now suggests that, prior to October 22, Moscow had given to the commander of Soviet forces in Cuba, Gen. Pliyev, predelegated authority to use nuclear armed tactical missiles in the event of an American invasion.

45. On Soviet alerts during the Cuban missile crisis, see Richard K. Betts, *Nuclear Blackmail and Nuclear Balance* (Washington, D.C.: Brookings Institution, 1987), p. 120, and Bruce G. Blair, *The Logic of Accidental Nuclear War* (Washington, D.C.: Brookings Institution, 1993), pp. 23–24. On the U.S. DefCon II alert broadcast in the clear contrary to regulations, see Lebow and Stein, *We All Lost the Cold War*, p. 341.

46. Sagan, *Moving Targets*, p. 146.

47. McNamara, in Blight and Welch, *On the Brink*, pp. 52, 195.

48. Allison, *Essence of Decision*, p. 224.

49. Paul Bracken, "War Termination," in Carter, Steinbruner and Zraket, eds., *Managing Nuclear Operations*, pp. 197–216.

50. Richard K. Betts, "Surprise Attack and Preemption," in Graham T. Allison, Albert Carnesale and Joseph S. Nye, Jr., *Hawks, Doves and Owls: An Agenda for Avoiding Nuclear War* (New York: W.W. Norton, 1985), pp. 54–79.

51. Stephen M. Meyer, "Soviet Nuclear Operations," in Carter, Steinbruner and Zraket, eds., *Managing Nuclear Operations*, pp. 470–534. See also Ghulam Dastagir Wardak, comp., and Graham Hall Turbiville, Jr., gen. ed., *The Voroshilov Lectures: Materials from the Soviet General Staff Academy*, Vol. I (Washington, D.C.: National Defense University Press, 1989), esp. p. 247; Meyer, "Soviet Pespectives on the Paths to Nuclear War," in Allison, Carnesale and Nye, *Hawks, Doves and Owls*, pp. 167–205.

52. John G. Hines and Phillip A. Petersen, "NATO and the Changing Soviet Concept of Control for Theater War," in Stephen J. Cimbala, ed., *The Soviet Challenge in the 1990s* (Westport, Conn.: Praeger Publishers, 1989), pp. 65–122. Notwithstanding my not very prescient title for this volume, a number of the individual chapters, including this one, retain value for reading into Soviet strategy in the latter Cold War years.

53. For Cold War Soviet views on terminating a nuclear, or other, conflict, see Raymond L. Garthoff, *Deterrence and the Revolution in Soviet Military Doctrine* (Washington, D.C.: Brookings Institution, 1990), ch. 5; and Garthoff, "New Soviet Thinking on Conflict Limitation, Control, and Termination," in Stephen J. Cimbala and Sidney R. Waldman, eds., *Controlling and Ending Conflict: Issues Before and After the Cold War* (Westport, Conn.: Greenwood Press, 1992), pp. 65–94. On the Soviet view of limited nuclear war as of the 1980s see Edward L. Warner III, *Soviet Concepts and Capabilities for Limited Nuclear War: What We Know and How We Know It* (Santa Monica, Calif.: RAND, February 1989), Marshal N.V. Ogarkov, *Vsegda v gotovnosti k zashchite Otechestva* (Moscow: Voenizdat, 1982), p. 16, and Ogarkov, *Istoriya uchit bditel'nosti* (Moscow: Voenizdat, 1985), esp. pp. 89–90. This author has heard nothing from Russian military sources to suggest that the skepticism expressed by Ogarkov, about the likelihood of keeping any nuclear war

in Europe limited, is now passe in the MOD or in any Russian arm of service holding nuclear weapons.

54. Despite Europeans' relative lack of enthusiasm for flexible response above or below the nuclear threshold, NATO's potential for repelling the initial stages of any Warsaw Pact attack was, in the 1980s, far from negligible. See Kurt Gottfried and Bruce G. Blair, eds., *Crisis Stability and Nuclear War* (New York: Oxford University Press, 1988), ch. 9, esp. p. 229.

55. For these and other World War II cases see Paul Kecskemeti, *Strategic Surrender: The Politics of Victory and Defeat* (Stanford, Calif.: Stanford University Press, 1958).

56. Bevin Alexander, *The Future of Warfare* (New York: W.W. Norton, 1995) provides some excellent cases and resumes of pertinent theory; see esp. pp. 86–147 and 160–175.

57. Douglas Porch, "The French Army in the First World War," in Millet and Murray, eds., *Military Effectiveness, Vol. I*, pp. 190–229, esp. p. 201 and pp. 216–217.

58. George F. Kennan, *Russia and the West Under Lenin and Stalin* (New York: Mentor Books/New American Library, 1960, 1961), esp. chs. 7–8.

59. Michael R. Gordon and General Bernard E. Trainor, *The Generals' War: The Inside Story of the Conflict in the Gulf* (Boston: Little, Brown, 1995), pp. 419–423.

60. Ibid., p. 423.

61. John S.D. Eisenhower, *The Bitter Woods* (New York: G.P. Putnam's Sons, 1969), pp. 172–174.

62. Allied and German order of battle data for the Ardennes (Battle of the Bulge) campaign from December 16, 1944 to January 16, 1945 is given in Trevor N. Dupuy, David L. Bongard and Richard C. Anderson, Jr., *Hitler's Last Gamble: The Battle of the Bulge, December 1944–January 1945* (New York: HarperCollins, 1994), Appendix D, pp. 424–457.

63. Thomas M. Nichols, *The Sacred Cause: Civil-Military Conflict over Soviet National Security, 1917–1992* (Ithaca, N.Y.: Cornell University Press, 1993), esp. pp. 21–32.

64. Jervis, *The Meaning of the Nuclear Revolution*, pp. 191–192.

Chapter 8

The Danger of Nuclear Weapons Spread

INTRODUCTION

Because nuclear weapons have not been fired in anger since the destruction of Nagasaki by the second American atomic bomb, some expert and lay opinion now assumes that nuclear deterrence is tantamount to perpetual peace. Arguments in favor of the spread of nuclear weapons to more states have been based on the assumption that the fear of mass destruction is a necessary and sufficient deterrent to potential disrupters of the international system, to aspiring regional hegemonies and to a variety of rogue states not otherwise deterred by the prospect of defeat in battle. In the face of concerns expressed by proliferation nay-sayers, the yea-sayers respond that nuclear deterrence worked well enough in the Cold War and there is no reason to suppose that it will not work in the future.

In this chapter we consider some of the arguments made by optimists about nuclear proliferation: either those who regard it as desirable or those who consider it unavoidable and confinable, if messy and risky. These arguments are sometimes expertly composed and subtly made and cannot be dismissed out of hand. Against optimism about nuclear weapons spread, we argue that the conditions that obtained in the twentieth century that made nuclear deterrence work will not repeat themselves. In addition, the reasoning of nuclear optimists on some basic issues of theory and policy in international politics is well intended, but wrong. The present chapter explains why the spread of nuclear weapons, other weapons of mass destruction (WMD) and delivery systems in the twenty-first century resembles nothing so much as a dead volcano poised to erupt against confidence in deterrence and complacency about nuclear arms control.

NUCLEAR AND OTHER REALISM

Some theorists and policy makers now predict that the slow spread of nuclear weapons can be made compatible with future international peace and stability by mixing the same ingredients: realism and deterrence.[1] The argument that the post–Cold War world may be compatible with a hitherto unknown, and unacceptable, degree of nuclear weapons spread rests on some basic theoretical postulates about international relations. These basic assumptions are derived from the "realist" or neorealist school of international political thought.[2] The temptation to parse these arguments for fine points that distinguish among old realists, new realists and hemi-, demi- and semi-realists will be resisted here. We are interested in the realist-derived assumptions that are specifically related to nuclear proliferation. Realist principles have considerable explanatory power and predictive utility at a very high level of abstraction: thus their appeal to scholars. Realism also has an inherent pessimism about some aspects of international relations: thus its appeal to worldly heads of state and military planners.

Proponents of international realism confronted nuclear technology with mixed reactions. The nuclear revolution separated the accomplishment of military denial from the infliction of military punishment. The meaning of this for strategists was that military victory, defined prior to the nuclear age as the ability to prevail over opposed forces in battle, now was permissible only well below the level of total war. And less than total wars were risky as never before. Nuclear realists admit that these profound changes have taken place in the relationship between force and policy. They argue, however, that the new relationship between force and policy strengthens rather than weakens some perennial principles of international relations theory. Power is still king, but the king is now latent power in the form of risk manipulation and threat of war, instead of power actually displayed on the battlefield. Peace is now guaranteed by threat of war unacceptable in its social consequences, instead of being dependent upon the defender's credible threat to defeat the attacker's armed forces in battle.

Despite some attempts to reconcile political realism with nuclear weapons, the union remained a shotgun marriage. Military professionals remained unimpressed with the substitution of manipulation of risk for the actual ability to prevail in combat. Strategic theorists were frustrated by mutual vulnerability based on assured retaliation and the apparent futility of any defenses against nuclear weapons during the Cold War. Political leaders kept demanding refinements in nuclear war plans that would somehow make them less than totally self-defeating, including options for graduated attacks and for the preservation of some measure of deterrence into nuclear war itself. Fortunately the Cold War ended before either the United States or the Soviet Union could test the assumption of limited nuclear war.

Notwithstanding these tensions, realism supported nuclearism during the Cold War by affirming the significance of international power politics for global stability. Realists are skeptical that international stability and peace can depend upon negotiation, trust or the exploitation of common interests among states. Peace is the result of fear of war, or, where victory in combat at an acceptable cost is not possible, fear of unacceptable societal consequences due to war. Nuclear deterrence thus closed with realism on the ability of a threatened state or alliance to pose the credible threat of assured retaliation against any attacker. Retaliation having been assured, no sensible or rational attacker would strike. This logic would apply across the board to any possessor of nuclear weapons regardless of its culture, ideology, or leaders.

Nuclear Realism

The nuclear version of international realism has a number of intellectual and policy-prescriptive weaknesses. Four problem areas are (1) whether the realist view is based on exceptional cases, (2) whether the economic theories on which some realist arguments about deterrence stability are based can be transferred from economics to international politics, (3) whether realism can account for both general and immediate deterrence situations, and (4) whether rational decision making as conceived by realists is dependable for explanation and prediction of arms race and war-provoking behavior.

Atypical Cases

First, realist arguments for the possibility of a stable nuclear multipolar world are based on the Cold War experiences of the United States and the Soviet Union. The supposition is that, just as the U.S. and the Soviet political and military leaderships worked out rules of the road for crisis management and the avoidance of nuclear war, so too will new nuclear powers among the current non-nuclear states. However, there are reasons to doubt whether the U.S. and Soviet experiences can be repeated after the Cold War. First, the U.S.-Soviet nuclear relationship between 1945 and 1990 was also supported by bipolarity and by an approximate equality, although an asymmetrical one, in overall U.S. and Soviet military power. Neither bipolarity nor, obviously, U.S.-Russian global military equity is available to support stable relations in the post–Cold War world; in fact, both are irrelevant so long as Russia evolves in a democratic, capitalist direction and prefers cooperative U.S.-Russian foreign relations.

A second reason why the U.S. and Soviet Cold War experiences are unlikely to be repeated by future proliferators is that the relationship between political legitimacy and military control was secure in Moscow and in Washington during the Cold War. A politically tame military cannot be assumed for some plausible future additions to the list of nuclear powers. The issue here is not whether democracies are less warlike than dictatorships are. The question is whether the regime can impose either assertive or delegative military control over its armed forces, and, if it does, the consequences for its crisis management and normal nuclear operations.

Assertive control implies a great deal of civilian intervention in military operations and management; *delegative* control, more willingness to let the military have their own way on operational and organizational issues. Strict rules about nuclear custody are an example of assertive control. For example, in the early years of the nuclear age, atomic weapons were withheld from the military under normal conditions. An example of delegative control is the understanding among U.S. Cold War policy makers that, in the event of a nuclear attack disabling the president and/or the civilian chain of command, the U.S. deterrent would not be paralyzed. Military commanders could, under carefully defined and admittedly drastic conditions, launch in response to unambiguous indications of attack.[3]

Organizational process factors and other decision-making attributes of states with small, new nuclear arsenals may push their militaries toward doctrines that favor nuclear preemption.[4] First-strike–vulnerable forces may invite attack on themselves. Newly acquired nuclear arsenals may not be "fail safe" against accidental launch or military usurpation of civil command prerogative. Among nuclear aspirants in 1998, several states, including North Korea, Iran, Iraq (temporarily thwarted by UN inspections) and Libya, the distinction between "civil" and "military" was as opaque to many outside observers as it was to some of their own poorly informed citizens. In Pakistan, a declared nuclear power since May 1998, the military has run the nuclear weapons development program from the time of its inception to the present. Neither Indian nor Pakistani nuclear release protocols are clear to outside observers, and uncertainty marks U.S. understanding of "first use" or "no first use" doctrines in New Delhi and Islamabad. The possibility cannot be excluded that nuclear command authority rests de facto in the hands of brass hats, unaccountable to civil control, in any one or more of the new nuclear powers or nuclear aspiring states. For example, according to one U.S. study prepared for Lawrence Livermore National Laboratory in 1991:

The nuclear chain of command is likely to reflect the military's dominance in Pakistani decision making. Thus, although formal authority to launch a Pakistani nuclear strike could be expected to reside with the President (as does control over the nuclear program today), the Pakistani military is all but certain to obtain *de facto* control over nuclear weapons and the decision to use them. A future civilian government could ignore the military's advice on nuclear use only at its own peril.[5]

Another reason why the U.S.-Soviet experience may not be normative for newer nuclear powers is that in the U.S.-Soviet case there were no pieces of territory or other vital interests for which one of the sides was committed to go to war rather than to suffer defeat or stalemate. The two sides were generally satisfied by *bloc consolidation* and by *internal power balancing* instead of external adventurism and zero sum competition for territory or resources. The preceding observation does not imply that Cold War crises, such as those which occurred over Berlin and Cuba, were not dangerous. They were dangerous, but the danger was mitigated by the awareness that neither state had to sacrifice a vital piece of its own territory or its own national values (allies were another matter) in order to avoid war. What was at stake in the most dangerous U.S.-Soviet Cold War confrontations was "extended" deterrence, or the credibility of nuclear protection extended to allies, and not defense of the homeland per se.

System as Dependent Variable

The second major set of theoretical problems with nuclear realism lies in the adaptation of arguments from microeconomic theory to theories of interstate relations. Kenneth Waltz explicitly compares the behaviors of states in an international system to the behavior of firms in a market. As the market forces firms into a common mode of rational decision making in order to survive, so too does the international system, according to Waltz, dictate similar constraints upon the behavior of states. The analogy, however, is wrong. The international system does not dominate its leading state actors; leading states define the parameters of the system. The international system, unlike the theoretical free market, is *subsystem dominant*. The "system" or composite of interactions among units is the cross product of the separate behaviors of the units.[6]

International politics is a game of oligopoly, in which the few rule the many. Because this is so, there cannot be any "system" to which the leading oligopolists, unlike the remainder of the states, are subject against their wishes. The system is driven by the preferred ends and means of its leading members on issues that are perceived as vital interests to those states or as important interests, although not necessary vital.[7] Realists, especially structural realists who emphasize the number of powers and their polarities as determinants of peace and war, assume that some "system" of interactions exists independently of the states which make it up. This is a *useful heuristic* for theorists, but a very mistaken view of the way in which *policy is actually made in international affairs*. Because realists insist upon reification of the system independently of the principal actors within the system, they miss the subsystemic dominance built into the international order. Napoleon Bonaparte and Adolph Hitler, for example, saw the international order not as a system that would constrain their objectives and ambitions, but as a series of swinging doors, each awaiting a fateful, aggressive push.

An important test of whether meaningful theory can proceed on the basis of the realist, or realpolitik, premise of "system" separateness, or whether domestic political forces must also be taken into account by theorists, is to test realist and domestic/constrained hypotheses against historical evidence. According to Bruce Bueno de Mesquita and David Lalman, the realist perspective as formalized in their models is not supported by the past two centuries' experience of interstate behavior.[8] The authors deduce an "acquiescence impossibility" theorem which shows that, in a logically developed game structure based on realist assumptions, it is impossible for one state to acquiesce to the demands of another "regardless of the beliefs held by the rivals, regardless of the initial demand made by one of the states, and regardless of initial endowments of capabilities, coalitional support, propensities to take risks, or anything else."[9] None of the deductions derived from the realist or neorealist versions of their international interactions game, according to Bueno de Mesquita and Lalman, were supported in the empirical data set that included 707 dyadic interactions.[10]

One might argue, in defense of realists on this point, that the assumption of system determinism is a useful falsehood. It allows for parsimony in expression and in focus on the essential attributes of the international system. But, again, the assumption of "apartness" of the system and its essential state or non-state actors is only useful, and methodologically defensible, if it leads to insights which are both accurate and not otherwise attainable. Neither exceptional accuracy nor exceptional attainability of insight has been demonstrated by realists for the assumption of system and actor "apartness." This is probably one reason why some realist thinkers did not exclude what Waltz, in another study, refers to as first and second image variables.[11] Realism fails to explain the high degree of international cooperation which takes place despite a legally anarchic international order because of the biased manner in which realism deals with imperfect information. According to Bueno de Mesquita and Lalman:

In the realist world, imperfect information can only encourage violence. Incorrect beliefs about the intentions of rivals can only steer disputes away from negotiation (or the status quo) and toward the blackmail inherent in a capitulation or the tragedy inherent in a war. Incorrect beliefs, secrecy, misperception, misjudgment, and miscalculation are routine features of human intercourse. In that sense, a realist world could be a dangerous world indeed.[12]

As Robert Jervis has noted, one can divide international systems theorists according to whether the "system" is treated as an independent variable, as a dependent variable, or as both.[13] Waltz contends that the most important causes of international behavior reside in the structure of the international system, (i.e., in the number of powers and in their positions relative to one another).[14] Jervis notes that Waltz's structure omits some important variables and processes that are neither at the system or actor level: for example, technology and the degree and kind of international interdependence.[15]

There is another difficulty inherent in Waltz's approach. System polarity is virtually identical with system structure in his analysis. But this near-identity of polarity and structure is flawed. Polarity is more the *result* of past state and non-state actor behaviors than it is the *cause* of future behaviors. Cold War bipolarity was the result of World War II, of nuclear weapons, and of the fact that leaders *perceived correctly* the futility of starting World War III in Europe. Leaders' perceptions of the balance of power are an intervening variable between polarity and outcomes such as stability, including peace or war. In other words, leaders' perceptions, including their risk aversion or risk acceptance, are the *efficient causes* for international behavior; "systems" and polarity are *formal* causes.

The difference between efficient and formal causes is important for theories that purport to be empirically testable. Formal causes are proved by an abstract process that follows a deductive chain of reasoning. Efficient causes are demonstrated by observation of temporal sequences and behavioral effects. International systems theorists who emphasize the importance of structure have been more successful at proving formal than efficient causes. There is merit in doing so, and Waltz and others who have argued from this perspective deserve credit for their rigor and for the insights derived from their perspective.[16]

The danger for international systems theorists lies in transferring inferences from the realm of deductive logic to the world of policy explanation and prediction. For example, Waltz argues both that (1) because there were only two Cold War superpowers, each had to balance against the other at virtually any point, and (2) disputes among their allies could not drag the United States and Soviets into war because they could satisfy their deterrence requirements through internal balancing, rather than alliance aggregation.[17] The first argument is at least partly inconsistent with the second, and neither is confirmed by Cold War evidence. The United States and Soviets sometimes conceded important disputes to one another in order to avoid the possibility of inadvertent war or escalation, as in the U.S. refusal to expand the ground war in Vietnam on account of expected Soviet and Chinese reactions. And allies sometimes did drag the superpowers into crisis and under credible threat of war, as the Israelis and Egyptians did in 1973.

General versus Immediate Deterrence

The preceding discussion also points to the third general set of problems with realist theories and nuclear weapons spread. The structure of the international system is not related to *general* deterrence in the same way as it is related to *immediate* deterrence. According to Patrick M. Morgan, the need for general deterrence is inherent in the normal day-to-day relations of states, based on the distribution of power and states' assumptions about one another's intentions. General deterrence is the latent possibility that any state may opt for war within an anarchic or non-hierarchical international order.[18] Immediate deterrence is a situation in which one side has actually made specific threats against another, the second side perceives itself threatened, and a significant likelihood of war exists in the minds of leaders in at least one of the two states. For example, the onset of a crisis often signifies a failure of general deterrence, but as yet immediate deterrence has not failed because states have not yet abandoned diplomacy and crisis management for battle.

It makes sense to assume that there might be a strong correlation between success or failure in general deterrence and system attributes such as distributions of actor capabilities and objectives. However, the relationship between international systems and failures of immediate deterrence is much more indirect. State and sub-state variables, including the attributes of individuals, groups and bureaucratic organizations, are among the filters through which any "system" forces must pass before those forces are manifest in state decisions and policies. The distinction between general and immediate deterrence helps to explain why perfectly logical deductions from deterrence theory based on rationality postulates often fly in the face of states' actual behavior.[19]

The significance of the distinction between general and immediate deterrence is illustrated by the Cuban missile crisis. The decision by Khrushchev to put Soviet medium and intermediate range ballistic missiles into Cuba was intended, among other objectives, to diminish the publicly acknowledged (by U.S. government officials) gap between U.S. and Soviet strategic nuclear capabilities. Khrushchev's decision, made in the spring of 1962 after consulting very few key advisors, represented a failure of general deterrence. The Soviet leadership had decided to risk the emplacement of its nuclear weapons outside of Soviet territory and in the Western Hemisphere for the first time. However, it was not yet a failure of immediate deterrence. Immediate deterrence was not involved in Khrushchev's clandestine deployment program because the deployments were deliberately kept secret. Had Khrushchev carried through his original plans, he would have completed the missile deployments and then announced their existence.

In that eventuality, the mere existence of Khrushchev's missiles on Cuban soil, however threatening it seemed to U.S. policy makers, would not have created a situation of immediate deterrence. Only the completion of deployments followed by a coercive threat would move the situation from a failure of general deterrence (Soviets make a dangerous move in the arms race) to one of immediate deterrence (for example, Soviets now demand that the United States and allies leave West Berlin immediately). The preceding supposition is of the "what if" or counterfactual kind; we may never know the full story of Khrushchev's motives for the missile deployments.[20] The actual shift from a general to an immediate deterrence situation took place on October 22 when President Kennedy ordered the Soviet missiles removed from Cuba, announced that the United States was imposing a quarantine on Soviet shipments to Cuba, and stated that a nuclear missile launched from Cuba against any target in the Western Hemisphere would call forth a full U.S. retaliatory response against the Soviet Union.

Realist perspectives help to explain the background to general deterrence failure in this instance, but they do little to clarify why the U.S. and Soviet political leaderships chose as they did. If the international power positions of states yield unambiguous inferences about their crisis management strategies, Khrushchev should never have dared to put missiles into Cuba. And the United States, once the missiles had been discovered, need not have hesitated to invade Cuba or to launch an air strike to destroy the missile sites, collocated air defense sites, and other nuclear-capable weapons platforms deployed in Cuba by Moscow.[21] Realists would argue, against the preceding statement, that nuclear weapons made the Soviets and the Americans cautious during the Cuban missile crisis. The danger created by nuclear weapons helped to end the crisis without war, following the logic and against my earlier argument.

However, realist arguments will not work in this context. Nuclear weapons did not make the crisis easier to manage, but harder. They added to the risk of escalation, to be sure, and leaders were well aware of these risks. The United States deliberately and, some would say, successfully manipulated the risk of escalation and war in order to force Khrushchev's withdrawal of the missiles. But the argument for nuclear coercion as the path to Cuban crisis settlement, will not work because nuclear weapons, and the Soviet sense of inferiority in the nuclear arms race, were major causes for the crisis.[22] If it is contended that nuclear weapons helped to resolve the crisis, that is true only as a historical tautology: having caused it or helped to cause it and by making it more dangerous, they played a part in ending it.

Realism aided by an appreciation for historical serendipity and indeterminacy fares better in explaining the Cold War relationship between nuclear weapons and peace. For example, John Lewis Gaddis contends that nuclear weapons influenced post–World War II international relations in at least four ways. First, nuclear weapons helped to support an already existing reluctance of the great powers to wage war against one another. Second, states that possessed nuclear weapons became more risk averse. Third, nuclear weapons did not create bipolarity after World War II, but they did prolong its life, and so, too, helped to prolong stability. Fourth, nuclear weapons helped to perpetuate the Cold War by saving the United States, the Soviet Union and their allies military expenditures on conventional forces, expenditures which, if necessary, might have forced rethinking of Cold War assumptions sooner.[23]

Paul Bracken has suggested that there were actually two cold wars, with respect to the relationship between nuclear weapons and international political stability.[24] The first period, until about 1967, was marked by a number of U.S.-Soviet diplomatic crises (Berlin, Taiwan Straits, Cuba, Middle East) and was extremely dangerous. It was during these first two decades of the nuclear age that the superpowers worked out rules of the road for crisis management and for avoiding unnecessarily provocative behavior that might lead to accidental or inadvertent war. In contrast, the interval from 1967 to the end of the Cold War is marked by fewer serious U.S.-Soviet crises (the 1983 "war scare" period being an arguable exception) and by evidence of nuclear learning on both sides, including their professional militaries, about the limits of brinkmanship. This author would, with due respect to Professor Bracken's point, prefer to establish the line of demarcation at 1964: the ouster of Khrushchev, on the heels of his disastrous Cuban missile gambit.

This summary shows that nuclear stability attributed by realists was purchased with significant trade-offs. For example, Gaddis' fourth form of nuclear influence acknowledges that *political* relations between the United States and the Soviet Union remained adversarial longer than necessary, in part due to ingrained habits of *military* hangover. To the realists' contention that nuclear weapons made war less likely because fighting became more dangerous, Gaddis' fourth argument for nuclear relevancy points to the downside of that contention. The very weapons of mass destruction which some would contend were instruments of deterrence or peace were also causes of U.S. and Soviet leaders' fears of devastating surprise attack. The capabilities of these weapons were so unprecedented that the very fact of their being targeted at another state made a relationship hostile in military-operational terms even when it had passed into a stage of nonhostility in policy.

Decision Rationality

As anticipated in our comments above, a fourth problematical aspect of realism as the basis for optimism about nuclear weapons spread is the question of rational decision making. The assumption of rational decision making is a necessary condition for making testable hypotheses and verifiable generalizations about social behavior. In and of itself, the rationality postulate does no harm. It becomes dangerous, however, when it is assumed that particular notions of rational decision making can be transferred from one culture or society to another. U.S. policy makers have on more than one occasion substituted assumptions for evidence or intelligence about the behavioral propensities or mind-sets of foreign leaders. For example, throughout the summer and early autumn of 1962, U.S. leaders simply assumed that Khrushchev would not dare to put Soviet missiles into Cuba because it was illogical and too risk acceptant, by U.S. reasoning, for the Soviet leader to have done so. As another example, American policy makers between 1965 and 1968 assumed that selective bombing of targets in North Vietnam would increase the pressure on the regime in Hanoi to withdraw its support from the National Liberation Front in South Vietnam.

When assumptions based on U.S. decision rationality are not supported by experience, leaders sometimes cling to the assumptions or to their supporting logic and blame the other side for "irrational" or illogical behavior. Khrushchev's deployment of missiles in Cuba in the face of U.S. warnings against doing so has been described as irrational by many American, and even some Soviet, sources. Yet in his memoirs Khrushchev gives two reasons: equalizing the balance of nuclear power and deterring U.S. attack on Cuba, which make plain sense from his political and military vantage point. Similarly, the North Vietnamese reaction to U.S. bombing from 1965 to 1968 was to increase their support to the NLF and their commitment to ultimate victory over the government of South Vietnam and its American supporters. The U.S. bombing could destroy value targets in North Vietnam, but it could not remove from Hanoi its capability to support insurgency in the south. Nor could bombing impose any unacceptable cost to North Vietnamese military capabilities for large-scale, conventional ground warfare, later put to use in the final push by Hanoi against Saigon in 1975.

U.S. policy makers assumed in July 1990 that it would not be prudent for Saddam Hussein to attack and occupy Kuwait. The Iraqi leader was thought by most American prewar assessments to be using coercive diplomacy against Kuwait on account of its uncooperative oil pricing behavior. Saddam Hussein also miscalculated Bush administration perceptions of U.S. and allied interests in the region, and he misestimated U.S. domestic politics as still being caught up in a Vietnam syndrome that would preclude President Bush from the actual use of force. Even after weeks of pounding from the U.S. and allied coalition air forces in January 1991, Saddam disbelieved that the United States would initiate a ground war on account of fear of excessive numbers of American and allied casualties.

Looking inside the heads of enemy leaders, especially those of idiosyncratic and impulsive dictators, is never easy. But the preceding examples hold some pertinent social science lessons. Explanatory and predictive approaches that may suffice for issue areas such as welfare, urban development, education and other largely domestic matters are not necessarily optimal for explaining behavior pertinent to war and peace. In these other issues with less than ultimate stakes, it makes sense to base predictions of future behavior on *typical* past behavior and on culturally shared norms and values. However, in international behavior related to war and peace, it is more important to be able to explain and predict *atypical* behaviors between states and leaders who do *not share* cultural norms and values. In other words, the marginal utility of being able to explain typical, as opposed to atypical, behavior declines as the situation moves from one of general to immediate deterrence (see above).

SPREADING MISSILES AND WEAPONS OF MASS DESTRUCTION

The Present Danger

The spread of nuclear weapons is not an isolated danger, but one heavily bound up with the proliferation of other weapons of mass destruction (chemical and biological) and of the means for their delivery. As Richard K. Betts has noted, the phrase "weapons of mass destruction" is something of a misnomer: these are not all of a piece. Nuclear weapons are highly destructive but difficult and expensive to make; chemical weapons, inexpensive and simple to make, but not on the scale of destructiveness of nuclear or biological weapons. Biological weapons are both easy to make (biotechnology capable of manufacturing pharmaceuticals also provides the tools for biological weapons) and capable of inflicting widespread societal damage even in small doses.[25] Biological weapons, like nuclear weapons but unlike chemical weapons, are not optimal against front-line troops but might be ideal war stoppers used against the logistics tail, communications and infrastructure that supports those troops. It's difficult to move and store ammunition, fuel, spare parts and communications gear when you are suited up in bio-hazard gear, even if you have escaped actual contamination.[26]

That having been said, the problem of nuclear proliferation is sufficiently serious in its own right. We first summarize (in Table 8.1) the status of nuclear proliferation as of this writing. We then consider some of the specific states of concern, with regard to possible threats to U.S. security or on account of their location in dangerous neighborhoods.

The status of North Korea has been mired in a complicated shell game of U.S. political relations with both Koreas, of bureaucratic politics on the American home front, and of a confrontationally oriented U.S. government approach to North Korea, up to the very edge of a near outbreak of war in 1994.[27] North Korea's standoff with the United States and the International Atomic Energy Agency (IAEA) over its nuclear production program, culminating in the Framework Agreement of 1994 intended to cap that program, is well known.[28] During the 1980s and 1990s, North Korea was able to develop a complete nuclear fuel cycle, including a capability for the production of plutonium at its Yongbyon nuclear research center. A plutonium production reactor became operational in 1986 with refueling in 1989, making available weapons-grade plutonium for at least one nuclear weapon. North Korea was also building a 50-megawatt reactor at Yongbyon and a 200-megawatt reactor at Taechon before construction was halted under the Framework Agreement. The 50-megawatt reactor could have produced enough plutonium for North Korea to fabricate between 7 and 10 nuclear weapons *per year*.[29]

North Korea was also developing a diversified industry for the production of ballistic missiles of various ranges, including missiles for export. North Korea in 1996 deployed with its forces several hundred SCUD-B and SCUD-C ballistic missiles with maximum ranges of 300 and 500 kilometers respectively. Its Nodong-1 medium range (estimated 1,000 km with a 1,000 kg payload) ground-mobile, liquid-propelled missile was first tested in 1990 and entered into service in 1994. By December 1994 according to some reports, between 12 and 18 Nodong-1 missiles were in service.[30] A follow-on Nodong-2 with increased range and reduced payload has been deployed: estimated range is 1300 to 1500 km with a payload from 500 to 750 kg.[31] North Korea has reportedly also deployed the Taepodong 1 medium range ballistic missile with an estimated range of 2,000 km with a single conventional or nuclear warhead.[32]

During the summer of 1998 North Korea test fired a three-stage ballistic missile rocket over the Sea of Japan. The DPRK government described the test as an intended satellite launch that was less than completely successful, but some U.S. observers drew the conclusion that

Table 8.1
Nuclear Proliferation: Status and Summary Indicators

Country	Delivery Systems	Warheads	Total Warheads
United States			
Deployed ICBMs and SLBMs	1,165	6,227	
Bombers (START I Counting Rules)	315	1,731	
Other Warheads Estimated		4,112	
Total Warheads			12,070
Russia			
Deployed ICBMs and SLBMs	1,392	6,454	
Bombers (START I Counting Rules)	117	908	
Other Warheads Estimated		15,138	
Total Warheads			22,500
China			
ICBMs and SLBMs	44	44	
Other Missiles	300–400	300–400	
Total Warheads			> 400
France			
Total Warheads			> 450
United Kingdom			
Total Warheads			260

India	
Total Warheads	~ 70
Israel	
Total Warheads	> 100
Pakistan	
Total Warheads	~ 15

Notes:

1. India and Pakistan declared themselves nuclear powers after each completed a series of tests in May 1998. India is estimated to have 60 to 80 weapons and Pakistan 10 to 15. Neither state is a member of the Non-Proliferation Treaty (NPT).

2. Israel is thought to have between 70 and 125 weapons. Israel is not a signatory of NPT.

3. North Korea's nuclear program is supposedly frozen under International Atomic Energy Agency (IAEA) safeguards. In 1994 Pyongyang signed the Agreed Framework with the United States, calling for North Korea to freeze and subsequently give up all parts of its nuclear weapons program. In return, the United States promised to arrange for North Korea to receive two 1,000-megawatt light-water reactors (LWRS), plus annual allotments of 500,000 tons of heavy fuel oil until the first LWR is completed. Implementation of the Agreed Framework has been assigned to the Korean Peninsula Energy Development Organization (KEDO), also including South Korea, Japan and the European Union.

4. Iran is a member of NPT. The United States suspects that Iran seeks a nuclear weapons program and has tried to prevent other states from providing Teheran with pertinent technology or know-how. Russia agreed in 1995 not to sell uranium enrichment technology to Iran, and China promised in 1997 to end civil nuclear cooperation with Iran.

5. According to UN Security Council Resolution 687, the UN Special Commission for Iraq (UNSCOM) and IAEA were to verify the complete elimination of Iraq's nuclear, chemical and biological weapons, its ballistic missiles, and its means for producing these weapons and delivery systems. After U.S. bombing attacks on Iraq in late 1998, Iraqi head of state Sadism Hussein ejected UNSCOM from the country and it is unclear as of this writing when, or if, inspections can resume.

6. Libya is a member of NPT, but the United States maintains that the regime nevertheless wants to acquire nuclear weapons.

Sources: Updated and adapted from: David B. Thomson, *A Guide to the Nuclear Arms Control Treaties* (Los Alamos, N.M.: Los Alamos National Laboratory, LA-UR-99-31-73, July 1999), pp. 318–319; Arms Control Association, Fact Sheet, *The State of Nuclear Proliferation* (Washington, D.C.: May, 1998); Scott Ritter, *Endgame: Solving the Iraq Problem—Once and for All* (New York: Simon and Schuster, 1999), esp. pp. 217–224; Commission to Assess the Ballistic Missile Threat to the United States (Rumsfeld Commission), *Report* (Executive Summary) (Washington, D.C., July 15, 1998); and Federation of American Scientists, *Nuclear Forces Guide*, http://www.fas.org.nuke/guide/china/index.html.

Table 8.2
North Korean Ballistic Missiles

Missile System	Range/Payload
SCUD-B	300 km/single conventional or chemical warhead
SCUD-C	550 km/single conventional warhead
Nodong-1	1,300 km/single conventional chemical or nuclear warhead
Nodong-2	1,500 km/single conventional chemical or nuclear warhead
Taepodong-1	2,000 km/single conventional chemical or nuclear warhead

Source: Patrick M. O'Donogue, *Theater Missile Defense in Japan: Implications for the U.S.-China-Japan Strategic Relationship* (Carlisle Barracks, Pa.: U.S. Army War College, Strategic Studies Institute, September 2000), p. 6.

North Korea had demonstrated a prototype capability for missile attacks well beyond the tactical or theater range. According to the Commission to Assess the Ballistic Missile Threat to the United States in its 1998 report to Congress, a North Korean decision to rapidly deploy the Taepodong 2 ballistic missile might not be known to U.S. intelligence very far in advance of the decision to launch. The capabilities of Taepodong 2 once deployed, according to the Commission, are potentially strategic in reach and impact:

This missile could reach major cities and military bases in Alaska and the smaller, westernmost islands in the Hawaiian chain. Light-weight variations of the TD-2 could fly as far as 10,000 km, placing at risk western U.S. territory in an arc extending northwest from Phoenix, Arizona to Madison, Wisconsin.[33]

A summary of some attributes of North Korea's currently deployed ballistic missiles appears in Table 8.2.

An important aspect of North Korea's ballistic missile program is that it is designed for export as well as for Pyongyang's own defense needs. Hundreds of SCUD missiles have been provided by North Korea to countries in the Middle East, including Iran, and North Korea is already marketing the Nodong for export. The U.S. Department of Defense estimates that, thus far, North Korea has not become an international supplier of nuclear, chemical or biological weapons technology, despite its aggressive marketing of missiles and missile technology. Pyongyang has a substantial chemical weapons capability and limited facilities for producing biological weapons.[34]

North Korea's ballistic missile export program has enhanced the threat to stability in Southwest Asia. Iran acquired SCUD-B missiles from Libya and North Korea and SCUD-C missiles from the latter in the 1980s. During just three years of the Iran-Iraq war, between 1985 and 1988, Iran fired almost 100 SCUD-B missiles at Iraq. In addition to obtaining ballistic missiles from North Korea, Iran is attempting to set up its own missile production capability. Acquisition of the North Korean Nodong missile would permit Iran to attack targets in Israel, much of Saudi Arabia and the Trucial States, Turkey, Russia and other former Soviet states, Pakistan and India.[35] Iran's original reason for acquiring ballistic missiles was to employ them in its protracted war against Iraq during the 1980s. Having acquired the taste for technology and having taken note of Iraq's post–Desert Storm weakness in the 1990s, Iran now reasonably aspires to the status of first-among-equals among Gulf states. In addition to its ballistic missile capabilities, Iran has Chinese-supplied cruise missiles, artillery and aircraft capable of delivering chemical and biological weapons, and Russian-built SU-24 fighter-bombers that can deliver nuclear weapons.[36] Rumors of Russian-Iranian nuclear cooperation and of leakage of nuclear weapons experts from the former Soviet Union into Iran are frequent in U.S. and other media sources.

The nuclear coming-out parties in Islamabad and New Delhi, added to Israel's de facto but unacknowledged nuclear status, add to uncertainty with regard to the relationship between nuclear weapons and regional conflicts. Pakistan and India have had several diplomatic crises growing out of their disagreements over the political status of Kashmir. This conflict is not likely to deescalate in the near term, although there is some evidence that the two sides have begun to discuss some rules of the road related to crisis management: e.g., mutual guarantees that neither will strike at the other's nuclear forces or facilities at the outset of an otherwise conventional war. Israel's nuclear deterrent also exists in a regional hot spot, and a Middle Eastern nuclear arms race between Israel and Iraq (or a possible war) was postponed by the latter's defeat in the Gulf war of 1991. Both Iran and Iraq still seek to become nuclear powers and Tehran is building toward a long-range ballistic missile force. Both Iran and Iraq consider the United States and Israel as enemies of first resort. On the other hand, each distrusts the other and aspires to regional hegemony. Life could get interesting in the Middle East/South Asia region during the next decade or two. Summary data on the suspected nuclear inventories of India, Israel and Pakistan as of the turn of the century appear in Table 8.3.

Can Deterrence Still Work, and When?

The marriage of nuclear and other weapons of mass destruction to long-range ballistic or cruise missiles expands the capabilities of aspiring regional hegemonies and of state or non-state actors determined for various reasons to undo the international status quo. Even with short-range

Table 8.3
Nuclear Arsenals of India, Israel and Pakistan, 1999–2000

Possible Nuclear Delivery System	Year Deployed	Maximum Range (km)	Launcher Total
		India	
Missiles			
Prithvi (Army/Air Force Version)	1995	150/250	100
Agni	Testing	2,500	unknown
Aircraft			
Jaguar	—	850	97
MIG-27 Flogger	1986	390	148
Strategic nuclear weapons (total) = 0; nonstrategic nuclear weapons (total) = 60+			
		Israel	
Missiles			
Jericho 1	1973	500	~ 50
Jericho 2	1990	1,500	~ 50
Aircraft			
F-4E 2000 Phantom	—	1,600	50
F-16 Falcon	1980	630	205
Strategic nuclear weapons (total) = 0; nonstrategic nuclear weapons (total) = 100+			
		Pakistan	
Missiles			
Hatf 1	~ 1995	80	18
Hatf 2	Testing	300	unknown
Hatf 3	Testing	820	unknown
M-11 (DF-11, CSS-7)	1992 (not deployed)	300	40
Shaheen 1	tested 1998	720	unknown
Shaheen 2	tested 1999	2,000	unknown
Ghauri	tested 1998	1,500	unknown
Aircraft			
F-16 Falcon	1983	630	34
Strategic nuclear weapons (total) = 0; nonstrategic nuclear weapons (total) = 15–25			

Source: Center for Defense Information, *Current World Nuclear Arsenals*, July 20, 2000, http://www.cdi/org/issues/proliferation and the author.

ballistic missiles of the SCUD-B or SCUD-C range and accuracy, states capable of producing chemical and biological, not to mention nuclear, weapons can wreak havoc against their regional neighbors. Iraq's military buildup prior to the Gulf war of 1991 is a case in point. The world was fortunate that Saddam Hussein's exhausted exchequer motivated his attack on Kuwait in 1990 instead of five years later. Iraq's massive military establishment included a multi-pronged strategy for acquiring nuclear weapons and a substantial chemical and biological weapons arsenal. Iraq's nuclear program was, according to authoritative sources, "massive" and "for most practical purposes fiscally unconstrained."[37] The pre–Desert Storm Iraqi nuclear program was also "closer to fielding a nuclear weapon, and less vulnerable to destruction by precision bombing than Coalition air commanders and planners or U.S. intelligence specialists realized before Desert Storm."[38] Coalition target lists on January 16 included two suspect nuclear production facilities; postwar UN inspectors uncovered more than 20 sites related to Iraq's nuclear program, including 16 described as "main facilities."[39]

In addition to the uncertainties surrounding Iraq's prewar nuclear weapons program, Saddam Hussein's mobile SCUD missiles played havoc with coalition intelligence during Desert Storm and threatened to cause a political crisis within the anti-Iraqi alliance. SCUD attacks on Israeli cities created the possibility that Tel Aviv might retaliate, thus bringing Israel directly into the war and giving Saddam a wedge issue to divide Arab members of the U.S.-led coalition from others. According to the U.S. Air Force commissioned *Gulf War Air Power Survey*:

Efforts by Coalition air forces to suppress Iraqi launches of Scud missiles against Israel, Saudi Arabia, and other Persian Gulf nations during Desert Storm ran into many of the same problems evident in the case of the Iraqis' nuclear weapons program. Key portions of the target set—notably the pre-surveyed launch sites and hiding places used by the mobile launchers—were not identified before 17 January, and, even in the face of intense efforts to find and destroy them, the mobile launchers proved remarkably elusive and survivable.[40]

Soviet exercises with SCUDs in Eastern Europe and Iraqi practices during the Iran-Iraq war suggested to coalition air war planners that a sufficient number of prelaunch signatures and adequate time might be available to permit attacks on mobile launchers, before they fired, by patrolling aircraft. Iraqi countermeasures disappointed these expectations: their Gulf war use of mobile SCUDs, compared to earlier cases, reduced prelaunch set-up times, avoided telltale electromagnetic emissions that gave away locations, and deployed large numbers of decoys in order to confuse coalition targeters.[41]

The case of Iraq is instructive for optimists about the stability of a new world order marked by proliferation of weapons of mass destruction and modern delivery systems. Consider how different the problem facing the United States would have been if Iraq had invaded Kuwait in 1996 instead of 1990. The United States in 1990 did not face an Iraqi adversary already equipped with usable nuclear weapons. The United States had available for Desert Storm the large, forward-deployed forces built up in the Cold War years for a theater-strategic campaign against the Soviet Union and its Warsaw Pact allies. The Soviet Union under Gorbachev decided with some reluctance to support the UN authorization for the forcible expulsion from Kuwait of its former ally in Baghdad. Iraq's unwillingness to employ chemical or biological weapons against the United States was probably related to its expectation that a U.S. nuclear retaliation might follow, to which Iraq could not respond in kind. An Iraq in 1996 (absent Desert Storm) possessing nuclear charges capable of delivery by air or missile, even over distances of several hundred kilometers, could have posed a threat against outside intervention by the United States and its NATO allies, or against regional antagonists like Saudi Arabia and Israel, very different from the threat it posed in 1990.

The preceding statement seems almost self-evident but there is more than a self-evident point built into it. Iraq successfully concealed from the most technically complex intelligence systems in the world the prewar location of most of the installations related to its nuclear weapons program. Iraqi mobile SCUDs confounded coalition air war planners to the extent that there exists not even a *single* documented case of mobile SCUD destruction by coalition fixed-wing aircraft.[42] Notably, this level of frustration marked the efforts of the winning side in a very one-sided military contest: an essentially post-industrial strategy for warfare against a static defensive strategy, accompanied by political ineptitude in Baghdad of the highest order.[43] In addition, the United States and its allies had five months to build up forces, collect intelligence and plan countermeasures against Saddam's anticipated moves while Iraqi forces inexplicably squatted down in the Kuwaiti Theater of Operations. All these considerations point to the uniqueness of the environment surrounding Desert Storm and contain tacit warnings about the potential mischief of a future Saddam, strategically tutored and more decisive.

The U.S. inability or unwillingness to deter Iraq's invasion of Kuwait in 1990 contains another warning about realist optimism and proliferation. The basic maxims of deterrence learned during the Cold War years may have to be rethought, or in some cases rejected outright, in the remainder of the century and thereafter. Nuclear weapons and war avoidance worked together during the Cold War because U.S.-Soviet strategic nuclear bipolarity enforced a *connection between basic and extended deterrence*. One could predict the degree of vulnerability to coercion to be expected of U.S. allies by deduction from the stability of the

U.S.-Soviet relationship itself. U.S. strategic nuclear forces were coupled to the fates of European and Japanese allies who could not then be coerced into submission by the Soviets, nor by third parties allied to the Soviets, without accepting unknown risks of escalation into confrontation with the U.S. deterrent.

The collapse of bipolarity after the Cold War diminishes the link between basic and extended deterrence: one can make fewer reliable predictions about states' behaviors on the basis of "system" variables. The significance of this theoretical construct for the practical problem of nonproliferation is illustrated by then Secretary of Defense William J. Perry's comment that future terrorists or rogue regimes "may not buy into our deterrence theory. Indeed, they may be madder than MAD."[44] Deterrence theory á la the Cold War, based on realist premises that assume risk-averse and cost-benefit sensitive leaders, may no longer hold tenable for leaders armed with weapons of mass destruction and motivated by "irrational" or "illogical" objectives by at least U.S. standards. As Keith B. Payne has explained:

Assuming that deterrence will "work" because the opponent will behave sensibly is bound to be the basis for a future surprise. I do not know whether our expectations of a generically sensible opponent will next be dashed by a so-called rogue state, such as North Korea, or by another challenger. That they will be dashed, however, is near certain. As we move into the second nuclear age and confront opponents with whom we are relatively unfamiliar, assumptions of a generically sensible foe almost certainly will ensure surprises.[45]

In addition, most academic or policy analyses have focused on dyadic relationships that are not complicated by triangulation or indirect deterrence.[46] Current U.S. strategy relies upon the ability to conduct one and one-half nearly simultaneous major theater wars against rogue states or aspiring regional hegemonies by exploiting the superior reach, battlefield knowledge and striking power of U.S. high-technology, conventional weapons. Future rogues or other regional aggressors might seek to neutralize the U.S. conventional deterrent by acquiring weapons of mass destruction and by threatening U.S. forces, regional allies, or even non-involved states. Threats to use nuclear weapons against noninvolved states' cities might play against U.S. or allied fears of civilian casualties. As Robert Harkavy has noted:

But conceivably, an Iraq or Iran could threaten to use nuclear weapons against other countries—perhaps those not aligned with the United States or nominally under its extended deterrence protection—banking on American reluctance to countenance massive civilian casualties anywhere. Either Iran or Iraq could indeed threaten to attack the other with nuclear weapons. Iraq could so threaten its own Kurdish cities; Iran could threaten cities to its north in the new Central Asian nations.[47]

Another reason why deterrence might not work in a post–Cold War, proliferated world is that reliable and timely intelligence and warning might not be available about the intentions or capabilities of rogues with WMD and ballistic missile capabilities. According to the Rumsfeld Commission, the U.S. intelligence community had great difficulty assessing the pace and scope of North Korea's Nodong missile program and may have very little advance warning of the deployment of Taepodong 2.[48] The commission report states that Iran has a nuclear weapons program intended to produce nuclear weapons as soon as possible, and the technical capability to demonstrate an ICBM-range ballistic missile similar to the TD-2 within five years of a decision by Iran to do so. Unfortunately, according to the Rumsfeld Commission, the United States is unlikely to know whether Iran has produced nuclear weapons "until after the fact."[49] An Iranian ballistic missile with a 10,000 km range "could hold the U.S. at risk in an arc extending northeast of a line from Philadelphia, Pennsylvania, to St. Paul, Minnesota."[50] The Rumsfeld Commission concluded, with regard to the possible dangers presented by short- or no-warning ballistic missile attacks and WMD proliferation:

A new strategic environment now gives emerging ballistic missile powers the capacity, through a combination of domestic development and foreign assistance, to acquire the means to strike the U.S. within about five years of a decision to acquire such a capability (10 years in the case of Iraq). During several of those years, the U.S. might not be aware that such a decision had been made. Available alternative means of delivery can shorten the warning time of deployment nearly to zero.[51]

The preceding arguments do not prove that deterrence, old style, can never work in the new world order, including deterrence based on nuclear weapons. But deterrence in the next century will be more conditional, culturally driven and less technology-oriented than it was during the Cold War. States owning weapons of mass destruction and ballistic missiles will present a mosaic of hard-to-read intentions that defy easy characterization by standard intelligence collectors. Deterrence, having been overdetermined in the Cold War, may lead the pack of under-achievers before the twenty-first century is very old.

CONCLUSION

Theoretically appealing and policy-relevant arguments can suggest that nuclear weapons spread is possibly compatible with international political stability in the twenty-first century. And these arguments may be correct. This author is doubtful. His suspicion is that the arguments are seductively wrong on the following counts. First, rational deterrence theory as understood by U.S. and other Western scholars and analysts may provide a poor basis for predicting the behavior of non-Western actors. Second, additional nuclear weapons states may have insecure or politically adolescent command and control systems. Third, the appeal of nuclear weapons as anti-deterrence deterrents, as against U.S. and allied power projection into troubled regions, spells trouble for American regional deterrence and war fighting strategy. Fourth, nuclear armed troublemakers do not need large or diverse arsenals in order to cause a great deal of crisis misperception and to raise the risk of accidental or inadvertent nuclear war. More is not better.

NOTES

1. Kenneth N. Waltz, *Theory of International Politics* (Reading, Mass.: Addison-Wesley, 1979). See also, and more specifically on Waltz's views of the relationship between nuclear weapons and stability, *The Spread of Nuclear Weapons: More May Be Better*, Adelphi Papers No. 171 (London: International Institute of Strategic Studies, 1981); "Nuclear Myths and Political Realities," *American Political Science Review*, No. 3 (September 1990): 731–745; and his chapters in Scott D. Sagan and Kenneth N. Waltz, *The Spread of Nuclear Weapons: A Debate* (New York: W.W. Norton, 1995). Other arguments for a positive association between the spread of survivable nuclear forces and international stability appear in Martin Van Creveld, *Nuclear Proliferation and the Future of Conflict* (New York: The Free Press, 1993).

2. Realists contend that power is based on tangible resources such as population, economic capacity and territory, and the most influential among them also believe that power is both a means and an end in international politics. See Hans J. Morgenthau, *Politics among Nations: The Struggle for Power and Peace* (New York: Alfred A. Knopf, 1948). Neorealists hold, as do realists, that the structure of the international system, especially system polarity, is the most important determinant of the context for state decision making. Neorealists, in contrast to realists, are more likely to acknowledge sources of power other than tangible ones, and to treat power as a means but not as an end in itself. Paul R. Viotti and Mark V. Kauppi divide international political theories into realist, pluralist and globalist schools, a taxonomy similar to that offered by Kalevi J. Holsti. See Viotti and Kauppi, eds., *International Relations Theory: Realism, Pluralism, Globalism* (New York: Macmillan, 1993), esp. ch. 1, pp. 61–227, and Holsti, *Peace and War: Armed Conflicts and International Order* (Cambridge: Cambridge University Press, 1991), p. 328. See also Holsti's comments on the roots of realism and neorealism, pp. 329–330. An excellent summary and critique of neorealist views is provided by Robert O. Keohane, "Theory of World Politics: Structural Realism and Beyond," in Ada W. Finifter, ed., *Political Science: The State of the Discipline* (Washington, D.C.: American Political Science Association, 1983), and reprinted in Viotti and Kauppi, eds., *International Relations Theory*, pp. 186–227.

3. The distinctions between assertive and delegative control are explained in Peter Douglas Feaver, *Guarding the Guardians: Civilian Control of Nuclear Weapons in the United States* (Ithaca, N.Y.: Cornell University Press, 1992), pp. 3–28 and passim. On U.S. nuclear predelegation during the Cold War see Bruce G. Blair, *The Logic of Accidental Nuclear War* (Washington, D.C.: Brookings Institution, 1993), pp. 46–52.

4. For arguments about the impact of organizational and decision-making variables on the relationship between nuclear weapons and stability see Sagan, in Sagan and Waltz, *The Spread of Nuclear Weapons*, pp. 47–91. See also Sagan, *The Limits of Safety: Organizations, Accidents and Nuclear Weapons* (Princeton, N.J.: Princeton University Press, 1993), esp. pp. 28–44.

5. Lewis A. Dunn, Sarah A. Mullen, Gregory F. Giles, Joseph A. Yager and James S. Tomashoff, *The Next Nuclear-Weapon States?* (McLean, Va.: Science Applications International Corporation, 1991), pp. 2–51.

6. The term "system" has many uses in international politics and in political science. Structural-realist theories of international politics emphasize the causal importance of system *structure*: numbers and types of units in the system and the distribution of military and other capabilities among those units. Other variations of systems theory emphasize the *interactions* among components of the system, including the *interdependence* of the actors or units. For a concise discussion of systemic theories of international politics, see James E. Dougherty and Robert L. Pfaltzgraff, Jr., *Contending Theories of International Politics*, 4th ed. (New York: Longman, 1997), pp. 100–134.

7. Vital interests as used here refers to interests over which states resist compromise and for which they are willing to go to war. See Donald M. Snow, *National Security: Defense Policy in a Changed International Order* (New York: St. Martin's Press, 1998), pp. 173–180.

8. Bruce Bueno de Mesquita and David Lalman, *War and Reason: Domestic and International Imperatives* (New Haven, Conn.: Yale University Press, 1992).

9. Ibid., p. 267.

10. Ibid., pp. 267–268.

11. Waltz, *Man, the State and War* (New York: Columbia University Press, 1959). The first image includes human nature and individual psychological attributes pertinent to decision making. The second image refers to state level decisions and behaviors.

12. Bueno de Mesquita and Lalman, *War and Reason*, p. 269. The authors acknowledge that, under conditions of imperfect information, states might mistakenly stumble into war as a result of misjudgments based on inaccurate information. But in a domestically constrained as opposed to a realist model of strategic rationality, leaders may also "mistakenly" avoid war and "stumble into negotiation or other peaceful solutions to their differences" (p. 269).

13. Robert Jervis, *System Effects: Complexity in Political and Social Life* (Princeton, N.J.: Princeton University Press, 1998), pp. 92–93 and passim.

14. Waltz, *Theory of International Politics*, p. 80.

15. Jervis, *System Effects*, p. 109.

16. See Morton Kaplan, *System and Process in International Politics* (New York: John Wiley and Sons, 1957), for an early and pioneering effort for its time. In-

ternational systems theories are classified and critiqued in Jervis, *System Effects*, ch. 3.

17. Waltz, "The Stability of a Bipolar World," *Deadalus*, vol. 93 (Summer 1964): 881–909; and Waltz, *Theory of International Politics*, pp. 170–171, cited in Jervis, *System Effects*, p. 118.

18. For the distinction between general and immediate deterrence, see Patrick M. Morgan, *Deterrence: A Conceptual Approach* (Beverly Hills, Calif.: Sage Publications, 1983). Or, as Hobbes explained it, it is a precept or general rule of reason that "every man, ought to endeavour Peace, as farre as he has hope of obtaining it; and when he cannot obtain it, that he may seek, and use, all helps, and advantages of Warre." Thomas Hobbes, *Leviathan* (New York: Washington Square Press, 1964), p. 88.

19. As Jervis explains, rationality assumptions are not necessarily falsified by cases in which leaders have chosen poorly. But in many other instances "the beliefs and policies are so removed from what a careful and disinterested analysis of the situation reveals that the failure is hard to fit into the framework generated by rationality." Jervis, introduction in Jervis, Richard Ned Lebow and Janice Gross Stein, *Psychology and Deterrence* (Baltimore, Md.: Johns Hopkins University Press, 1985), p. 6.

20. See Raymond L. Garthoff, *Reflections on the Cuban Missile Crisis* (Washington, D.C.: Brookings Institution, 1989 rev. ed.), pp. 6–42.

21. U.S. officials at the time of the Cuban missile crisis underestimated significantly the size of the Soviets' conventional forces deployed on that island (actually some 40,000). Nor did they realize that, in addition to warheads for medium- and intermediate-range missiles deployed in Cuba, the Soviets also deployed nuclear warheads for tactical weapons launchers. At the time of the crisis, U.S. leaders were uncertain whether *any* Soviet warheads actually arrived in Cuba. Raymond L. Garthoff, "The Havana Conference on the Cuban Missile Crisis," in *Cold War International History Project Bulletin* (Washington, D.C.: Woodrow Wilson Center, Spring 1992), pp. 1–4. According to Bruce Blair, actual orders to the senior Soviet commander in Cuba specifically precluded the use of any nuclear weapons without prior approval from Moscow (Blair, *The Logic of Accidental Nuclear War*, p. 109).

22. U.S. leaders were not well informed about the actual Soviet nuclear force deployments in Cuba in October 1962. See Gen. Anatoli I. Gribkov and William Y. Smith, *Operation ANADYR: U.S. and Soviet Generals Recount the Cuban Missile Crisis* (Chicago: Edition Q Publishers, 1994).

23. Gaddis, "The Essential Relevance of Nuclear Weapons," in his *The United States and the End of the Cold War* (Oxford: Oxford University Press, 1992), pp. 105–132.

24. Paul Bracken, *Fire in the East: The Rise of Asian Military Power and the Second Nuclear Age* (New York: HarperCollins, 1999), pp. 99–101.

25. Richard K. Betts, "The New Threat of Mass Destruction," *Foreign Affairs*, No. 1 (January/February 1998): 26–41, esp. p. 32.

26. Bracken, *Fire in the East*, p. 43.

27. Leon V. Sigal, *Disarming Strangers: Nuclear Diplomacy with North Korea* (Princeton, N.J.: Princeton University Press, 1998), esp. pp. 3–14.

28. See Michael J. Mazarr, *North Korea and the Bomb* (New York: St. Martin's Press, 1995), passim.

29. Office of the Secretary of Defense, *Proliferation: Threat and Response* (Washington, D.C.: U.S. Government Printing Office, 1996), pp. 6–7 provides background on the North Korean nuclear program.

30. Jane's Strategic Weapons Systems, September 30 1998, http://janes.ismc.sgov.gov/egi-bin...h_janes/.

31. Ibid.

32. Patrick M. O'Donogue, *Theater Missile Defense in Japan: Implications for the U.S.-China-Japan Strategic Relationship* (Carlisle Barracks, Pa.: U.S. Army War College, Strategic Studies Institute, September 2000), p. 6.

33. Commission to Assess the Ballistic Missile Threat to the United States (Rumsfeld Commission), *Report* (Executive Summary) (Washington, D.C.: July 15, 1998), p. 9. Pagination may be inexact due to variations in electronic transmission.

34. Ibid.

35. See map, *Ranges of Current and Future Ballistic Missile Systems* (Iran), in Office of the Secretary of Defense, *Proliferation: Threat and Response*, p. 17.

36. Ibid., p. 16.

37. Thomas A. Keaney and Eliot A. Cohen, *Revolution in Warfare? Air Power in the Persian Gulf* (Annapolis, Md.: Naval Institute Press, 1995), p. 67. This is a revised version of the official U.S. Air Force *Gulf War Air Power Survey* (GWAPS) first published in 1993.

38. Keaney and Cohen, *Revolution in Warfare*, p. 67.

39. Ibid.

40. Ibid., p. 72.

41. Ibid., p. 75.

42. Ibid., p. 78. Special forces teams may have destroyed some mobile SCUDs.

43. Jeffrey Record, *Hollow Victory: A Contrary View of the Gulf War* (Washington, D.C.: Brassey's, 1993), pp. 71–73.

44. Secretary of Defense William J. Perry, *On Ballistic Missile Defense: Excerpt from a Speech to the Chicago Council on Foreign Relations*, March 8, 1995, p. 1 (mimeo), cited in Keith B. Payne, *Deterrence in the Second Nuclear Age* (Lexington: University Press of Kentucky, 1996), p. 58.

45. Payne, *Deterrence in the Second Nuclear Age*, pp. 57–58.

46. Robert E. Harkavy, "Triangular or Indirect Deterrence/Compellence: Something New in Deterrence Theory," *Comparative Strategy*, No. 1 (1998): 63–82.

47. Ibid., p. 74.

48. Rumsfeld Commission, *Report* (Executive Summary), p. 10.

49. Ibid., p. 11.

50. Ibid.

51. Ibid., p. 22. The Rumsfeld Commission cannot be dismissed by skeptics as an alarmist group. Its membership included, in addition to former Secretary of Defense Donald Rumsfeld who chaired it, noted experts on nuclear technology, strategy and policy representing a variety of policy views and professional backgrounds.

Conclusion

INTRODUCTION

The nuclear era is over, but nuclear weapons, strategy and arms control remain important. Failure to recognize the continuing risks of nuclear war, or of nuclear arms races that can lead to war, by politicians, planners and pundits in the next century, is a near certainty. The 1990s were a decade, at least in the United States and in the high-tech parts of other "first world" countries, of unprecedented rapid economic expansion and political euphoria. Along with this went the kind of hubris that regards military threats to U.S. security as an afterthought. Indeed, the U.S. Department of Defense in the 1990s found that it was mainly in the business of enforcing peace, as opposed to fighting war.

The U.S. armed forces were tasked in the 1990s with more than 30 peace operations. Some were called "peacekeeping" and demanded only a low-maintenance form of military policing and presence. Others were humanitarian rescues, pure and simple. But others moved beyond peacekeeping or humanitarian missions into the more politically complicated, and militarily committing, arena of "peace enforcement." The United States and/or its allies (sometimes with UN blessing, sometimes without) would impose a peace or impose a halt to ethnic cleansing resulting from civil war. Now this author intends no brief against peace operations per se, provided they are based on clearly defined and militarily attainable objectives. But at the level of the "grunts" who must train for war, retrain for deployment for peace operations, and retrain again for war, confusion and disappointment were understandable. And for those at or near the top of the military service chain of command, they might be forgiven if their attention spans and radars became de-sensitized to the possibility of large-scale conventional or nuclear wars. The larger the war, the less urgent it seemed as the 1990s ended in a global celebration of the end of war, the end of autocracy and the end of days.

If my reading of history is correct, the 1990s will eventually be written about as a decade of glib detachment from the realities of military threat and power politics. And the most surprised of all may be the power that seemed politically, economically and militarily invincible from the end of the Cold War until the end of the millennium: the "sole remaining superpower" with its one-of-a-kind global military reach and its nearly hegemonic leadership in the globalization of information, finance and investment. What could possibly derail this U.S. Express from its contin-uing preeminence in the appeal of its democratic institutions, its Dow-blasting economy, and its apparently intimidating qualitative and quantitative military power? History says that great powers can be brought down by misestimation of their own strength and their oppo-nents' weaknesses. The United States in the 1930s disparaged Japan's growing military and naval strength on the basis of cultural bias that assumed Japanese could only copy technology applied to war from oth-ers. U.S. leaders also assumed that Japan would not dare take on the American Pacific fleet in its lair, nor that Dai Nippon would blow like a typhoon over the remnants of the British and Dutch empires in south Asia. Japan was thought to be a small country with big ambitions, lack-ing in stamina, resolve and innovation. These assumptions were put to the test on December 7, 1941, and for many months thereafter, and found wide of the mark. Were the events of September 11, 2001 a case of déjà vu?

THE FIRST NUCLEAR AGE

Japan's defeat in 1945 was expedited by the first use of an atomic bomb in anger. The "nuclear era" or first nuclear age begins with the U.S. bombing of Hiroshima in 1945 and ends with the end of the Cold War and the collapse of the Soviet Union. The post-nuclear era or second nuclear age begins in the 1990s and carries forward into the twenty-first century.[1] The nuclear era from 1945 to 1991 is one in which a bipolar distribution of international military power, combined with a two-sided ideological competition between capitalism and communism, over-shadows all other military activity. The nuclear era is the era of military persuasion through the selective application of threat of force, mixed with reassurances that the threatened party can escape punishment by acquiescing to the demands made upon it. The use of the most powerful weapons in actual war fighting would be self-destructive. So, instead, for most of the Cold War the Americans and Soviets used those weapons as instruments of political influence short of war.

Two means of influence were predominant among those chosen by policy makers and their advisors in bringing military instruments to bear on problems short of war: deterrence, and coercive diplomacy. The first, deterrence, is the more passive of the two: it aims to prevent an action that a hostile state has not yet taken but appears to be seriously considering. Deterrence is before the fact. The second, coercive diplomacy, is the more active form of influence by means of threat of force and, possibly, selective reassurances. Coercive diplomacy, as Alexander L. George has explained, is intended to stop an action already in progress or to undo and reverse an action already completed.[2] It therefore requires more exertion and commitment on the part of the threatener, and it also usually requires of the threatened party, in order to comply with the threatener's demands, to make a greater adjustment in its current behavior compared to deterrence. President John F. Kennedy's demand that Soviet Premier Khrushchev remove his missiles from Cuba in October 1962 is an example of the application of coercive diplomacy in order to stop, and then undo, an action regarded as contrary to U.S. national interest. Kennedy first imposed a naval blockade around Cuba to prevent the shipment of additional Soviet missiles there (the "stop" aspect of coercive diplomacy). In addition, he demanded that the Soviet Union remove the missiles previously deployed in Cuba as soon as possible (the "undo" aspect).

The Cuban missile crisis displayed the two-sided character of nuclear weapons when employed as instruments of military persuasion. Enormous coercive power could be derived from the threat of nuclear first use or escalation even if the threat was not explicitly stated in the course of an international negotiation. On the other hand, the devilish paradox of nuclear deterrence was that, for deterrence to be credible, both the willingness and the capability to use nuclear weapons had to be apparent to the other side. Capabilities could be measured and, after the deployment of reconnaissance satellites, counted with reasonable fidelity. But intentions were another matter. Intentions were contingent upon the exigent circumstances of the moment as much as they were derived from any generalized mind-set of a state's leadership. Thus, U.S. leaders might assume that Soviet Cold War aims included political expansion backed up by selective military pressure. But this assumption about Soviet mind-sets in general did not tell U.S. intelligence whether Khrushchev would deploy missiles to Cuba, nor whether he would pull them out attendant to a U.S. crisis-time demand to do so.

This duality of nuclear weapons, enticing for their coercive potential and dangerous on account of their capacity to destroy modern civilizations in several hours, made it of first importance for policy makers and commanders to grapple with the concept of escalation. If a conventional war in Europe began, could it be stopped short of nuclear first use? If not, could some stopping point between nuclear first use and Armageddon be agreed to as NATO and Warsaw Pact armies clashed on the Central Front? Did the Soviets even recognize any concepts such as "escalation control" and "war termination" as discussed in the U.S. deterrence and arms control literature?[3] The matter of escalation, like the coercive power potential of nuclear weapons, was Janus-like. If escalation from conventional to nuclear war, or from smaller to larger nuclear wars, were *certain to occur*, then no rational head of state would start either a conventional or nuclear war, at least, not in Europe. On the other hand, if escalation were *guaranteed not to happen* and states were confident that "firebreaks" could be preserved between conventional and nuclear war, or between limited and total nuclear war, then states would be free to play with fire either at the level of conventional war or within a spectrum of nuclear wars.

But, to the confounding of nuclear theory, neither condition was certain: neither the absence of escalation nor its presence could be foreseen. The uncertainty of escalation in any particular case was the effective deterrent as much as the firepower behind it. While this might provide interesting speculative material for applied psychologists, it drove military planners to distraction and drove scholars and policy advocates in either of two directions: toward more insistent demands for nuclear arms control and/or disarmament, or toward more insistent demands for increased nuclear war preparedness. During the early years of the Kennedy administration, these two theoretically opposed sets of demands actually coincided in time and space, with large clusters of expert and lay opinion weighing in on both sides.

When all of the dust had cleared after four decades or so of actually operating nuclear forces, of conducting arms control negotiations, and of reaching various agreements to prevent accidental nuclear war or escalation growing out of incidents between American and Soviet forces, it fell to Soviet President Gorbachev and U.S. President Reagan to bell the cat. Nearing the end of the Cold War, both acknowledged from different perspectives that the basic issues of the first nuclear age had been thought through and fought out. Those shared understandings from the archdeacon of capitalism and the last dying emperor of Soviet socialism, held with more or less reluctant acquiescence by their respective militaries, were as follows:

1. Nuclear war could neither be fought nor won in the traditional (pre-nuclear) sense. Victory was not attainable at an acceptable cost in any nuclear war involving more than a few demonstration shots at noncritical targets.

2. No technology then in existence or immediately foreseeable could provide an effective defense of the U.S. or Soviet national territories against large-scale attack (Reagan's Strategic Defense Initiative called for a research and development program for a *future* (read: futuristic) nationwide defense system, not for imminent deployment of one as some misperceived).

3. It was in the interest of both the United States and the Soviet Union, as well as in the interest of the civilized world, that nuclear weapons spread be confined to the smallest number of state actors (and, preferably, to no non-state actors, such as terrorists).

4. The safe and secure operation of nuclear weapons and forces, including the alerting and crisis management of nuclear capable forces, was a requirement for maintaining peace and security in the Cold War and for stabilizing the nuclear relationship between Washington and Moscow (accordingly, both sides worked out "rules of the road" to reduce the possibility of misunderstanding, such as prenotification of test missile launches within certain geographical areas).

5. Although NATO was a voluntary alliance of democratic states and the Warsaw Treaty Organization was not, the American and Soviet leaderships both agreed that neither wished to be dragged by allies into a catalytic nuclear war. Accordingly, the nuclear potential of allies or erstwhile allies was limited by multilateral agreement and diplomatic persuasion (as in NATO), by imposition of Soviet military domination (as in the Warsaw Pact), or by a combination of sticks and carrots (as between the Soviet Union and China).

These were important areas of agreement during the first nuclear age. Not a single one of them can be taken for granted as a policy consensus shared by nuclear or nuclear-aspiring powers as the second nuclear age enters the twenty-first century. Why not?

THE SECOND NUCLEAR AGE

First, the two "policemen" or principal constables of the Cold War antiproliferation system, the United States and the Soviet Union, have been reduced to one. This subtracts from the strength of regulatory forces.

Second, the nuclear successor state to one of the two Cold War constables, Russia, has financial and other incentives to join the ranks of nuclear and missile technology suppliers. There is considerable evidence that she has already done so. Russia has aided in the development of the nuclear industry and missile technology infrastructure in North Korea. U.S. intelligence cannot say for certain how much weapons-grade material (plutonium or enriched uranium) has leaked from holdings in Russia into the hands of other states or terrorists.

Third, on account of the condition of its conventional military forces in the 1990s, Russia became more reliant on its nuclear weapons to cover a variety of contingent threats to its security. These threats were not limited to nuclear attack on Russia or on a Russian ally. Overlapping with growing nuclear dependency in Russia was NATO's decision to enlarge its membership to include Poland, the Czech Republic and Hungary in the spring of 1999. Although NATO declared that it had no "intention, plan or reason" to station nuclear weapons in any of these newly admitted members, NATO enlargement brought the alliance's nuclear guaranty up to the doorstep of the Ukraine and the Baltic states.

Nor was this all. NATO attempted to mollify Russian President Yeltsin about its decision for enlargement by offering Russia membership in a NATO-Russia consultative arrangement on security issues, according to the NATO-Russian Founding Act of 1997. However, much of the good will that might have been created by this was dissipated when NATO, on the heels of its enlargement decision in 1999, waged its first war ever against a sovereign state in its air campaign against Yugoslavia, a traditional Russian ally.

Fourth, and related to nuclear uncertainties surrounding U.S. relations with Russia, the United States has cast doubt on the viability of the ABM Treaty of 1972 by pushing forward with plans for a limited national missile defense (NMD) system. The Clinton administration declared in 1999 that it would make a decision by summer of 2000 whether to deploy the first phase of a system of defense interceptors, radars and command/control systems based on exoatmospheric, hit-to-kill technology. Much of the U.S. arms control community remained opposed to deploying any missile defense system, but pressure from the U.S. Congress (including several pieces of legislation passed during Clinton's second term) and more pessimistic threat assessments about possible ballistic missile attacks on U.S. territory built momentum in favor of defenses. President George W. Bush settled the issue in December 2001 by officially withdrawing the United States from the ABM Treaty, thus removing legal obstacles to NMD deployment.

For its part, Russia remained, under President Putin as well as former President Yeltsin, skeptical that any modification of the ABM Treaty would be to its advantage. Russia lacked competitive technology with the proposed American NMD system. But more fundamentally, Russian military and arms control experts feared that any U.S. nationwide defense would overturn stable deterrence based on offensive retaliation that had served the Soviet Union well during the Cold War. There was some irony in Russia clinging to a doctrine that the Cold War Soviets had first opposed vehemently, and then reluctantly embraced as a way to slow down the Americans in the arms race. Now Russia feared that the United States might invent its way into a defense technology that would be good enough to negate Russia's nuclear retaliatory strike, even if it could not defeat a surprise first strike. If Russia's retaliatory strike were up for grabs, then Russia in a political crisis might be forced to operate its nuclear retaliatory forces on a hair trigger.

Fifth, and related to the preceding point, it was not only "assured destruction" based solely on offensive retaliation that was in danger of falling out of favor in the twenty-first century. Equally unclear was the fate of deterrence itself as a central concept for understanding the arms debate, and as a policy-prescriptive tool for organizing alternatives. Deterrence had grown up with the Cold War and nuclear weapons. It provided a common nomenclature within which academics, policy makers, military planners and others could debate military and political options. Deterrence, to paraphrase Clausewitz, became not only a common grammar of reference for inter-elite nuclear debates, but also a logic unto its own for answering virtually any question about strategy and military policy. Eventually deterrence was even extended downward on the ladder of escalation into the bowels of so-called "low intensity conflict" of unconventional warfare.

As deterrence became an all-purpose talisman by which virtually any policy or strategy could be analyzed, its ubiquitous application came at the expense of explanatory or predictive power. All deterrence analyses or forecasts were made equal. By the time two decades of the nuclear age were history, it had been forgotten that the theory of deterrence (unlike the practice of it, which had existed since the beginning of human interpersonal conflict) had grown up under very special conditions in the early years of the nuclear age, when policy makers needed advice about how to deal with these new weapons of unprecedented destructiveness. Thus, large debates were held in academic journals and at conferences in the 1980s, for example, as to whether "conventional deterrence" on the Central Front in Europe would suffice to preclude an outbreak of war, ignoring the inescapable commingling of nuclear and conventional forces in both Soviet and NATO forward deployments and war plans.

But the major weakness of deterrence was not conceptual overstretch, important as that was. A more important limitation of the theory of deterrence, relative to the probable practices of states in the twenty-first century, was inherent in its assumptions about rational decision making. When deterrence theory worked as an explanation or prediction for real political phenomena, it "worked" because heads of state or other political leaders behaved according to a simplified rational policy model. The model assumed that individuals in a competitive bargaining game behave according to a certain game-imposed logic that requires them to engage in value-maximizing behavior within a set of carefully drawn rules. Change the rules or the assumption of value-maximizing behavior, as defined by the observer, and all bets are off. In other words, deterrence is a quasi-experimental, open system subject to fluctuation in behavior to the extent that the mice choose to cooperate, or not, with the designers of the maze.

The assumption of rationality on which deterrence theory was based was itself criticized for being politically naïve, but this criticism was sometimes overstated. One had to make some assumptions, and rationality was not the worst place to start. A more important limitation in deterrence models was the assumption of a U.S. or Western kind of rationality in decision making—the assumption that "they" think like "we." So it was assumed by some policy makers and analysts, for example, that the Soviets would look upon nuclear weapons and nuclear arms control from the same frame of reference as did their U.S. and allied Western counterparts. When, in the event, this expectation of strategically identical "apes on a treadmill" was proved wide of the mark, Soviet leaders were disparaged for their inability to comprehend the realities of the nuclear age.

Even more challenging to deterrence theory were the so-called low-intensity conflicts, mostly unconventional wars, raging in a variety of states in the Third World outside of U.S. and Soviet direct political control and military influence. A common misunderstanding is to see this mostly Asian, African, and Middle Eastern landscape as relatively pacified by the Cold War superpowers until the breakup of the Soviet Union and the end of the Cold War. Here there is a collective memory loss. In fact, neither the Americans nor the Soviets, nor the former colonial powers numbered among U.S. allies, succeeded very well in applying deterrence theory to the practice of preventing or "deterring" revolutionary-guerrilla warfare. The U.S. policy and strategy of extending containment to Southeast Asia crashed and burned in Vietnam. The Soviets invaded Afghanistan in 1979 with the expectation of quickly imposing their will on a scattered rabble of Afghan mujahideen opposition; they withdrew in embarrassment and defeat a decade later. The French were driven first from Indochina and then from Algeria, although the latter was legally defined as part of metropolitan France, and French withdrawal provoked part of the army to mutiny.

One could argue that revolutionary-guerrilla and other unconventional warfare is embedded in local causes too numerous to generalize about, and, therefore, that it lies outside the ambit of deterrence theory. This may be so, but it was not only deterrence that failed in the cases listed above, but also the inability of policy and strategy to resolve the matter once a state of war had supplanted a state of peace. U.S. officials who were responsible for committing American forces to the war in Vietnam between 1965 and 1973 now acknowledge, for example, that they misunderstood in fundamental ways the politics, society and culture of Vietnam. This phenomenon was not isolated during the Cold War or since.

Not understanding the "otherness" of states in the new world order includes not understanding how new nuclear powers might view their arsenals, compared to the five original and officially sanctioned members of the nuclear "club" (also permanent members of the UN Security Council). In the United States and in NATO, nuclear weapons are now treated as weapons of last resort and something of a post–Cold War embarrassment. Since the Gulf war of 1991, the weapons of first choice for the United States and others who want to play in the league of major powers have been the high-technology, information-based conventional weapons for long-range, precision strike; stealth technology; and advanced systems for C4ISR (command, control, communications, computers, intelligence, surveillance and reconnaissance). This "Revolution in Military Affairs" is thought by some to have established a dividing line between those states that can afford to play in this high-tech military world of "smart" or future "brilliant" weapons and those who cannot afford the price of entry.

On the other hand, it is entirely possible that those who cannot afford the price of entry into information-based warfare, of which "information warfare" or cyberwar is a subspecies, will play other strategies consistent with their history, strategic culture and available options. Iraqi leader Saddam Hussein, for example, was widely discussed in the West in 1991 as someone who had "lost" the Gulf war because his forces had been expelled from Kuwait and decimated by U.S. smart firepower. This is the outcome of the war as seen from a U.S. perspective. But it is not the only possible vantage point. From Saddam Hussein's perspective and that of some others in the Middle East, Iraq had successfully stood off a coalition of thirty states headed by the world's sole superpower and survived with its regime and much of its modern army intact. True, a peace was imposed on Iraq that required it to dismantle many of its weapons of mass destruction in the 1990s (although not all) and UN-imposed sanctions cut drastically into its economy (most notably, restraints on its ability to export oil).

Moreover, Saddam Hussein remained in power in the year 2001 long after George Herbert Walker Bush had departed the presidency and in time to watch President George W. Bush, son of the former president, assume office. Repeated air attacks by the Clinton administration and a widely known if officially unacknowledged CIA effort to dislodge Hussein from power, by fomenting a rebellion among dissident Kurds in northern Iraq, failed to change the regime in Baghdad. So who "won" in Iraq in the 1990s? The answer all depends upon the perspective by which one defines winning and losing. And those states or revolutionary movements fighting against the top dogs in any international system, including the international system of the next two decades, may calculate "winning" or "losing" with a calculator powered by the batteries of faith, nationalism, or simple warrior mentalities that are unfamiliar to law-regarding and casualty-averse Western audiences.

In this regard, the availability of ballistic missiles and nuclear weapons to new powers from the Middle East to the Pacific Rim should cause U.S. policy makers and strategic planners to rethink their military-strategic geography. One reason for this is inherent in the technical properties of missiles apart from culture. Medium- and long-range ballistic missiles shrink the geography over which conflicts can be fought quickly and, if those missiles are carrying weapons of mass destruction, with much greater devastation than hitherto. But more important than the technical properties of ballistic missiles are the variations in the way that missiles can be used, depending on the imagination of the user.

Western military experts tended during the Cold War to disparage the utility of early generation ballistic missiles sold to countries outside of NATO or the Warsaw Pact on account of those missiles' low accuracy. The measure of a missile's value was, in addition to its range, its ability to strike with high accuracy against military forces, i.e., counterforce targets. But non-Western leaders had other ideas. During the Iran-Iraq war of the 1980s, both sides fired conventionally armed ballistic missiles at one another's cities as terror weapons, like the German V-2 rockets fired at London during World War II. And during the Gulf war of 1991, Iraq used its SCUD missiles to launch terror attacks against Israeli cities: although the missiles carried no chemical or biological weapons, U.S. and Israeli intelligence knew that Saddam Hussein had deployed some SCUDs that were capable of launching chemical or biological weaponized warheads. Hussein undoubtedly knew that the United States and Israelis knew, and exploited this knowledge in his effort (unsuccessful but nonetheless energetic) to try to divide the coalition.

Hussein's SCUDs during the Gulf war were also a weapon of terroristic counter-deterrence. On account of the possibility that they might be mated to some chemical or biological warheads, especially the latter, they could be used to checkmate especially any opportunistic expansion of war aims on the part of the United States and its victorious allies. Subsequent to the expulsion of Iraq's invading armies from Kuwait, some contended that the United States had ended the war too soon. It was felt by critics of the U.S. decision to terminate the ground war after 100 hours that additional pursuit of Iraq's fleeing forces might have destroyed additional components of the crack Republican Guard armored forces that were vital to Saddam Hussein's postwar survival. Other critics of the prompt war termination were unhappy that the United States and its allies did not persevere until the entire power structure of Hussein's regime was forced out of office or destroyed. But the United States suspected that Saddam Hussein would pull out all stops to stay in power, including an apparent willingness to have prepared SCUDs with biological weapons pretargeted at cities in Israel and in Kuwait. In the event of an enemy storming of Baghdad to dislodge the regime, the deadly missiles armed with germ weapons would fly automatically.[4]

The willingness to employ biological and other weapons of mass destruction stamps Asian and Middle Eastern leaders as backward in the eyes of Western advocates of precision, information-based warfare. But this sort of thinking misses the leverage that WMD may confer on aspiring hegemons who seek to dominate their regions and to keep outside powers like the United States from interfering. For actors of this type, the lack of accuracy of SCUD missiles, for example, may not be dissuasive. These Soviet-designed ballistic missiles may not provide the pinpoint accuracy of smart weapons, but they are adequate to target the rear echelon forces and supporting bases of American expeditionary forces. Knowing this, the United States may be deterred from forcible entry into hostile zones. As Paul Bracken has explained:

The great administrative and technical intricacies of the Western military effort are not seen at the tip of the military spear, but at its shaft. The tip—the frontline units—needs ammunition, fuel, and spare parts for its complex vehicles, radars, and radios. Biological weapons attack the shaft, the long, vulnerable part of the Western spear, comprising trucks, parts inventories, repair shops, and air and sea transportation. The shaft of the spear is not nearly as well protected as the tip is.[5]

If cultural dissimilarity will impede Western understanding of the strategies that adversaries in Asia and the Middle East armed with ballistic missiles will pursue, another potential vulnerability lies in asymmetrical information strategies available to opponents both above and below the threshold of mass destruction. One potential U.S. vulnerability is the casualty aversion in the mind of the U.S. public, media and Congress that has grown up with the advent of the all-volunteer force and the spectacular success of American and allied arms in Desert Storm. This casualty allergy can be manifest in two ways: it can enhance the counter-deterrent effect of the enemy's threat to employ nuclear or biological weapons against intervening American forces or their bases of support; or, second, it can be used to intimidate the American public by running up casualties in protracted conventional, or unconventional, conflicts. Iraq's strategy for deterring U.S. military attack in 1990 and 1991 was to threaten a ground war of attrition that would cause tens of thousands of U.S. casualties, as predicted even by some American sources. This strategy failed because superior U.S. airpower and knowledge-intensive warfare blinded and deafened Iraq's war machine, allowing its head to be disconnected from its body so that it flailed helplessly to self-destruction. However, the strategy of exhaustion of the U.S. body politic by means of casualty attrition worked for North Vietnam and the Viet Cong from the Tet Offensive until the withdrawal of American combat forces in 1973.

More recently, the Clinton administration was moved to withdraw combat forces from Somalia in the wake of a shootout with the unconventional warriors of warlord Mohammed Farah Aideed in October 1993, that resulted in 18 U.S. and hundreds of Somali deaths in Mogadishu. But the most recent showcase for policy planners motivated by casualty aversion was NATO's war against Yugoslavia (Operation Allied Force) in the spring of 1999. Political leaders, including President Bill Clinton, ruled out a ground offensive at the outset of the air campaign. Knowing this, Yugoslav President Slobodan Milosevic was unimpaired in accelerating his ethnic cleansing of Albanians resident in the Serbian province of Kosovo. In addition, the NATO air sorties against targets in Serbia were mostly held above 15,000 feet in order to minimize the loss of pilots (in the event, no pilots were killed by hostile fire). But one result of this limitation on air tasking was that ground targets, including tanks and armored personnel carriers, were difficult to identify clearly and to hit precisely. After-action reports compiled by the NATO staffs were unable to verify more than about 20 destroyed tanks, despite claims by the U.S. Joint Chiefs of Staff and high NATO officials that the air campaign had actually knocked out hundreds of tanks and APCs.

Admittedly these examples are not examples of deterrence or counter-deterrence by means of WMD, but that is precisely the point. In the case of NATO, we had a nuclear armed alliance centered around the sole global superpower at the end of the twentieth century, and collectively disposing of about two-thirds of the world's gross national product, in one corner. In the other corner, we had the state of Yugoslavia, whose government was under siege from within and was unprotected by its former superpower patron, the now defunct Soviet Union. From the standpoint of military-strategic capability, it was a most unequal match. However, strategy can confer additional points of advantage, or disadvantage, on military combatants and the policy makers they work for. NATO's no-casualty strategy left the Milosevic regime on the ground to accomplish its war aims of expelling Albanians from Kosovo, after which Milosevic agreed to say "uncle" and negotiate an end to the fighting. Thereafter, NATO found itself embroiled in a peace operation that required the restraint of Albanians who, having returned to Kosovo, sought to get even with their erstwhile Serbian oppressors.

The preceding discussion has covered reasons why the nuclear past, incorrectly interpreted, offers a misleading guide to the nuclear future. The burden of our argument has been that nuclear proliferation outside of Europe will create a new map of geostrategy, especially in the Middle East and in Asia. In addition, deterrence as practiced in the Cold War was insufficiently cognizant of the importance of cultural and social variables in comprehending the mind-set of other state and non-state actors.

In the next section, we consider a third aspect of the attempt to project the twenty-first-century role of nuclear weapons: technology.

MISSILE DEFENSES: BRINGING BACK CLASSICAL STRATEGY?

In the first nuclear age, military traditionalists were frustrated by the dominance of offensive over defensive technology. Anti-bomber defenses were developed and deployed by the United States in the 1940s and 1950s with mixed success. Once ballistic missiles became the dominant arm of the Soviet strategic nuclear forces, air defenses seemed superfluous and the United States energetically pursued a variety of research programs on missile defense. The ABM Treaty of 1972 between the United States and the Soviet Union permitted each side to deploy ABM (anti-ballistic missiles, the then-preferred acronym for BMD, ballistic missile defense) systems at two sites: one to protect the national command authority and one other. The United States chose to deploy its Safeguard system at Grand Forks, North Dakota, in the early 1970s to defend an ICBM field, but Congress chose to dismantle the system in 1975.

From the mid-1970s, the issue of missile defenses remained off the radar of the U.S. policy debate until the Reagan administration. President Reagan in 1983 called for a research and development program to create national missile defenses for the U.S. territory, and Congress authorized the creation of the Strategic Defense Initiative office in the Pentagon to review a number of technology and policy issues related to the president's directive. SDIO spent a considerable amount of money and time on the problem, but the technology was not available, nor imminently foreseeable, to fulfill the president's ambitious objective. But the Reagan proposal and SDIO did keep the issue alive into the next administration.

Recognizing that neither the money nor the political support for Reagan's original and ambitious Strategic Defense Initiative would be available to his successors, President George H.W. Bush and Secretary of Defense Dick Cheney downsized and reoriented the missile defense research and development program toward the goal of limited rather than comprehensive national missile defense. The Bush program was intended to defeat small attacks of nuclear missiles caused either by accidental launches or by deliberate strikes from "rogue" states such as North Korea, Iraq, Iran or Libya. The Clinton administration later adapted the downsized Bush program as its own, with less apparent enthusiasm but in recognition of the sunken costs already invested, of the Congressional support from members of the Congressional Republican majority in 1994, and as a hedge against an uncertain threat environment created by the proliferation of weapons of mass destruction and ballistic missiles.

The Clinton missile defense program (or the Clinton-Congress, approach-avoid program, to be more truthful) was intended to provide the option to deploy a light missile defense system within three years after suitable technology became available and a credible threat materialized. This timetable was accelerated by external forces (North Korean missile tests, Iraqi resistance to UN inspections, Iranian interest in nuclear weapons) and internal forces (Congressional resolutions and demonstrations of intent to press for some kind of limited NMD program). Clinton indicated that he would make a final decision in the summer or fall of 2000 whether to approve deployment of a first phase system of interceptors at a site in Alaska, to be completed by 2005. The president said approval of any funding for deployment would be dependent upon (1) the threat environment, (2) competency of available technology, (3) countermeasures available to defeat the defense, (4) probable cost.

The Russians were predictably wary of U.S. missile defense plans. They recognized that the United States could not soon deploy any missile defense system that deflected Russia's first or retaliatory strike down to acceptable levels of mass destruction. But Russia feared that U.S. defense technology might improve significantly over the next several decades and that the symbolism of the United States having the only workable defense system would reduce Russia's credibility in claiming to be the second strongest nuclear military power. European political leaders also expressed some misgivings about the Clinton program, wondering if they would be isolated from coverage provided by a U.S. NMD system and what that might mean for NATO alliance solidarity. In addition to Russians and U.S. European allies, a third source of public disquiet about American NMD was China. PRC leaders warned that they might be forced to increase the size of their relatively small (compared to the United States and Russia) ICBM force and engage in other nuclear modernizations in response to any U.S. missile defense. U.S. diplomats would have their work cut out selling NMD as a benign technology.

Clinton was almost boxed in on missile defense by pressure from Congress, from defense contractors, and from the apparent uncertainty of the new world order. But the ripeness of NMD technology was still in dispute, even after President George W. Bush assumed office in 2001 and resolved all arguments with his firm decision for deployment. The difficulty in arbitrating debates about missile defense is that the applied scientific research was so embedded with political advocacy. This has been true since the earliest U.S. debates about missile defense in the Cold War. The 1980s were an especially active decade of aggressive confrontation between proponents and opponents of BMD. I recall vividly a case in point. Michael Altfeld, then at Michigan State University, and I decided to collaborate on a research project called "Closing the Window of Vulnerability" in response to some claims that the American land-based missile force was becoming vulnerable to a Soviet first strike. The col-

Table C.1
Possible Technology and Threat Environments for Ballistic Missile Defense

Simple defense technology/simple threat environment	Simple defense technology/complex threat environment
Complex defense technology/simple threat environment	Complex defense technology/complex threat environment

Source: Author.

laboration was fruitful because he was more-or-less sympathetic to missile defense and I was more-or-less doubtful. Our research asked whether the so-called "window of vulnerability" for U.S. ICBMs could be closed at lower cost and with simpler technology than the Reagan-proposed SDI program. We showed that, if policy makers really cared about closing the "window," and it was not just a debating point, then they could do so by combining mobile, deceptive ICBM basing with simple silo defenses at the missile sites.[6]

This analysis pleased neither liberal arms controllers nor conservative Reaganauts. The Reaganauts were not interested in a cost-effective so-lution to ICBM vulnerability: they aimed to overturn deterrence based on offensive retaliation entirely. Liberals, on the other hand, distrusted any research that supported defenses of any kind, for fear that this would play into the hands of the Reagan administration.[7] The debate about missile defenses in the 1980s, in the public domain and to some extent in the academic community, became so polarized that analysis devoid of cant and partisanship was a relatively scare commodity. So professors as well as pundits venturing into this terrain in the twenty-first century have no one but themselves to blame for entering the heart of darkness yet again.

How to sort out the technology and policy issues attendant to BMD or NMD? Let us try some provisional constructs for categorizing two important aspects of the problem: the technology and strategy environ-ments within which current and future policy makers will have to de-cide. First, let's compare possible present and/or future conditions with regard to the technology available for missile defense. Of course, we are not merely interested in the technology as a test bed, but in how well defense technology compares to the evolving threats that it is expected to meet. The possibilities that present themselves are summarized in Ta-ble C.1.

Numbering the cells from left to right and from top to bottom, we can see that cells two and three (simple technology–complex threats, or com-plex technology and simple threats) are *asymmetrical* conditions in which either the defense (cell three) or the offense (cell two) is favored. Cells one and four, on the other hand, present *symmetrical* conditions in which offensive and defensive technologies are more or less in balance. Let us define symmetrical and asymmetrical more precisely. A symmetrical condition is one in which neither the offense nor the defense can leap ahead by a generation and outperform its rival so much that the nuclear stalemate is broken and first-strike capability is within reach for one or more nuclear armed states. Symmetry is a frozen woolly mammoth in your cellar: interesting to look at, and not disruptive of existing living arrangements. An asymmetrical situation, in contrast, is a condition such that one or more states have been able to leapfrog a generation ahead in offenses or in defenses, thus placing at risk the second-strike capability of one or more other actors. In an asymmetrical situation, your woolly mammoth has thawed out, come back to life, and now remembers the hunger pangs that it had before being frozen. In other words, a symmetrical relationship between technology and threat environment is probably going to be stable (i.e., less prone to war); an asymmetrical relationship, more war prone.

Notice, however, that symmetrical and asymmetrical conditions describe a *relational* attribute between technology and threat environment, not technology itself. We might have, as some have done, compare the probable state of offensive and defensive technology 5, 10 or 15 years from now. But comparing technology with technology misses the point. We are less interested in offensive and defensive missile technology than we are in the *strategy* or military uses for these technologies. Offensive technology (long-range ballistic missiles) can be used to support a defensive strategy, as we saw during the Cold War: deterrence was based on *retaliation* (a defensive strategy) after having absorbed an offensive first strike. Conversely, it would be possible to use missile defense technology as part of an offensive strategy: launching a nuclear first strike and then using defenses to mop up the other side's ragged retaliation.

What makes a threat environment complex or simple? A simple threat environment is one that is more or less predictable based on available intelligence and one for which existing or near term technology provides an appropriate and available response. A complex threat environment, on the other hand, is a condition that is difficult to predict on the basis of existing intelligence and for which no available or near term technology provides an appropriate response. What makes a threat environment complex as opposed to simple is not necessarily how complicated the technology is; it is the degree of ingenuity of exploitation of the technology on the part of the users that matters. Thus, for example, Germany leaped ahead of Britain and France between the world wars in its ability to wage tank warfare not on account of superior technology (British and French tanks were better in some respects) but due to Germany's superior concept of armored warfare, including uniquely constituted panzer divisions, specially tasked supporting tactical air power, and radio communications that allowed superior information flow up and down the chain of command.

By analogy, it is not necessarily the first power that parks weapons in space that will dominate the future of anti-missile technology, but the power that incorporates space-based weapons into an overall strategy for the denial of mission superiority and political coercion to its opponent. Space-based weapons may be vulnerable to prompt kill from anti-satellite weapons (ASATs) or to degradation or spoofing from information warfare. Or, the leading edge state in space-based weapons may nevertheless be intimidated from employing its weapons by the superior fanaticism or ruthlessness of its opponent. Say, for example, that the United States deploys some first generation, space-based kinetic weapons and says to a potential aggressor: if you launch a ballistic missile in the direction of U.S. territory or that of our allies, we will blow it out of the sky with our space-based weapons and then consider strikes against your armies or cities. The response might be: you do that, and we will launch hundreds of mobile ballistic missiles and cruise missiles with biological warheads at the cities of your allies and at your own cities. In addition, we will set off twenty prelocated biological weapons already set on "command detonate" in twelve American cities. Europe and North America will suffer plagues for which there are no existing cures.

The scenario is imaginary but the illustration of a relationship between technology and strategy points to a more enduring reality. Nuclear weapons and anti-nuclear defenses will either contribute to the avoidance of twenty-first century warfare, or to its greater likelihood, on the basis of the policies laid down by governments and the strategies preferred by their national security managers. The relationship between war and peace, or in nuclear deterrence theory between offense and defense, is both relational and paradoxical. In order to understand why a war broke out, you have to explain why peace broke down. And vice versa—an explanation for why peace happened is tantamount to at least part of the explanation for why war did not. Explaining a failure of deterrence presumes that you have already defined some standard for the successful practice of deterrence: explaining why deterrence worked in a particular case implies that you have some concept of a deterrence failure. In each case, in order to have a viable research hypothesis, one must have an equally robust "null" hypothesis with which to juxtapose, and contradict, it.

It follows that missile defenses may make nuclear deterrence more stable, or less stable, depending on how the investigator defines premissile defense experience. If the history of the first nuclear age, covering approximately the same years as the Cold War, is regarded as mostly stable and peaceful, then that appraisal will be used as a marker to cast doubt on the contribution of missile defense to stability, or, to say it another way, to predict that missile defenses will make the international system less stable. Conversely, if the assessment of the observer is that nuclear deterrence in the Cold War was more precarious than many judge it to have been, then the observer is likely to be more willing to entertain the possibility that missile defenses could improve, instead of detract from, stability. Most experts would agree that the twentieth century ended with the burden of proof resting on the advocates of missile defenses. They have shown little reluctance to assume that burden of argument, making the opening decades of the twenty-first century an interesting time for Americans, for Russians and for others interested in the relationships among nuclear weapons, arms control and international security.

NOTES

1. The concept of "second nuclear age" is developed and explained in Colin S. Gray, *The Second Nuclear Age* (Boulder, Colo.: Lynne Rienner, 1999), esp. pp. 5–9. See also Keith B. Payne, *Deterrence in the Second Nuclear Age* (Lexington: University Press of Kentucky, 1996).

2. Alexander L. George, "Strategies for Crisis Management," in George, ed., *Avoiding War: Problems of Crisis Management* (Boulder, Colo.: Westview Press, 1991), pp. 377–394, esp. pp. 384–387. George's definition of coercive diplomacy corresponds to Thomas C. Schelling's concept of "compellence." See Schellling, *Arms and Influence* (New Haven, Conn.: Yale University Press, 1966), pp. 69–78.

3. On this issue see Raymond L. Garthoff, *Deterrence and the Revolution in Soviet Military Doctrine* (Washington, D.C.: The Brookings Institution, 1990), pp. 174–185.

4. Paul Bracken, *Fire in the East: The Rise of Asian Military Power and the Second Nuclear Age* (New York: HarperCollins, 1999), p. 40.

5. Ibid., pp. 42–43.

6. In essence, we took a variation of Carter's proposed "racetrack" basing scheme for land-based missiles and added Richard L. Garwin's so-called "simple novel" defenses for silos. The Carter-proposed basing scheme moved each ICBM around a track of some 23 shelters: enemy targeters would never be certain which shelter held the real missile at any particular time. Garwin's simple-novel defenses were located contiguous to ICBM silos and, in essence, fired a hail of pellets at incoming reentry vehicles as they neared their targets.

7. A notable exception to the political typecasting was the Princeton scientist Freeman Dyson, who advocated building down offenses and phasing in missile defenses, but with a very different political agenda from that of the Reagan administration.

For Further Reading

Arquilla, John and David Ronfeldt, eds. *In Athena's Camp: Preparing for Conflict in the Information Age.* Santa Monica, Calif.: RAND, 1997.

Bellamy, Christopher. *Knights in White Armour: The New Art of War and Peace.* London: Hutchinson, 1996.

Blair, Bruce G. *The Logic of Accidental Nuclear War.* Washington, D.C.: Brookings Institution, 1993.

Davis, Paul K., ed. *New Challenges for Defense Planning: Rethinking How Much Is Enough.* Santa Monica, Calif.: RAND, 1994.

Feaver, Peter Douglas. *Guarding the Guardians: Civilian Control of Nuclear Weapons in the United States.* Ithaca, N.Y.: Cornell University Press, 1992.

Gaddis, John Lewis. *We Now Know: Rethinking Cold War History.* Oxford: Clarendon Press, 1997.

Gareev, M.A. *M.V. Frunze: Military Theorist.* New York: Pergamon-Brassey's, 1988.

Garthoff, Raymond L. *Deterrence and the Revolution in Soviet Military Doctrine.* Washington, D.C.: Brookings Institution, 1990.

Garthoff, Raymond L. *Reflections on the Cuban Missile Crisis.* Rev. ed. Washington, D.C.: Brookings Institution, 1989.

George, Alexander L., ed. *Avoiding War: Problems of Crisis Management.* Boulder, Colo.: Westview Press, 1991.

George, Alexander L. and William E. Simons, eds. *The Limits of Coercive Diplomacy,* 2nd ed. Boulder, Colo.: Westview Press, 1994.

Gray, Colin S. *Modern Strategy.* Oxford: Oxford University Press, 1999.

Gray, Colin S. *The Second Nuclear Age.* Boulder, Colo.: Lynne Rienner, 1999.

Holloway, David. *Stalin and the Bomb: The Soviet Union and Atomic Energy, 1939–1956.* New Haven, Conn.: Yale University Press, 1994.

Huntington, Samuel P. *The Clash of Civilizations and the Remaking of World Order.* New York: Simon and Schuster, 1996.

Jervis, Robert. *The Meaning of the Nuclear Revolution*. Ithaca, N.Y.: Cornell University Press, 1989.

Keaney, Thomas A. and Eliot A. Cohen. *Revolution in Warfare? Air Power in the Persian Gulf*. Annapolis, Md.: Naval Institute Press, 1995.

Klare, Michael. *Rogue States and Nuclear Outlaws: America's Search for a New Foreign Policy*. New York: Hill and Wang, 1995.

Kokoshin, Andrei. *Soviet Strategic Thought, 1917–91*. Cambridge, Mass.: MIT Press, 1998.

Kolodziej, Edward A. and Roger E. Kanet, eds. *Coping with Conflict after the Cold War*. Baltimore, Md.: Johns Hopkins University Press, 1996.

Libicki, Martin. *What Is Information Warfare?* Washington, D.C.: National Defense University, ACIS Paper 3, August 1995.

Martel, William C. and William T. Pendley. *Nuclear Coexistence: Rethinking U.S. Policy to Promote Stability in an Era of Proliferation*. Montgomery, Ala.: Air War College, April 1994.

May, Ernest R. and Philip D. Zelikow. *The Kennedy Tapes: Inside the White House during the Cuban Missile Crisis*. Cambridge, Mass.: Harvard University Press, 1997.

Metz, Steven and James Kievit. *Strategy and the Revolution in Military Affairs: From Theory to Policy*. Carlisle Barracks, Pa.: U.S. Army War College, June 27, 1995.

Payne, Keith B. *Deterrence in the Second Nuclear Age*. Lexington: University Press of Kentucky, 1996.

Sarkesian, Sam C. and Robert E. Connor, Jr. *The U.S. Military Profession into the Twenty-First Century*. London: Frank Cass, 1999.

Sigal, Leon V. *Disarming Strangers: Nuclear Diplomacy with North Korea*. Princeton, N.J.: Princeton University Press, 1998.

Talbott, Strobe, ed. and trans. *Khrushchev Remembers*. Boston: Little, Brown, 1970.

Tarr, David W. *Nuclear Deterrence and International Security: Alternative Nuclear Regimes*. White Plains, N.Y.: Longman Publishing Group, 1991.

Van Creveld, Martin. *Technology and War: From 2000 B.C. to the Present*. New York: Macmillan, 1989.

Van Creveld, Martin. *The Transformation of War*. New York: The Free Press, 1991.

Wardak, Ghulam Dastagir, comp., and Graham Hall Turbiville, Jr., gen. ed. *The Voroshilov Lectures: Materials from the Soviet General Staff Academy*, Vol. I. Washington, D.C.: National Defense University Press, 1989.

Index

About the Author

STEPHEN J. CIMBALA is Distinguished Professor of Political Science at Pennsylvania State University (Delaware County). He has contributed to the literature of international security, defense studies, and nuclear arms control for more than 20 years. He is the author of numerous books, including *Nuclear Strategy in the Next Century* (Praeger, 2000). He serves on the editorial boards of various professional journals and has served as a consultant to various agencies of the U.S. government and policy think tanks.

1877.